Working Knowledge

Working Knowledge

The New Vocationalism and
Higher Education

Edited by
Colin Symes and
John McIntyre

The Society for Research into Higher Education
& Open University Press

Published by SRHE and
Open University Press
Celtic Court
22 Ballmoor
Buckingham
MK18 1XW

email: enquiries@openup.co.uk
world wide web: www.openup.co.uk

and 325 Chestnut Street
Philadelphia, PA 19106, USA

First published 2000

Copyright © The editors and contributors, 2000

A catalogue record of this book is available from the British Library

ISBN 0 335 20571 2 (hb)

Library of Congress Cataloging-in-Publication Data
Working knowledge: the new vocationalism and higher education/edited by Colin
Symes and John McIntyre.
       p.   cm.
Includes bibliographical references and index.
ISBN 0-335-20571-2
    1. Education, Higher – Economic aspects.   2. Knowledge management.
3. Organizational learning.   I. Symes, Colin, 1945–   II. McIntyre, John, 1946–

LC67.6. W67 2000
378′.013–dc21

00-035994

Typeset by Graphicraft Limited, Hong Kong
Printed in Great Britain by Biddles Limited, Guildford and Kings Lynn

Contents

Notes on Contributors

David Beckett is a senior lecturer in the Faculty of Education at the University of Melbourne. Adult education, as it is apparent in leadership and professional development, policy analysis and workplace and lifelong learning, is the main focus of his teaching. Research interests include philosophy of education and policy analysis. With Paul Hager he edited a recent issue of *Education Philosophy and Theory* dealing with Practical Reasoning, and he is currently writing a book on learning at work.

David Boud is Professor of Adult Education and Assistant Dean of Research in the Faculty of Education at the University of Technology, Sydney. He is the author of numerous books on adult learning of which the most recent is a co-edited collection entitled *Understanding Learning at Work* (Routledge). His current research deals with universities and work-based learning.

Clive Chappell is a senior research fellow with the Research Centre for Vocational Education and Training in the Faculty of Education at the University of Technology, Sydney. His current research deals with the impact of contemporary social, economic and political discourses on the identities of teachers and students in vocational educational and training.

Stewart Clegg is Research Professor in the School of Management at the University of Technology, Sydney. He has previously held professorships at the Universities of New England, Western Sydney and St. Andrews. He is the author of many books on sociology and management theory of which *Changing Paradigms: The Transformation of Management Knowledge for the 21st Century* (Harper-Collins) is the most recent.

Lesley Farrell is a senior lecturer in the Faculty of Education at Monash University. Her research is concerned with language, education and social change. She has an interest in language and education in cross-cultural contexts and co-edits the *International Journal of Intercultural Studies*.

John Garrick is a senior lecturer in the Faculty of Education at the University of Technology, Sydney. He is an academic consultant for Work-based Learning in the Faculty of Business at the UTS. He is the author of *Informal Learning in the Workplace: Unmasking Human Resource Development* (Routledge 1998) and co-editor of several books on research, learning and work.

Paul Hager is Professor of Education in the Faculty of Education at the University of Technology, Sydney. His current research projects involve examinations of informal workplace learning, professional practice, and generic skills. He has published widely on these and related topics.

John McIntyre is Director of the Research Centre for Vocational Education and Training at the University of Technology, Sydney. He has been Principal Researcher on a range of national projects in Australian adult and vocational education. His current interests are in participation studies and the relationship of education research and policy in the contemporary state.

Hermine Scheeres is a senior lecturer and programme coordinator in the Faculty of Education at the University of Technology, Sydney. Her work brings together expertise in discourse analysis with an analysis of the changing workplace. Her current research focuses on the construction of identities in restructuring workplaces.

Nicky Solomon is a senior lecturer and senior research fellow in the Faculty of Education, University of Technology, Sydney. She is also Programme Manager for Work-based Learning at UTS. Her current research interests focus on the relationship between workplaces and universities. She has contributed chapters to a number of recent books on adult education.

Colin Symes is a research fellow in the Faculty of Education at the University of Technology, Sydney and a lecturer at the Queensland University of Technology. He has recently co-edited a book entitled *Taut Bodies* (Peter Lang) and is currently researching textual mediation in the workplace.

Mark Tennant is Professor of Adult Education at the University of Technology, Sydney. He is the author of several books on adult learning and adult education. The most recent is *Psychology and Adult Learning* (Routledge). He is currently researching the nature of expertise among professionals.

Robin Usher is Professor of Education and Director of Research and Consultancy in the Faculty of Education, Language and Community Services at the Royal Melbourne Institute of Technology University. He is the co-author of *Postmodernism and Education* (Routledge) and *Globalisation and Pedagogy* (Routledge). His current research is on the cultures of learning in the contemporary workplace and their implications for research in universities.

Foreword

Ronald Barnett

Across the world, universities are being ever more closely integrated into the wider world. For some, this movement is overdue; the only problem is that progress in this direction is far too slow. For others, it is a matter of concern: the new order threatens many of the values for which higher education has stood. The significance of this timely volume is that it disentangles many of the issues involved and, between the chapters that it offers, presents a balanced treatment of the issues.

The key issue that the contributors confront might be summarized in this way. In the knowledge society, the production of knowledge and its transmission – even high status knowledge – is not confined to a special institution such as the university but is, by definition, distributed throughout society. The knowledge society values, produces and transmits knowledge. Immediately, therefore, the purpose of universities is placed in some difficulty: it now has rivals. This loss of the monopoly over knowledge production is commonly remarked. Less commonly remarked is a second sense in which the university has rivals for its position as a knowledge producer. Not only is knowledge produced and passed on across society, but the very forms of that knowledge challenge the definitions of knowledge for which universities have come to stand. In essence, it is no longer what one knows that counts; it is what one can do through one's knowledge.

Knowledge, to gain its spurs, has to be put to work; it has to be seen to work. Even more than this, it has to be *in* work. Work of any significance has to be able to show that it has a knowledge base; but that knowledge might be tacit, not easily susceptible to being made explicit. Expertise comes to be understood as founded on a mix of knowledges (plural). Work and knowledge, accordingly, come to stand in a complex set of relationships to each other. The idea of 'working knowledge', in turn, emerges as nicely ambiguous.

How should institutions of higher education respond to this challenge? After all, it strikes at the heart of their purposes as producers and transmitters of knowledge. Should they embrace their new rivals? Should they form alliances with places of work and construct their curricula around work-based learning? In the process, of course, the curricula would no longer be theirs but would in part be constructed by others, more representative of work itself. Or should they resist such opportunities, seeing in them the end of knowledges as such; at least, the reflexive and critical forms of knowledge for which they have stood?

Overall, this volume takes a positive line. Frequently, the reader is pointed to the positive opportunities that the new order heralds, in wider definitions of knowledge, in worthwhile new forms of collaboration between higher education and work, in curricular innovation and in academic identities. For some time, higher education has worked within narrow definitions on all these fronts, as it defined its key concepts and activities in its own image. Now, it has opportunities to unfreeze these self-understandings. But the contributors also point to possible dangers in enthusiastically embracing the new order. Forms of closure may lie in wait, especially if the new knowledges lack criticality and self-reflection.

A continuing theme in the volume is that of work-based learning. In work-based learning, as the contributors make clear, we see many of the ambiguities and challenges of the new order. Does it refer to work-oriented elements within curricula or does it refer to curricular elements that are situated in workplaces? To what extent might it imply new forms of knowledge? Can practical wisdom and creative making (to take but two possibilities) be granted the status of formal knowledge? What of tacit knowing which, by definition, is hardly even observable? Can such forms of knowing be securely assessed? What weight should they be accorded in the framing of a curriculum?

This volume does not pretend to give definitive answers to these – and many other – questions that it raises. Its merit is that it raises the questions, from a range of different points of view. It gives us something to work on.

The sub-title of the volume is 'The New Vocationalism and Higher Education'. Perhaps the key term here is the adjective 'new'. It reminds us – as do some of the chapters – that higher education has, since its inception in the middle ages, been vocational, both overtly *and* more discreetly, through the more general personal and intellectual powers that it sought to offer. In other words, there should be no resistance on the part of higher education to the new order on account of its being vocational. There may be other grounds, if not for resistance, then for hesitancy, for careful appraisal and, perhaps, for some kind of constructive negotiation. It just may be that the new order offers continuities with past understandings of higher education in its power to engage with the wider world. It may even offer new opportunities to realize more fully those past understandings of higher education in the working world of today.

Acknowledgements

Books are strange creatures, which once in existence often have a life of their own, with their own idiosyncrasies, patterns of development and growth phases. This one is no different. It began its life as a core project of a research group at the University of Technology, Sydney (UTS). Collectively known as the Research into Adult and Vocational Learning (RAVL), this group is one of the university's designated research strengths. Had it not been for this and the funding that was attached to the designation, this book, in all probability, would not have transpired. Our first thanks, then, are to UTS, whose funding has enabled the group to meet on regular basis, host seminars and travel to conferences, to rehearse some of its ideas and insights. It was such rehearsals that form the foundations of this volume and its companion, to be edited by David Boud and Nicky Solomon, which will also appear from the Open University Press. In this connection we would also like to thank Professor Robin Usher of the Royal Melbourne Institute of Technology University, who in May 1999 agreed to host a two-day seminar dealing with 'working knowledge'. This event helped to consolidate, and led to some reformulation of, the book's themes. We would also like to thank the School of Culture and Language Studies, Queensland University of Technology, who allowed Dr Colin Symes a period of extended leave to work as a Research Fellow with the RAVL group. Finally, a sad note: during the time in which the idea of this book was being developed one of its projected contributors and a foundation member of RAVL, Geof Hayton, died. We would like to dedicate this book to his memory.

1

Working Knowledge: An Introduction to the New Business of Learning

Colin Symes and John McIntyre

Let's work without thinking about it. It is the only way to make life bearable.
(Voltaire 1958)

The direction that work has taken in the last two decades has made life unbearable – that is, if Voltaire is to be believed. More than ever before, work is subject to theorization on a number of fronts, at least that is the thesis of this volume. But this is a volume more than about work: it is about the connection, which is an increasingly close one, that is now beginning to emerge between education and work. Of course this connection has always been evident in various ways – although its expression has been somewhat more oblique in the past than its contemporary forms. The origins of universal schooling, for example, took their impetus from the industrial revolution. Schools came into being first to quarantine children from exploitative labour practices, and second to instil within them the essence of the work ethic (Bauman 1998). In more recent times the focus was on reproducing the divisions in the labour order. These centred on gender, around the idea that the work of men was different from that of women, and around the Taylorized divide between workers who did things with their hands and workers who did things with their heads. National systems of education, with specific forms of schooling earmarked to produce the patterns of mentality associated with each form of labour, were developed (Gellner 1994).

In the 1980s and 1990s the patterns of human capitalism, which underpin the principles of labour regeneration through education, have assumed a new form. Once again the impetus stems from economic change, from the emergence of new modes of production that are more specialized and dependent on continuous innovation, research and development. This regime of 'flexible specialization' has seen the demise of mass production and its replacement by specialized products and services matching demand from an increasingly heterogeneous market. Hence the new work order associated with these smaller scales of production is often called post-Fordism.

Though some remain lukewarm about this notion, and suggest it does not apply to the bulk of the workforce who continue to labour under Fordist conditions that are, if anything, more intensively deployed than in the past, its underlying principles inform much policy in education. This has at its heart a type of 'instrumental progressivism', which stresses a student-centred style of education that is individualized and flexible, and is designed to enhance the individual's opportunities for employment. Unlike previous forms of progressivism that were inner-directed, their revamped forms are outer-directed, and are tethered to the goals of performativity rather than reflexivity. This shift is especially apparent in the universities, which are now more student-centred and less subject-centred, more oriented to satisfying the labour market demands.

None of these changes is internally driven. Many of them have been imposed on institutions by governments responding to changes that are also beyond their control. One of the most signficant of these is the globalization of the economic order, which has made nation-states increasingly vulnerable to sudden shifts of capital and the vagaries of the international money markets. The ascendancy of neo-liberalist policies, particularly in economies that have derived their models from the US and the UK, has shifted the sovereignty of determination from the state to the market. The consequences of this shift are manifold but principally centre on a radical attenuation of the public sector, now evident in a generalized impoverishment of education and health services, and patterns of wealth distribution marked by increased disparities between the highest and lowest echelons of society. The complexion of civil society is an increasingly individualistic one, where the principle of self-investment underwrites the working of the meritocracy, where the regime of affordability determines access to education and health. The arithmetic of these manoeuvres proceeds in the following fashion: as the state minimalizes its functions, it can reduce the burden of tax on individuals who then have more discretionary income to advantage their situation rationally and, in the long run, increase their levels of happiness. In exchange, the state gets human capital on the cheap.

The latest addition to these upheavals is the so-called 'knowledge economy', to which education at the policy and practical levels is now responding with alacrity. Much of the response has been obsequious as educational institutions, in an effort to boost their pecuniary circumstances, see alliances with business and industry as initiating new income streams. Governments see such collaborations as good for the economy, and that, as embodiments of intellectual capital par excellence, academics needs to be 'incorporated' into the real world. Others are not so sanguine and regard such flirtations with capitalism as pernicious, regarding them as symptomatic of the growing commodification of learning and knowledge. Unless carefully monitored such developments could threaten the independence of the university and academic freedom. This book tries to provide a more measured response and suggests that the values of education need not be irretrievably debased if it participates more fully in the knowledge economy.

From the outset it is important to recognize that education has always been at the forefront of the knowledge economy. For almost a millennium, universities have been the centres of knowledge accumulation and dissemination, where old and new pathways of knowing have been explored, accredited, documented and institutionalized. And although much of the knowledge involved was arcane and recondite, it did produce economic outcomes of sorts that were exemplified in the publishing industry to which academic literature was a signficant contributor, and in and around the economic infrastructure of educational institutions. Universities, for example, are large enterprises and the mainstays of economic activity in many communities, where the pockets of prosperity are otherwise few and far between. In some instances – Stanford is the most notable example – they have helped to create new sectors of industry that the R & D ethos of the university has helped to inspire and supply with a constant stream of innovations (Robertson 1999).

In the current era the epistemological preoccupations of the university have, since the advent of information technology, begun to pervade many areas of economic endeavour. Knowledge is no longer the fruit of idle curiosity, pursued in the spirit of open and disinterested inquiry, but is something which now invokes use-value and application. In this more mercenary context, the principle of Newtonian knowledge has been suspended in favour of forms of knowing in which utility is uppermost. A number of commentators have drawn attention to the changing nature of knowledge production in the academy and the world at large, and identified its various characteristics. Gibbons *et al.* (1994), for example, in a work that has attracted considerable attention and commentary, describe the ascendancy of Mode 2 knowledge. They characterize such knowledge, which is also produced outside the academy, as that which is useful to government, industry and society.

In this book, we prefer to use the term 'working knowledge' – which is not by any means original – partly because it is more semantically telling and partly because, through its various ambiguities, it is able to convey the range of meanings inherent in the new epistemological formulations of knowledge. Of these, the idea that knowledge can be put to work is the dominant one. But in the traditional sense of the phrase, this often meant not understanding the procedures and processes involved. Working knowledge was precisely that: a form of knowledge that was sufficient to get things done, to produce a certain end or outcome; it was enough that it worked. There was no need to inquire into the reasons why. Indeed many workers, particularly those working in manufacturing, and with materials and tools, have always known much more than they could tell or speak of – a fact that has enabled various thinkers, Polanyi (1972) being the most prominent, to differentiate tacit from explicit forms of knowing. The essence of this distinction is that there are forms of knowing which can be formulated and textualized, whereas there are others which transcend articulation. In contradistinction to the former, which is mostly acquired in educational institutions, tacit knowledge can only be acquired 'on the job', through coming into close 'communion' with its materials and tools, and gaining a deeper understanding of their characteristics and nature. One of the reasons why explicit knowledge, particularly in its academic forms, is so often disparaged, is that its generality expunges those specific understandings that make such knowledge workable and applicable.

In the last few years, capitalists have popularized the notion that learning can be profitable for business and that organizations which encourage their employees to educate themselves are likely to be more competitive ones (Drucker 1993). In conjunction with the fact that 'working knowledge' is more than ever being academicized through competency approaches to learning, the principles of Taylorism, which saw learning as inhibiting productivity, are being spurned. One of the more significant features of this change is the degree to which over the last decade universities have been vocationalized, and are now offering more occupationally specific credentials (Symes 1999).

But there are dark sides to these developments. One is that many types of work have undergone or are undergoing digitalization, and that jobs which were once performed by human beings are fast being automated, often with devastating consequences for their communities. Another is that the advent of the digital society (which is more often celebrated than damned) is leading to increased surveillance and control in avenues of life that were formerly spared these intrusions. Our productive and consuming habits are now subject to datafication on a grand scale, and we now live in world of pan-panopticism, where most of our actions are transparent and visible. The neo-Sloanist character of contemporary capitalism means that is more than ever exigent that corporations decode the cultural logic of consumers in such a way as to know their tastes but also to develop them. Ironically, many of the jobs that are emerging in call centres and data processing companies are concerned with garnering information that will make individuals more manageable and manipulable (Robins and Webster 1999). The knowledge economy cuts both ways: it liberates but also oppresses.

This is the context, then, in which this collection of chapters has been compiled. Its contributors are located at Australian universities, which have been at the forefront of the developments that are the subjects of their reflection and analysis. The collection had its genesis at the University of Technology, Sydney (UTS), and was prompted by a series of seminars dealing with 'working knowledge' which in their turn had been stimulated by an article written by David Boud (1998), dealing with work-based study in the university. In this article Boud examines a relatively new form of higher education, mainly to be found in the UK at some of its newer universities, in which 'work is the curriculum'. He notes that its emergence, which coincides with the increased demand for higher education and the legitimation of flexible delivery as a way to meet this demand, grants opportunities to those who might not otherwise benefit from university study by allowing them to incorporate their working knowledge into a degree programme.

At the University of Portsmouth, which was a pioneer of work-based learning, students with no formal qualifications as such can enrol in a variety of so-called partnership programmes, all of which can be cross-credited with more conventional degree subjects. Thus through customization of projects students can embark on courses of learning that meet the requirements of degree study but also have some direct utility in their workplaces and which are flexible enough to accommodate their work schedules. These are all symptoms of instrumental progressivism, of customizing courses to benefit the student and, in the long run, their employers. One of Portsmouth's students, who at the time was employed by a local engineering company, developed a diagnostic procedure for estimating the costs of reconditioning aircraft engines which reduced company costs substantially. To develop this procedure, the student studied corrosion chemistry, superalloys and electron microscopy (University of Portsmouth 1999).

Boud's analysis is extensive and raises many provocative issues, including the matter of evaluation and assessment, and whether such courses will ever enjoy parity of esteem with more conventional degrees. Yet his chapter stops short, as he freely admits, of undertaking a broader critique of work-based learning in the context of globalization and a changing labour market. The chapters in this collection, which are far-reaching and diverse, dealing with everything from workplace identities to the virtual university, provide this critique. They are written from a variety of disciplinary perspectives and fields, and reflect the diverse background, histories and theoretical propensities of their authors.

The next chapter in the collection is by David Boud and Colin Symes who examine work-based learning as an educational encapsulation of working knowledge. They suggest that this radical innovation in higher education has challenged many of the orthodoxies and preconceptions associated with university pedagogy and its administration. They list these challenges and suggest that work-based learning could transform much of what we have taken for granted about university education, particularly in relation to assessment and curriculum practices. In particular they suggest that these practices are based on assumptions derived from Mode 1 knowledge (Gibbons *et al.* 1994), whereas work-based learning emerges from the context of Mode 2 knowledge. This poses diffficulties for the academics who served their apprenticeship in the Mode 1 traditions and who find the transition to more outward-looking forms of pedagogic and epistemological practice a threat to their identities.

The chapter written by Colin Symes takes a step back from the contemporary moment and suggests that the emergence of work-based learning cannot be divorced from its historical antecedents and their ongoing legacy. He argues that the policy locus of higher education flies in the face of this legacy that the modern university inherited from the nineteenth century and which was, on the surface at least, antagonistic towards professional courses of study. In order to clarify the nature of these traditions and their conceptual parameters, he identifies four discourses of higher education around which the nexus between the university and work has been variously formulated. He argues that the current policy locus is fashioned around human capital discourse and that work-based learning is the most dogmatic expression of this discourse. But he also suggests, like Usher in a later chapter in the collection, that the differences between vocational and liberal discourses (which lie at the heart of his double-binary) are more those of emphasis than outcome. He notes for example that even the most die-hard apologists of liberal education recognized that it exhibited vocational elements, albeit through its ability to foster generic attributes such as ethical capacity which were useful in most professions. Notwithstanding these overlaps, the utility of Symes's discourses derives from their capacity to draw attention to the pedagogic chain of events inherent in the links between education and work. The third discourse, for example, is a human capital one but with a critical dimension added; it argues work should form the basis of the curriculum but only insofar that the curriculum also includes study linked to the political economy of work. In the end Symes suggests that an education system wholly driven by the imperatives of human capital, such as a work-based one would entail, is shortsighted.

The next chapter is by Paul Hager, who argues that work-based learning has radical ramifications for understanding the ways in which knowledge is produced and created. Like Symes, he argues that the university is undergoing radical re-engineering. He suggests that the traditional foundations of higher education have either been abandoned or are in the process of reconstruction in the light of imperatives such as the move to mass higher education, the emergence of the knowledge society and so forth. In this context it is important to reconsider the nature of the knowledge which forms the foundation of university study. Interrogating Ronald Barnett's (1997) 'new conception of education', which re-envisages the university curriculum in terms of an 'unknowable world', Hager argues that Barnett's various epistemological assumptions are flawed and fail to recognize the continuum that exists between academic and everyday knowledge. The strong streak of scepticism that impels Barnett's preferred model of knowing, which is discourse-based and which denies any permanency to knowledge at all, Hager suggests has severe limitations. First, it is unmistakably Cartesian, and second, it seems to deny a world of action, where bridges are built, individuals cross rivers, and where some certainties prevail. Hager's own knowledge scenario, which is derived from studying working knowledge in situ, is centred on the capacity to exercise judgements. This involves the capacity for acting in and on the world, embodied and tacit knowledge: the very elements that would lie at the heart of a properly constituted work-based approach to learning.

One theme to which Hager draws attention is the virtualization of the university. This is a theme that David Beckett explores in somewhat more detail in his chapter. In its initial section Beckett's chapter examines the trends inherent in corporate culture. He sees these trends in a somewhat more positive light than some other contributors to this collection – most notably Garrick and Clegg – especially when compared with some of those that are now endemic in universities. Beckett is most critical about the latter, and suggests that the move, in particular, to computer-mediated pedagogy is leading to a reaffirmation of Cartesianism. He suggests that such mediated pedagogy is 'disembodied', and stresses approaches to education that place the mind ahead of the body. Whereas the rest of postmodern culture is celebrating the body, the university is denying it! Indeed, Beckett argues that the workplace is fast becoming a place where proper learning, in all its bodily forms, is being affirmed, is given (to use corporeal jargon) a workout. In fact, Beckett uses a classical source to reinforce his argument: Aristotle, who argued for the importance of *techne* as a key action of human beings. If universities abandon embodied learning in favour of informatized pedagogy they risk losing out to the corporate world which, as many examples now demonstrate, is more than able to conduct its own programmes of learning.

The next three chapters in the collection explore other themes relating to the organization of work-based learning. John McIntyre and Nicky Solomon – both experienced practitioners in work-based learning – in their chapter suggest that the impact of work-based learning can only be understood if the context from which it springs is elucidated. They suggest that this context is dominated by the 'forces of globalization' – which other contributors to the book also recognize as being salient. They argue that these forces, which are now being felt by many institutions and organizations in the nation-state, are enacted through policy that is framed, increasingly, by international bodies such as the Organisation for Economic Co-operation and Development (OECD) and the International Monetary Fund (IMF). Much of their chapter is concerned with delineating the features of globalization and the way these features are articulated in the locus of policy making at the nation-state level. They note the degree to which the institution of higher education has been subject to corporatization and the academy has embraced a more businesslike ethos. Adaptation of courses to accommodate the demands of businesses and industries is but one feature of this ethos, which is also associated with internationalization of courses, knowledge commodification and the commercialization of educational services. Thus the differences between the academy and the 'real world', which were once relatively pronounced, have been elided as the processes of corporatization have gathered momentum. The university as a workplace and studyplace is not that different from other workplaces. This 'convergency' has added cogency to work-based approaches to learning.

The academization of these approaches, to which McIntyre and Solomon then turn their analysis, has assisted to create a 'performative university'. This has reshaped the alliance between the academy and work, whose antecedence can be traced to a number of quarters, many of them beyond the realm of the university. McIntyre and Solomon suggest, for example, that the boundaries between work and the academy are increasingly permeable ones, marked by more flexibility and greater accommodation to the work demands of students. They suggest that the emergence of the learning organization and increased concern about human resource development has created a domain that is conducive to work-based approaches to higher learning. In order to satisfy the curriculum bureaucracy of the university, this has led to the epistemological codification of the labour process.

These issues are explored further in Solomon and McIntyre's second chapter, which utilizes perspectives drawn from the sociology of knowledge, particularly those of Basil Bernstein. They use his various codifications of knowledge to suggest that work-based learning has manifold repercussions for understanding the boundaries between work and learning, which are now being erased. They note how work-based learning is a logical extension of pedagogic practices that were already evident in professional courses such as teaching and medicine, where practicums were an adjunct of the curriculum. The difference between these more traditional forms of work-based learning and their present incarnations is the degree to which work is an integral part of the curriculum, around which all other academic experiences are organized. In that it legitimates the principle at the core of deschooling, namely, that individuals should learn from the world, not about the world (Illich 1971), work-based learning challenges the dominant code of the university, which was disciplinary-based, culturally concentrated and restricted. That it does so, and gives due recognition to the fact that more knowledge is embodied in the community at large (which is the point Hager makes in his chapter) than ever resides in the university, is one of the more progressive aspects of work-based learning. Yet at the same time, the advent of work-based learning carries risks, that outside the arena of academy learning becomes unmanageable and unruly, risk-laden and anarchic – qualities upon which, incidentally, the new corporate culture is said to thrive.

Robin Usher's chapter complements those of McIntyre and Solomon. It provides a more excoriating analysis of Gibbons *et al.* (1994). This reveals a number of weaknesses in the epistemological foundations of their argument. He argues that the binaries they employ mask the degree to which there is more continuity than difference between them. Further, their analysis, because it has been the object of so much commentary, is assisting to create the very phenomenon of which it speaks! Indeed, some of their language is already permeating the 'talk' of the academy. A recent undergraduate course being promoted at UTS, for example, is described as a 'transdisciplinary' course. Yet as Usher indicates, the more diversified conditions of the new university have created a more flexible arena, offering scope for new empires of practice to be created within the expanded domain of teaching, research and administration. In the context of change, there has been a tendency to look back nostalgically at the academy of the pre-1990s and to forget that it was a monolithic and elitist enterprise, whose structures discouraged innovation. The new structures permit diversity and opportunity and far more 'play', to use Usher's term, than the university of old. Too much regulation, it is Usher's contention, which universities might deploy as a reaction to deregulation, could asphyxiate the potential for innovation now existing in the re-engineered university. Unmanageability might not be such a bad thing after all.

The final three chapters, though exploring it from different perspectives, coalesce around a single theme, that of identity and the degree to which the work-based approaches to learning exercise an influence on its formation. Mark Tennant's chapter argues that this is the case and that in the wake of these new learning identities pedagogical practices are being produced that are compatible with the demands of the new workplace. Following a view that has become orthodoxy among post-structuralists, Tennant holds that identity is a more protean entity than in the past when more essentialist views held suggested that once identity had been formed it was not subject to re-creation or re-production. He suggests that under the press of the new work order it is work rather than culture that provides fulfilment and that education is becoming the key moral technology in career preparation. Tennant, like some of the other contributors to this volume, regards such trends with suspicion and is particularly cautious about what he sees as reductionist tendencies in work-based learning. In particular, he suggests that such approaches are necessarily narrow and incompatible with the generation of more communal and civic capacities such as those relating to social justice and respect for the environment. He encapsulates this by suggesting that work-based approaches have seen a shift in the university away from education to learning. Indeed, he is right to be circumspect about these developments on the long-term character formation of individuals. Sennett (1999) has suggested that the new work order is corrosive in its impact on character, emphasizing individualism at the expense of more communal virtues. Universities should be places that arrest these trends and provide sanctuaries from the neo-Fordist values that are fast enveloping other social formations.

The next chapter in the identity trilogy, which is written by Clive Chappell, Lesley Farrell, Hermine Scheeres and Nicky Solomon, provides a series of 'cases' of work-based learning in action. They argue that the new work order, of which work-based learning is a constituent part, is assisting to create 'new social identities'. Under the new capitalism, knowledge and learning have become privileged discourses in workplaces, where they were once disparaged. As Chappell *et al.* demonstrate in their snapshots, which range over a number of sites including universities and factories, the emergence of knowledge capitalism as a distinct economic form is transforming the identity condition of workers in profound ways. They argue that the conditions of epistemological production are contradictory: they are more unruly than they were but they are also more subject to regulation and scrutiny, meterage and measurement. This is particularly the case in universities where academics enjoy more freedom as knowledge producers yet are also most subject to more accountability. Analogous contradictions exist in other sectors of the educational workforce, most notably among vocational teachers in the Technical and Further Education (TAFE) sector – the

second of the snapshots of Chappell *et al.* – who have traditionally fashioned their pedagogic identities around working knowledge. Yet in a world
where the conditions of production are subject to constant change and
restructuring, they face death by anachronism. Hence, the emergence of
workplace educators who can more directly increase the 'skill base of the
workforce'. The last two snapshots demonstrate how such educators ensure
that the practices of learning are integrated into the production cycle and
are used to assist with the creation of the new work order.

The final chapter in this collection also deals with matters of identity but
in a more expansive and contextualized way than the two previous chapters.
Its authors, John Garrick and Stewart Clegg, representing a business perspective on working knowledge, provide a detailed analysis of the labour
market, which they see as characterized by a number of features: globalization, informatization, de-differentation. Like other authors in this collection they note the emergence of knowledge and information as critical
elements of capacity building, facilitated by the creation of the learning
organization and opportunities for work-based learning. But unlike many of
the enthusiasts for these developments, who see them as humanizing the
workplace, Garrick and Clegg are less sanguine about their potential and
argue that their seductive surface masks some disturbing undercurrents.
Like Zuboff (1988) and other perceptive commentators on the knowledge
economy, they argue that there is a dark side to the information revolution
now sweeping the globe. This resides in the capacity of information technology to 'digitalize' even forms of knowledge, such as the aforementioned
tacit knowledge, which once defied explication, and which could only be
acquired in a social context. Hence Garrick and Clegg's vampiric metaphor: of a rapacious organization, creating opportunities for workers to
learn which become opportunities to donate via a Count Dracula – one of
Fairclough's (1996) 'discourse technologists' – their expertise to the organization's knowledge bank. And once secured, they become expendable. For
learning organization read learning transfusion! Yet there is a smidgen of
optimism in Garrick and Clegg's gothic tale. All organizational revolutions
cause insurrectionary forces to mobilize, and to create a 'space of resistance'.

* * *

To conclude this introduction, it seems fitting to try and frame some of the
leading questions that seem to emerge from the chapters that follow. It
seems particularly useful to think in terms of questions that point to the
outstanding theoretical issues – and of course to matters that invite empirical investigation. It will be useful to do this in a way that helps to highlight
some of the key categories that seem to be 'at work' in the various chapters.

Much of the following discussion will assume that work-based learning
as it is defined in this book is by and large a positive development and is
one rich in potential for rethinking our educational institutions and our
educational practice in general – not only those practices that have been
thought to be the domain of adult and vocational education. Indeed, the

leading subtext to the volume is the view that old distinctions between the general and vocational education (or education and training) are, or will be rendered, increasingly irrelevant in this century. Work-based learning is taken to be a harbinger of fundamental change in institutions and not a temporary aberration or fashion that will hopefully disappear without doing too much damage to established institutions or making too many demands on educators to change their thinking. The associated subtext is that learning at work has for too long been undervalued for what it might teach professional practice in formal education.

It is from the promise of work-based learning that the book attempts to draw out some possibilities for this task of rethinking educational philosophies and practices that better acknowledge the realities of the workplace as a site of learning.

1. *Questions about the conditions bringing about work-based learning.* How might it be possible to conceptualize the broad social and economic changes that are bringing about new partnerships between corporations and the academy and endorsing work-based learning programmes as a leading educational innovation? To what extent is the state-led restructuring of educational institutions forcing this accommodation, and to what extent is it conditioned by other pressures for a 'convergence' of developments in the corporation and the academy and, indeed, in society at large in a globalizing world?
2. *Questions about the nature of working knowledge.* In attempting to conceptualize the nature of working knowledge, or knowledge at work, what understandings of 'knowledge' are we working with? How does work-based learning challenge our existing theories of knowledge, particularly as these have been shaped by academic experiences that have been traditionally at odds with workplace learning? How might the idea of the 'production' of knowledge through learning at work offer a perspective on the formation of human capital as well as a basis for understanding learning at work?
3. *Questions about knowledge formation and learning at work.* How might current approaches to workplace learning be reconceptualized better to take into account concepts of knowledge production? How can workplace learning be theorized in terms of the way knowledge is taken up and transformed through professional judgements and other processes at work? How do the demands of the contemporary workplace demand higher order cognition in this way?
4. *Questions about academic institutions and their knowledge codes.* If it is true that work-based learning challenges those knowledge codes that have historically been the basis for framing the formal curriculum, what new knowledge codes are required by the different conditions of learning in the workplace? To what extent are concepts such as productive learning necessary or useful to the task of designing educational practice around a 'curriculum of work'? What might be some of the implications for

education in general (that is, general education) from rethinking curriculum knowledge codes in the light of work-based learning? If work-based learning represents a 'weakening' of boundaries of work and education, to what extent will the strong divisions between higher and further education institutions be sustained in the future?

5. *Questions about contemporary knowledge formation.* Much of the argument takes as its reference point current theorizations of 'new modes' of knowledge production. There are questions about the adequacy of this theory of contemporary knowledge formation, including how the supposed shift to knowledge production in its contexts of application is to be understood. What might the debate about knowledge production imply for the rethinking of educational institutions and the formal curriculum? How does this debate provide a broader context for arguments about workplace learning as situated knowledge production?

6. *Questions about working identity.* Given the changing parameters of work and learning implied in the foregoing, what is entailed for the management of identity in workplaces? How does work-based learning present limits and possibilities for defining working identity? How can working knowledge be understood as including the processes by which employees manage their identities as workers? What kinds of capacities or competencies must workers have developed to take advantage of opportunities in the 'humanized workplace' to be able to fashion work identities? To what extent are current theories of learning from experience useful in this task? How do power and authority relationships govern the processes involved? How in its nature is 'working identity' accomplished in specific workplaces and in terms of local and situated working knowledges?

It will be apparent on any reading of the following contributions that this summary only begins to suggest the wealth of material that the development of work-based learning is now generating. This is partly because, as many contributors argue, the developments bring into question at many points the orthodoxies of education as they have been long practised. Running through the above questions are some key and interlinked categories – knowledge, identity, work, learning, curriculum. Work-based learning as an innovation offers an important opportunity to explore anew these categories which tend to be taken for granted in our educational thinking. If we do this, then education might be considerably ameliorated. We began with Voltaire; it seems fitting therefore to end on this panglossian note.

References

Barnett, R. (1997) A knowledge strategy for universities, in R. Barnett and A. Griffin, (eds) *The End of Knowledge in Higher Education*. London: Cassell.

Bauman, Z. (1998) *Work, Consumerism and the New Poor.* Buckingham: Open University Press.

Boud, D. (1998) How can university work-based courses contribute to lifelong learning?, in J. Holford, P. Jarvis, P. and C. Griffin (eds) *International Perspectives on Lifelong Learning.* London: Kogan Page.

Drucker, P. F. (1993) The new society of organisations, in R. Howard (ed.) *The Learning-imperative: Managing People for Continuous Innovation.* Boston: Harvard Business Review.

Fairclough, N. (1996) Technologisation of discourse, in C. Caldas-Coulthard and M. Coulthard (eds) *Texts and Practices. Readings in Critical Discourse Analysis.* London: Routledge.

Gellner, E. (1994) *Encounters with Nationalism.* Oxford: Blackwell.

Gibbons, M., Limoges, C., Notwotny, H. *et al.* (1994) *The New Production of Knowledge: The Dynamics of Science and Research in Contemporary Societies.* London: Sage.

Illich, I. (1971) *Deschooling Society.* Harmondsworth: Penguin.

Polanyi, M. (1972) *Personal Knowledge: Towards a Post-critical Philosophy.* London: Routledge and Kegan Paul.

Robertson, D. (1999) Knowledge societies, intellectual capital and economic growth, in H. Gray (ed.) *Universities and the Creation of Wealth.* Buckingham: SHRE/ Open University Press.

Robins, K. and Webster, F. (1999) *Times of the Techno-culture: From the Information Society to the Virtual Life.* London: Routledge.

Sennett, R. (1999) *The Corrosion of Character. The Personal Consequences of Work in the New Capitalism.* New York, NY: Norton.

Symes, C. (1999) 'Working for your future': the rise of the vocationalised university. *Australian Journal of Education,* 43 (3), 243–58.

University of Portsmouth (1999) Welcome to the Partnership Programme, http://www.port.ac.uk/-partner/cs 3. htm.

Voltaire, F. M. A. de (1958) *Candide ou l'optimisme.* London: University of London Press.

Zuboff, S. (1988) *In the Age of the Smart Machine: The Future of Work and Power.* New York, NY: Basic Books.

2

Learning for Real: Work-based Education in Universities

David Boud and Colin Symes

Personalities which became effective in action were bred and tested in the medium of action.

(Dewey 1900: 4)

Introduction

In several countries including Australia and the UK, work-based learning degrees are being established in which learning occurs primarily in the workplace, with work as the curriculum. These are not extensions of cooperative education and sandwich courses but a radically new approach to what constitutes university study. They provide a new framework for organizing and structuring a university award. In this respect, work-based learning needs to be distinguished from workplace learning, that form of learning that occurs on a day-to-day basis at work as employees acquire new skills or develop new approaches to solving problems. No formal educational recognition normally accrues to such learning, whether or not it is organized systematically. The emergence of work-based learning acknowledges that work, even on a day-to-day basis, is imbued with learning opportunities (Garrick 1998), heretofore not recognized as educationally significant or worthwhile. Work-based learning gives academic recognition to these opportunities, when suitably planned and represented.

In specific terms work-based learning has come to be used as a description of accredited university courses in which a significant proportion of study, if not all, is undertaken in the workplace whose issues and challenges form the principal focus of study. At present, the majority of learners enrolled in work-based learning programmes are engaged in full-time employment. Work-based learning courses, which have been pioneered at such universities as Portsmouth and Middlesex (Boud 1998), are typically not a new mode of study or a substitute for existing part-time courses, but a new approach to higher education which extends its accessibility and flexibility.

It is becoming apparent, though, that there is no one form of work-based learning, that its current incarnations are a reflection of the contemporary moment, and that in different circumstances, work-based learning might have a different character altogether.

In this chapter we examine work-based learning in both old and new universities in the United Kingdom, where work-based learning has been somewhat more elaborated as a practice than, say, in Australia where work-based learning is still in its infancy. This is in part because the Department for Education and Employment (DfEE) in the UK has been more active than some other countries' governments in promoting the vocationalization of its system of education. Its recent enthusiasm for the University for Industry – potentially another version of work-based learning – is typical of its support for extending the ambit of higher education into the workplace. Work-based learning is beginning to be implemented in some Australian universities, most notably at the University of Technology, Sydney, where the authors of this chapter are located.

It is of note that there are similar developments to work-based learning in the Technical and Further Education (TAFE) sector in Australia (see ANTA 1999). It seems probable that over time there will be a loosening of the boundaries between higher education and other sectors of post-compulsory education, as well as the boundaries between undergraduate and postgraduate education.

In this chapter though, the main focus is university education, and the challenges that the introduction of work-based learning alongside more orthodox forms of study pose to the academic and administrative environment of the university. We describe the way in which work-based learning has been accommodated into the higher education system and argue that this accommodation has not always been a comfortable one. In many respects its accommodation has been facilitated by the changing context of higher education and policies that have fostered more 'realistic' forms of university curricula designed to meet the needs of the changing workforce. 'Learning for real' is a now a powerful force in the formation of the university as has been the force of access. Their combined impact is producing a style of higher education in which the fulfilment of career aspiration has become an important goal. This will come about as the essentially arbitrary structural arrangements of institutions are challenged over the need for more seamless educational opportunities by learners applying the principle of consumer demand.

Work-based learning: a new pedagogy for new times

Work-based learning is, in many respects, an idea whose time has come. As a new mode of education it epitomizes much of the dramatic change which has been occurring in and around higher education. For example, work-based learning has come to prominence during a period when universities have been undergoing a process of 'realization'; that is, they have been encouraged to develop closer alliances with business and commerce, industry and the public sector. This has been part of a broader policy agenda centring on economic reform that has focused on, among other matters, the need, if they are to take advantage of the emergent knowledge economy, for nation-states to intellectualize their labour forces. Higher education, because it is a central player in human capital formation, has been regarded as a vital part of this reform. Thus a cult of relevance has begun to sweep through the sometimes arcane tendencies of the academy, which has resulted in universities updating their epistemological profiles and organizational structures in line with what they perceive to be the world's best practice. This has not been easy. For example, some of the elite institutions (not all by any means) and some faculties are staggeringly untouched by these developments and have resisted these modernizing trends. They are badly infected with legacy inertia, which makes it difficult for them to liberate themselves from the stranglehold of their traditions.

Thus the advocacy of work-based learning has tended to be strongest in universities which have always had more pragmatic outlooks. It is no accident, for example, that it has been strongest in those institutions which were formerly polytechnics, or institutes of technology as they were called in Australia, and which always championed closer relationships with industry and commerce than the universities. Part of the charter of such institutions, as Symes argues in his chapter, involved establishing such links, and foregoing some academic aspirations in favour of more applied approaches to learning. However, work-based learning is not confined to such institutions as can be testified by pioneering work at the universities of Leeds and Cambridge (see Boud and Solomon, forthcoming).

But recent support for work-based learning is also symptomatic of a more generalized shift towards to what has been called 'instrumental progressivism' across the whole spectrum of education which is marked by a number of features. These include an emphasis on accessibility, transferable skills, competency formation, modularized educational programmes, student profiling and the development of reflective practitioners (Robins and Webster 1999). In direct contrast to the approaches to learning which emphasized inflexibility and the attenuation of capacity, and which were commensurate with Taylorist patterns of work, the new emphasis is on the cultivation of the flexible individual, possessing a range of symbolic and numerical capacities.

The trend towards 'instrumental progressivism' is driven by radical changes to the nature of work. The move from mass production to flexible specialization has created a labour force in which the major input is intellectual rather than muscular. Whole categories of employment have been created in the last two decades or so, which did not exist before the era of information technology; at the same time, many areas of work have declined or, in some instances, become extinct. There have also been dramatic changes to the demographics of work – more women in the labour force, for example – and to the temporalization of work. Individuals work longer and harder, but also in jobs that are of shorter duration and have a project focus (Sennett 1999). It is now a case of several careers in a lifetime, not one, for which individuals can expect to have to upgrade and extend their credentials, often through self-financed education.

These changes have placed new demands on the nature of university study. Universities were always to a degree vocational institutions, particularly in terms of the high-status professions such as law and medicine, but in the last few years this vocationalism has become more pronounced, reflecting the growth in knowledge-based employment, particularly in the service and financial sectors. But these developments have also brought into question the efficacy and appropriateness of front-end education and training, comprising a degree followed by work.

The rise of work-based education emerges from the phalanx of forces now driving higher education. The reforms of the 1980s in UK and Australia acquiesced to these, leading to a questioning of the very nature of the university as 'academic'. The term has come to have pejorative overtones denoting something that is not applicable to the real world. Indeed, in recognition of the fact that during the 1960s and 1970s universities had become too ivory-towerish, most have begun to promote themselves as belonging to the real world, dealing with issues that really matter and that are useful (Symes 1998). Although much of the language is rhetorical and relates to the way institutions are positioning themselves in the new context, and has actual substance in the 'real' world (see Robin Usher in this volume), there are telling points in the rhetoric. Universities are keen to underline the point that their degrees are useful and will enhance employment opportunities. The fact that work-based learning has caused no obvious consternation, as it might have done in the ivory-tower university, is a mark of the shift to a more 'realized' university.

But the impetus for work-based education is not just instrumental. The clarion calls of access and equity are ones to which higher education has also had to respond not only on social justice grounds. Much of the access and equity rationale has a human capital underlay, that of better utilizing the talent pool of the population and making available the highest forms of education to the disadvantaged (Taylor and Henry 1994). This has led to the transformation of higher education from an elite to a mass system. At a time when universities have been encouraged to extend their access to sections of the community that were under-represented in their populations, it has made sense to diversify the ways of undertaking university study. The virtualization of the university is one current version of this diversification. Yet it is one which has its limitations and also dangers. Although on-line courses might facilitate teaching much of the content in a degree course, it is difficult to see how more personal and social skills can be acquired on-line. Also, most high school leavers want to experience the university in some real way, if nothing else for its social life.

Work-based learning diversifies the study repertoire of the university in such a way, as Beckett argues in this volume, to affirm the real. More to the point, it also facilitates access in a different sense from the policies of inclusion that have seen minority groups admitted to the university. Access in this case refers to those at work, who are not disadvantaged in any orthodox sense but might be disadvantaged in terms of access to higher education by being at work. This might mean that they are not available for existing forms of study or, perhaps, are unable to meet the disciplinary demands of the university's knowledge structures. Work-based learning aims to mitigate both types of disadvantage. First, it recognizes that workplace experiences are potentially 'knowledgeable' ones, which contain countless opportunities for learning and development, the acquisition of expertise and so on. There is no reason to suppose that classrooms and lecture theatres are the only venues in which pedagogical experiences may be located. This means that individuals who are at work and who would not ordinarily have considered going to university are able to do so and, moreover, able to incorporate some aspects of their work experience as part of their study for a degree. Second, this makes it easier for those who have been out of the schooling system (often because they were excluded from it) for some time to re-embark on study through the 'academization' of what they know and learn at work.

The intensification of work makes time an increasingly precious commodity, but it also makes its 'academization' one of the more seductive features of work-based learning. Accrediting work as a legitimate area of learning means reduction of time on-campus; that already 'overtimed' students do not have to leave their workplace or their home for study. That many work-based students are on-line as part of their normal work means that they can also take advantage of the virtual learning opportunities through university study, including open learning.

In many ways work-based learning is adult education in a new guise, one that uses work as an alternative point of entry into the higher education system. As such, it presents an extremely grounded version of the postmodern challenge to higher education, which is leading to a more student- and less discipline-centred university. Indeed, this shift from the product to the consumer of educational services is symptomatic of the specialization of services in postmodern culture, which are increasingly mapped around the particular needs of the individual and designed accordingly. The diversification of university study has normalized the notion that there should be different modes and ways of obtaining a degree. The context of flexibility is a mark of the more student-centred university. This has meant attending to the needs of the consumers of education (who after all are paying for much of their higher education) in a more direct way.

The discourse of free choice that undergirds the marketization of higher education has also caused universities to use the market as the place to test the viability of their courses. This has also meant attempting to determine the logic of the consumer of education services, which is one reason (apart from the obvious pedagogic ones) why there has been an upsurge in interest in work-based learning. A degree gained in the workplace and for the workplace makes sense for the employee and the employer alike, who are also consumers, albeit in a more indirect way, of educational services. On both grounds, then, work-based learning satisfies the logic of consumption and production: it purports to produce a more productive worker and a more satisfied educational consumer.

In summary: work-based education is demand-driven, arising from a number of significant imperatives. These include:

- *students* who want recognition for what they have already learnt, would like to develop their emergent interests through study, and require more flexible modes of study to do so, including the opportunity to make work the major focus of their study;
- *employers* who want to harness more effectively what they see to be the considerable under-utilized potential of universities and to emphasize learning as part of new forms of productivity;
- *governments* which want to increase the measure of satisfaction among students and employers regarding the outcomes of higher education, and to shift costs away from the public purse;
- *universities* which want to be less dependent on the purse strings of government, to provide more relevant courses of learning for their students and to engage in partnerships with new sites of knowledge production.

The problems of implementing work-based learning

Although there is much that makes pedagogic sense in work-based learning, its implementation in universities has been fraught with academic and administrative difficulties. While universities have had their structures corporatized in the last decade or so, their administrative mechanisms are still highly bureaucratic and are not conducive to pedagogic approaches such as work-based learning which challenge established procedures in a variety of ways. Universities are, for example, extremely territorial in terms of their faculty operations and epistemological advantages. This means that they are often less favourably disposed to strategies of learning which challenge traditional areas of understanding and knowledge.

For example, at a quite mundane level, work-based learning often runs into problems with the university calendar which, unlike that of work, is fragmented into semesters and contains extended periods of time when, on the surface at least, no academic action takes place. Work-based learning is often incompatible with the time units of the university, and the way these are allocated. Of more significance is the fact that work-based problems and projects do not correspond to the disciplinary structures of the university or even the structures of practice associated with professional courses of learning. Learning at work is not necessarily labelled history or physics but can involve a variety of disciplinary or, even, no disciplinary experiences at all. The boundaries of knowledge involved, where they exist, are far more amorphous than those associated with the traditional university, which are often inflexible and not easily abandoned. When learning challenges are created from the exigencies of work there is often no pre-existing map that represents the territory of knowledge being explored.

Other problems are posed by learners who do not want to study what they have already learned. Therefore genuine recognition of prior learning is needed: not just a process of jumping through the criteria referencing of acquired competencies to demonstrate equivalence with particular university courses, but providing real credit for learning gained at work. This may not relate to an existing university course but it must relate to a programme of work-based learning. As we have already argued, work is a potentially rich environment of learning. But what in the world of work can really be equivalent to Psychology 1?

Work-based learners may not be very interested in ceasing their employment and studying full-time. This is understandable given that jobs may be few and far between; but they are also not even interested in weekly attendance at lectures in the part-time mode, which is increasingly impractical given the time-intensification of contemporary work.

Moreover, many work-based learners are not thrilled to study content packaged in a way to suit disciplinary or professional knowledge interests. Work-based learning challenges the existing categories of knowledge that underline the organization of content. These are inappropriate to the needs of the workplace. Thus universities need to offer courses that are not attendance-dependent, that measure course participation in some other way. Indeed, the whole notion of a course of study linked to semesters and pre-requisites is anachronistic, and out of step with the temporal revolution that has occurred in the post-Fordist workplace (Symes 1999). It is ironic that the regime of diversity and access has done little to change the basic parameters of university education, which are much the same, notwithstanding the addition of summer and winter schools, as they were two decades ago.

This also extends to assessment. Work-based learners typically want to be assessed in ways and on matters that are related to their work needs and interests; they want to demonstrate their competencies and have them recognized and legitimated in an academic form. Therefore new forms of assessment need to be devised that are tailored to these new work-related modes of learning but yet at the same time preserve the integrity of the university qualification.

There is thus much involved in work-based learning that challenges the whole framework of university learning. That these issues are not widely canvassed in relation to such learning is, perhaps, a reflection of the fact that the numbers of students involved are relatively small. Yet the questions that work-based learning poses could easily be transposed to the university as whole, which needs a thorough educational reappraisal, particularly as it faces competition from the virtual or corporate university and other providers of quality education. For example, we need to be able to determine what is essential about university education and what cannot be replicated elsewhere without compromise or degradation. Is it, as Barnett (1997) has recently suggested, the critical life? Unless universities can identify the characteristic features of their education that are not readily replicable by other institutions then there is no reason why they should continue to enjoy their autonomy or their control over the provision of higher learning.

These are not matters for armchair speculation. Already one Australian university has been approached by one of the largest engineering management organizations in the world and by one of Australia's largest multinational financial institutions to provide courses of learning for their organizations. The university could not accommodate the first and so the corporation has approached one of the oldest and most traditional universities that could do so. Plainly, such overtures are becoming more common and in the climate of fiscal restraint, universities cannot afford to reject them. Indeed, the trend towards work-based education is beginning to develop a momentum of its own and what appears to be a small experiment at the moment could very quickly grow into something much larger. The challenge then for work-based educators in the university is to develop a framework which neither compromises academic standards nor preserves them in such an inflexible way as to make the potential of work-based learning hard to realize.

Work-based learning in the best possible of worlds

As has been discussed, work-based learning is a radical approach to university education in which students undertake study for a degree or diploma through activities conducted primarily in their workplace and in topic areas which may have no immediate equivalence to university subjects. The learning opportunities found in work-based learning programmes are not contrived for study purposes, but arise from the normal work situation. The role of the university is to equip 'unqualified' individuals already in employment to develop lifelong learning skills, not through engagement with existing disciplines or programmes of study defined by university teachers, but through a curriculum which is customized for each individual and each context. This borrows its pedagogic form from the independent studies programmes that were prevalent in the 1970s at several UK polytechnics (Percy and Ramsden 1980; Stephenson 1988). What is significant, though, in these approaches to work-based learning is that work is not a discrete and limited element of study, as is familiar in sandwich courses and internships – the immediate ancestors of work-based learning. Neither are issues arising from problems encountered in work used merely as subjects of assignments as is common in many other forms of flexible provision which use learning contracts. In work-based learning degrees, work is quite literally the foundation of the curriculum (Boud 1998); the activity from which learning arises and by which learning is defined.

Work-based degrees have been embraced by employers across industry and business, the public and community sectors. The appreciation of their value, generally attributed to the fact that such learning advances the cause of their enterprises, is expressed to the extent of granting financial support to work-based students and entering into formal partnerships with universities. Nonetheless, the university continues to enforce its controls over work-based programmes through determining what is ultimately acceptable in the way of a work-based award. But this does not mean that the content of courses is ever fixed and absolute. Each work-based programme is designed to suit a particular work situation. Students are expected to take a more active role in negotiating their learning than is the case in conventional courses. This negotiation usually involves three parties: student, academic adviser and workplace supervisor, the last of whom provides specific guidance on learning how to learn and work-based learning skills. Through such negotiations entry requirements into courses can be adjusted according to the prior qualifications and current competencies of the students. Learning outcomes are performance-related, not time-related, which means students can exit courses whenever they have reached or demonstrated an appropriate level of learning.

In order to do this, it is necessary to have an explicit framework for assessment and the determination of what constitutes a given level of achievement, including generic learning outcomes. Thus in many respects work-based learning is not less regulated than a conventional university course; if anything, because it involves more variables and unexpected contingencies, it is subject to more regulation, more accountability and scrutiny (see Usher and Solomon 1999). Typically, in a work-based learning course there is an amalgam of the following educational elements:

- units from existing university courses and those specially designed for the programme;
- recognition of current competencies to establish how much needs to be studied for a particular course;
- accredited subjects offered by the employing or any other organization;
- work-based learning studies;
- a learning agreement or contract which specifies the above and ensures that the various partners involved adhere to it.

Throwing down the gauntlet to the mainstream university

Work-based learning, by its very nature, throws down the gauntlet to the mainstream university, many of whose pedagogic practices such as the lecture were originally developed during the Middle Ages. These practices served a culture in which books were few and far between, and have hardly altered much in spite of the fact that books are no longer a rare commodity. We have already mentioned that universities have undergone massification, and are no longer the elite institutions they were in quite the same sense of catering to the intellectual 'aristocracy' of the nation. This said, work-based learning is still undergoing evolution. Indeed, in many respects, work-based learning is still an idea in search of a practice, a pedagogy that is undergoing development as it accommodates itself to the exigencies of the workplace and the university. We want to discuss some of the ways in which this is occurring and how work-based learning is mounting a challenge to existing conceptions of university education. In doing so, we will focus on a limited number of examples which exemplify work-based learning at its most advanced. We will ignore those approaches which are essentially flexible versions of existing courses with a small component of workplace learning. Instead we will focus on some of the challenges to conventional university education which are posed by those forms of work-based learning in which the majority of study takes place at work and does not involve existing course units.

One of the more important of these challenges is that of acceptance, of establishing the credentials of work-based learning and gaining its legitimacy in the university setting. Unless a work-based award is in some sense equivalent to other qualifications and accepted as such, the reason for having the university involved lessens, and other institutions will burgeon to take its place without, perhaps, its ethical and critical concerns. This, then, raises the question, what is required for any programme of work-based study to meet the requirements of a university degree? Ultimately, this matter is linked to the question of assessment. Obviously, in a programme which is solidly based in work, assessment needs to be related to practice. Competence frameworks, though far from infallible, are well developed in terms of assessing capacity in professional domains (Gonczi 1994), and many universities experimenting with work-based learning have turned to them.

A more holistic approach to assessment is that developed by Richard Winter at the Anglia Polytechnic University in Cambridge. Originally established for work-based learning in social work, the generic features of this approach enabled it to be translated with relative ease into an automotive engineering course used with the Ford Motor Company. The approach adopted a set of seven Core Assessment Criteria that are in effect dimensions of a model of professionalism. The criteria involved included effective grasp of professional knowledge, intellectual rigour and flexibility and continuous professional learning. These were then matched against field-specific Elements of Competence for each course module whose achievement had to be demonstrated (Winter and Maisch 1996).

Work-based learning and the new knowledge production

One of the ongoing problems relating to work-based learning concerns the matter of proprietorship and ownership. In the traditional university courses were owned by the academy, which defined the parameters of assessment, determined who taught the course, and in what manner and with what types of course materials. In work-based learning these issues are more amorphous, and therefore more subject to contestation and debate.

In fact, many of these concerns are not peculiar to work-based learning courses. Earlier it was argued that the emergence of such learning epitomized many of the issues and problems experienced by the university at all levels of its operation. The mechanisms of knowledge production, which are undergoing radical change, are just another of them. Knowledge production, for example, is obviously no longer monopolized by the university but is being produced in other sites such as corporations and by industry in general. In the context of product and service development characteristic of the post-Fordist economy, knowledge and information have become increasingly valued commodities. They have become valued assets in most workplaces, not just academic ones. Recognition of the changing nature of knowledge production has been the subject of much recent commentary (e.g. Gibbons *et al.* 1994), and is discussed more fully by other contributors to this volume.

Gibbons and his 'globalized' team of academics have argued that knowledge practices are increasingly transdisciplinary ones, which have broken out of the boundaries of the academy and are employed across a variety of social and economic contexts. For example, much of this new knowledge production occurs in think tanks such as the Friends of the Earth or the Evatt Foundation. They argue too that the scientific frameworks of knowledge, which gave rise to the disciplinary categories of the modern university, are also fast being abandoned. They are being replaced by more permeable boundaries of knowledge production, in which teams of experts representing a variety of disciplinary backgrounds pool their wisdom and insights. This is because many of the problems that society now confronts are complex, and involve empirical as well as ethical issues. Gene technology is a case in point and is typical of the new epistemological conditions, which make demands on molecular biologists and ethicists who must balance the pursuit of biological understanding against the possible abuse of such understanding. Hence, Gibbons *et al.* (1994) differentiate two modes of knowledge production. The first they call Mode 1, which they typify as disciplinary knowledge and which is culturally concentrated and institutionalized within universities. The second they call Mode 2, which is knowledge that is useful to governments, industry and society. They see it as involving fields of understanding rather than disciplines. It is typically communicated through professional networks rather than academic journals and monographs. This means that it is more accessible and socially distributed than Mode 1 knowledge.

In terms of this differentiation, work-based learning exemplifies Mode 2 type knowledge. It acknowledges that the workplace is a site of knowledge production – knowledge that is difficult to compartmentalize in terms of the traditional epistemological frameworks associated with university study. This is one of the reasons that it poses so many difficulties for the university which remains, for the most part, a Mode 1 construct, still organized along disciplinary lines and following the paradigm of research production displaying Newtonian features. Moreover, academics for the most part – although this is beginning to change – are socialized into Mode 1 forms of knowledge production, and much of their academic identity is tethered to maintaining the values and protocols of such production. Hence, many academics remain rightfully perturbed about the directions of the academy as it embarks on mercantile ventures, sometimes at the expense of academic freedom (Buchbinder 1993).

Academic identity is particularly threatened by work-based learning, when academic knowledge has to be tested in the workplace and where it can be made to look vulnerable and non-viable. In such a scenario, academics find their academic and professional identities challenged. Their perceived capacity to be useful is reduced when supervising a work-based student who is often more in command of the knowledge environment of work than an academic can ever hope to be. The new work situation, which has been reconfigured in ways which the academy has yet to come to terms with, is much less subject to control than the professional or disciplinary context. Work-based learning challenges the traditional codifications of knowledge: for working knowledge is often unbounded, unruly, and much less subject to disciplinary control (an issue explored by Solomon and McIntyre in Chapter 8). This means that those who advise work-based learning studies have to have more affinity with the 'practising epistemologists', that emergent category of academics who are more 'in-the-world and of-the-world' than the Mode 1 academics who have tended to pride themselves on 'being out-of-the-world' (Barnett 1997: 148).

The challenge to identity is not just that of the teacher. Learning in a work context takes the learning interactions from the private to the semi-public domain. No longer is it something that is apart from normal work interactions, but it is a potentially significant part of them. Therein lies the potential for examining and questioning relationships and assumptions about work. There is also the question of who are one's peers. There is probably a need to establish peer learners in a work context as a necessary part of work-based learning rather than assume that learning at work can just be an add-on and not be disruptive.

The challenge to academic identity can easily become a challenge to academic professionalism. Some of the people with whom we have spoken have been far more relaxed than we would be about the supervision of learning projects being undertaken by staff not employed as academic staff and in some cases not qualified to do so. We do not mean here industrial staff with technical expertise – these certainly have a role – but non-professional and often part-time employees of universities. If we are demanding greater professionalism of academics in teaching and learning for conventional courses – which is certainly required – we should demand at least as much from those who have not even been socialized into their role of fostering learning.

If work becomes the curriculum, how do we think about it and negotiate our way through it? What must necessarily be included, what is of lesser significance? Does it involve workplace research or workplace learning? How do we ensure that students are equipped as broad, lifelong learners when the curriculum is potentially narrow? In sorting through these dilemmas the academy needs to maintain control over the educational qualities of work-based learning otherwise it risks becoming a debasement of the educational process, conducted on the job with only a minimal contribution from the university.

Although work-based learning offers opportunities for those who, for various reasons, might not otherwise be able to take advantage of tertiary study, and thus assists to improve the inclusiveness of the university, there is a need to be cautious about some aspects of its provision. One area of caution relates to the knowledge frameworks within which work-based learning are located. Without careful consideration this can tend towards a narrowness of specialization that flies in the face of the traditional function of the university, which is to expose individuals to an environment in which many disciplinary 'conversations' are taking place (see Oakeshott 1967). Universities are sites where a number of communities of inquiry exist alongside one another. Work-based learning can be remote from these communities and through its focus on individualized and localized inquiry can create the impression that knowledge is a thoroughly individualistic creation with only local and very specific features. Yet more than ever enquiry, as was argued earlier, is trandisciplinary and involves conversations between different specialists and communities. Universities have always been places where the aspiration was that knowledge experiences were generalizeable rather than specific, which is where most of their value has been derived: that the skills acquired in doing philosophy and history, for example, can be transferred to other domains. Although the issue of transferability is a hotly debated one, there are still good reasons for ensuring that students encounter a variety of ways of understanding which can help them interrogate their work experience. For example, work-based learning may include, if appropriate, general studies of the contemporary workplace as an increasingly complex organizational unit, involving organizational theory, equity and access policies, ethical decision making, health and safety issues. Alternatively, work-based learning studies may necessarily need to encompass studies of multiple sites of activity using different perspectives if the traps of the individual and the local are to be avoided.

There is much more to work than simply being productive, and work-based learning, if it is to be authentic and useful in the fullest sense, must encompass these areas. One of the major pitfalls for work-based learning is that it could degenerate into short-term training or the fixing of immediate problems. This means that the skills that are acquired in a work-based degree are so narrow that once the job associated with them disappears – and we live in fast-changing working environment – the student will have to embark on another work-based degree, and so on, ad nauseam.

Another is that employers, the partners in work-based learning, start to stake a more manifest interest in the learning of the university in such a way that its benefits are directed entirely at the workplace. Work-based learning thereby becomes a way of underwriting the efficiency and productivity of the workplace, which reduces the cogency of courses of learning that do not obviously do this or that, worse still, begin to raise difficult questions about the practices inherent in a workplace. Here, then, matters of academic freedom are being compromised, and the whole condition of epistemological conduct, which requires openness and untrammelled access to sensitive issues, is being threatened. This is because the value systems of the academy and workplaces are not always in accord. Here again the university needs to operate with responsibility to ensure that work-based learning takes place in workplaces that are suitable for learning and contain appropriate ethical measures designed to protect the worker/student from exploitation. Universities need to vet partnerships carefully to ensure that minimum standards can be met in fostering learning in the workplace and to ensure that partners are aware of the potential challenges of work-based learning studies in the organization.

The way forward

In this chapter we have argued that work-based learning poses challenges for contemporary universities – challenges which they have no option but to embrace if they are not to decline in influence. Work-based learning is perhaps a greater test than that of reduced funding because it touches the very heart of what a university represents.

Innovation in work-based learning involves balancing the often conflicting forces involved in its realization. So far educational strategies have been assembled from well-tried approaches in the adult learning area (recognition of prior learning, negotiated learning contracts, action learning sets and so on), and have built on the practices in independent studies. But the major challenge involves appreciating the constraints and limitations of these approaches and making them work in a context where there is considerably less direct influence over learning than exists in a conventional university course. It is likely that new pedagogic innovations will also be required to deal with the epistemological conundrums of Mode 2 knowledge and new ways of thinking about 'criticality' developed in the context of work.

Work-based learning puts an important new focus on learning as distinct from teaching: it is called work-based learning *not* teaching. Ultimately, all that counts is the learning outcome. How this is achieved is not important, and protecting cherished disciplinary territory is in these circumstances now less meaningful. This offers the potential for new links between teaching and research through the common ground of learning. Courses are becoming more like investigations and the activities in which staff engage are more like research supervision. This is indeed one of the headaches for cost-conscious university administrators: work-based learning is expensive in terms of the cost of its supervisory arrangements. Unless care is taken in rethinking the role of the academic adviser, making good use of workplace supervision and peer learning, the costs can rival those of supervising research students. Work-based learning is certainly not, as many administrators and employers often see it, a way of realizing human capital on the cheap!

An obvious trap is applying existing pedagogies to the supervision of work-based learning. It is possible that some of the ways of approaching research students might be translated unthinkingly to work-based students, pushing work-based learning in the direction of work-based research. In itself this is no bad thing and research courses of this kind are valid in their own terms. However, the full range and potential of work-based learning may be lost if the research model becomes too dominant.

While some of the dilemmas and challenges are apparent, it is not clear what the political and social circumstances will be in which we respond to them. Will the momentum towards work-based learning be so great that there will be an unholy rush to offer such programmes? As with on-line learning (the current 'unholy rush'), this could result in programmes which are poorly conceptualized and formulated by staff who have not faced the educational challenges which are presented. The alternative is to be more cautious in the development of work-based programmes and to take time and effort to produce frameworks and processes of learning that have real cogency and potency and lead to good-quality programmes of which we can be proud. Anything less and we risk abandoning the visionary aspects of work-based learning to the academic opportunists.

References

ANTA (1999) *The ARF at Work. Australian Recognition Framework.* Brisbane: Australian National Training Authority.

Barnett, R. (1997) *Higher Education: A Critical Business.* Buckingham: SRHE/Open University Press.

Boud, D. (1998) How can university work-based courses contribute to lifelong learning?, in J. Holford, P. Jarvis and C. Griffin (eds) *International Perspectives on Lifelong Learning.* London: Kogan Page.

Boud, D. and Solomon, N. (forthcoming) *Work-based Learning: A New Higher Education?* Buckingham: SRHE/Open University Press.

Buchbinder, H. (1993) The market oriented university and the changing role of knowledge. *Higher Education,* 26: 331–47.

Dewey, J. (1900) *School and Society.* Chicago, IL: University of Chicago Press.

Garrick, J. (1998) *Informal Learning in the Workplace: Unmasking Human Resource Development.* London: Routledge.

Gibbons, M., Limoges, C., Nowotny, H. *et al.* (1994) *The New Production of Knowledge: The Dynamics of Science and Research in Contemporary societies.* London: Sage.

Gonczi, A. (1994) Competency-based assessment in Australia. *Assessment in Education*, 1 (1), 27–44.

Oakeshott, M. (1967) *Rationalism in Politics and Other Essays*. London: Methuen.

Percy, K. and Ramsden, P. (1980) *Independent Study: Two Examples from English Higher Education*. Guildford: SRHE.

Robins, K. and Webster, F. (1999) *Times of the Techno-culture: From the Information Society to the Virtual Life*. London: Routledge.

Sennett, R. (1999) *The Corrosion of Character. The Personal Consequences of Work in the New Capitalism*. New York, NY: Norton.

Stephenson, J. (1988) The experience of independent study at North East London Polytechnic, in D. Boud (ed.) *Developing Student Autonomy in Learning*. London: Kogan Page.

Symes, C. (1998) Education for sale: a semiotic analysis of school prospectuses and other forms of educational marketing. *Australian Journal of Education*, 42 (2), 133–52.

Symes, C. (1999) Chronicles of labour. A discourse analysis of diaries. *Time and Society*, 8 (2), 357–80.

Taylor, S. and Henry, M. (1994) Equity and the new post-compulsory education and training policies in Australia: a progressive or regressive agenda? *Journal of Education Policy*, 9 (2), 105–27.

Usher, R. and Solomon, N. (1999) Experiential learning and the shaping of subjectivity in the workplace. *Studies in the Education of Adults*, 31 (2), 155–63.

Winter, R. and Maisch, M. (1996) *Professional Competence and Higher Education: The ASSET Programme*. London: Falmer Press.

3

'Real World' Education: The Vocationalization of the University

Colin Symes

... (in) education geometry and poetry are as essential as turning laths.
(Whitehead [1932] 1962)

Trading places

The university is at a watershed point in its long history. In the century that has seen this oldest of institutions become established throughout the world and accessible to a larger proportion of the population than ever, the university now faces unprecedented changes. Most of these changes stem from the fact that governments, with some considerable pressure from international bodies such as the OECD (Bengtisson 1993), have sought to reduce the economic burden of expensive educational institutions. To compensate for the savage cuts that have been incurred, universities have adopted the behaviour of corporations, streamlining their operations and supplementing their contracting budgets with income from whatever sources seem agreeable to underwrite their operations and activities. These have included fee-paying students, the export of education, partial privatization, the pursuit of lucrative consultancies, applied research, endowments, sponsored chairs and so on. Its capacity to generate income is increasingly the criterion by which an activity is valued or not by the academy (Peters 1992; Marginson 1997; Slaughter and Leslie 1997; Symes 1999). The rules of market in conjunction with an ethos of pragmatism have produced a context for university education that is ever more businesslike, and which the recent fiscal stringency and press for deregulation has compounded. Nor is such deregulatory pressure likely to decline; if anything, it will become stronger as local universities face competition from their counterparts overseas, and from private and internet providers.

Surprisingly, these changes have not received the attention they deserve (Smyth 1995). Their compound impact, which might take some decades to fully 'express' itself, is likely to result in a very different kind of university from that of the present. Though it might be difficult to apprehend the nature of this putative university, it is, arguably, already immanent in the ethos of the millennial university. It has been suggested, for instance, that the Humboldtian idea of the university, that of an institution charged with identifying and preserving a nation's culture, has been superseded by the university as corporation, whose dominant concern is excellence (Readings 1996). Yet this is a somewhat monolithic reading, obscuring other discourses that the university, in responding to market forces, has incorporated. It is also a reading that is over-generalized, failing to account for the fact that, even in this era of globalization, universities retain their own national characteristics. The university of North America for example (which owes much to the German model) has always been a far more pragmatic enterprise than its British and Australian counterparts (Ashby 1974). Yet this is now beginning to change and universities across the globe are becoming far more diversified institutions, taking on functions once regarded as antipathetic to the university endeavour. Of these, that of vocationlization is paramount and seems likely to emerge as a dominant trait of the university in the early part of this century.

In this chapter I shall argue that this vocationalization is not incompatible with the idea of a university, as some thinkers have argued; nor has it ever been. What is distinctive about its most recent incarnation is the context in which it has arisen and which is marked by a number of distinctive features. These include the emergence of a new order of work associated with a smarter labour force; policy settings with a strong human capital accent; and more student-centred systems of education that are characterized by flexibility, responsiveness to equity considerations and so forth. It is also associated with the ascendancy of working knowledge, knowledge that bridges the divide between theory and practice, and which has the potential to produce a significant reconciliation between those most antithetical forms of education, the liberal and vocational (Silver and Brennan 1988; Beck 1990; Lewis 1994; Wirth 1994). While these developments continue to attract criticism on the grounds that they could lead to the complete collapse of academic values in the university, it is plain that they also afford the opportunity for the university to be recreated into a more egalitarian and relevant institution.

Ivory or concrete towers: the discourse architecture of education

The discourses framing the formation of the university have always been in flux, subject to argument and counter-argument, particularly at times of change. The present is, arguably, one such period, when the nineteenth-century university, the 'cultured' university, which had superseded the 'theocentric' university, has been undergoing 'vocationalization', and is being turned into an institution whose primary goals are economic, servicing the knowledge-based industries. The matter of whether university education should be subsumed to economic interest is a theme around which much educational thought continues to oscillate (Minogue 1973). In fact, it is another one of those footnotes to Plato, of which the history of Western philosophy, including that of education, it has been said, is a series. Plato's aversion to excessive educational instrumentalism was, in the main, epistemological and grounded in the belief that true knowledge can only be achieved through transcending the mundane. Vocational education, because it deals with managing the mundane, thwarts the true purpose of education, which involves placing individuals in touch with timeless and incorrigible values; it is therefore to be disparaged.

The emphasis on the incorrigible, which lies at the heart of liberal education, has meant that many education systems have been circumspect about specific training[1] and have focused their attentions instead on the 'accumulated treasure of the thoughts of mankind' (Mill 1971). Such thinking has resulted in a long-term stigmatization (only now being thwarted) of vocational education, which has held low status in most education systems at all levels of their expression.

The origins of the antithesis between vocational and liberal education are also classical and can be traced to Aristotle's belief that the leisure classes should be free to pursue activities of the mind without being hampered by the exigencies of the mundane. In modern societies this legacy persists in their social arrangements, which hinge on the differential distribution of cultural capital in relation to the allotment of occupational roles (Bourdieu and Passeron 1977). This is turn reflects education's broader function in the reproduction of an unequal social and cultural order, and which the rigorous defence of a liberal education has only served to consecrate. For the mechanics of credentialism, under the smokescreen of meritocracy, have operated in such a way as to protect the cultural codes of the middle classes and ensure that access to them remains restricted (Brown and Scase 1994). At the same time, they have also served to hide the degree to which education has always played a role in the preparation for work: assisting young people to desire a 'job' in accordance with their capacities and to comply with its moral protocols.

The general arguments[2] appertaining to vocational as opposed to an allegedly more educative form of education are important antecedent discourses, framing the polemics of higher education. They are simple to summarize and constitute four distinctive narrative streams in the history of educational thought, sometimes imbricated, sometimes at loggerheads with one another and, at others, coming together.

- The first is that educational institutions ought to be quarantined from instrumentalism and provide courses of learning that are intrinsically worthwhile, done for their own sake, and not shackled to the imperatives of the workplace. The core of this discourse is the liberal approach to education, which centres on the cultivation of the self within a framework of high moral and ethical ideals. The most celebrated modern apologist of this view, at least in the context of the university, was Cardinal Newman ([1852] 1947), who regarded the 'professionalization' of the university as a distortion of its true purpose and mission.[3] Universities existed to cultivate a sense of mind and intellectual grace that was marked by moderation, calmness and freedom; they were to teach a way of life rather than a way of learning, and were to encourage an appreciation of knowledge for what it is rather than what it does. They were to be places that provided a 'moratorium from practical life', places that enabled individuals to focus on the inward rather than outward, and to enlarge their 'moral imaginations'. This occurred through general rather than specific studies (Arcilla 1995). The cultivation of personality rather than utility was the overriding goal then of education. Indeed, Newman's model, which is a Cartesian one, consciously sets the liberal arts apart from 'servile work', which he defined as activities in which the mind plays next to no part. This model also excludes commercial education, not because it lacks mental attributes, but through its 'failure to stand on its own pretentions' (Newman [1852] 1947: 95–6).

- The second discourse removes the moratorium on the practical, and places utility ahead of moral enrichment as the principal goal of education. In this model of education performativity assumes far more importance than reflexivity. Educational instrumentalism is to be applauded, not derided. The idea that education should be useful has its provenance in the Scottish Enlightenment. It was espoused by, among others, John Locke who, in direct antithesis to Newman, placed utility ahead of that which was 'intrinsically worthwhile' and argued that the lath, in his experience, was a far more natural element of education than geometry or poetry. The most radical expression of this idea that education should be useful is human capital theory whose underlying assumption is that investment in education is a predicate of economic expansion and development (Schultz 1961). The nation that squanders its human resources and fails to exploit its intellectual talent pool will founder in the global economy. At least, this has been the prevailing view among international policy makers for the last decade or so. Education thus becomes a mechanism for marshalling the mental energies of populations, for supplying the intellectual capital required by modern industry and commerce, and without which productivity of the contemporary economy cannot be sustained.
- The third discourse accepts that a nexus between education and work is an inevitable part of any economy, and that schools and universities have always facilitated the reproduction of labour power (see Braverman 1974; Bowles and Gintis 1976). It also accepts that work is an inevitable part of the human condition, and that due recognition of this fact could ameliorate pedagogy. From this discourse springs the idea that labour should be brought into accommodation with education through making work a pivotal part of the curriculum as in those socialist approaches to education that originated at New Lanark with Owen (Castles and Wüstenberg 1979). This discourse is also underpinned with a radical

epistemology, one that links theory to practice, and that overturns the distinction between mental and servile labour. Recent attempts to instigate more work-oriented approaches to education (such as those which are the subject of this volume) but without an enlightened approach to the political economy of work have led some to champion approaches that stress the critical (see Kincheloe 1995). Their fears that an unfettered instrumentalism can, if not contained, be counter-educational have their roots in John Dewey. He argued that there was much to be gained in giving an occupational basis to the curriculum – for work, in Dewey's view, provided the proper foundations of civilization. However, Dewey was careful to distinguish being educated about work from being educated to work. The former involved the cultivation of an 'industrial intelligence' much broader in character than the 'technical efficiency' associated with the latter. This was not only supposed to equip workers with the powers of 'readaptation' necessary to stop them being the blind and willing participants of capital accumulation but was also part of a programme of general and democratic social reconstruction (Dewey [1916] 1966, 1997) which education had previously retarded. This was because its foundations were built on aesthetic and literary values – mainly Whitehead's geometry and poetry – that were fundamentally alien to a tradition of popular education.

• The fourth discourse recognizes that the only adequate system of education is a synthesis of the first and second discourses, a conjunction between vocational and liberal elements. In effect, it rejects any hierarchy of knowledge based around professions and occupations, and argues for a 'liberal vocationalism' (Silver and Brennan 1988). Philosophically, it opposes the implied 'separation of powers' as groundless: there is no practical life that does not also contain liberal elements. Vocational education is not therefore an oxymoron – a contradiction in terms. One of the most fervent advocates of this view was A. N. Whitehead (1962) who railed against any education that did not balance the technical with the liberal, and that emphasized contemplation at the expense of the action or the reverse. Too much of the one or the other, in Whitehead's view, resulted in the attenuated development of human beings. To offset this likelihood, he argued for an approach to education in which the domain of performance is tempered by that of reflection and vice versa, where 'technique' and 'vision' inform each another.

Knowledge for what it is

In reality these benchmark discourses are more interlocking than is implied in the above distinctions, since not even the most diehard advocate of liberal education could suggest that it is not a preparation for some form of educational 'after-life'. Thus even at the earliest phase of their development, the theocentric, when universities were dominated by scholasticism, their students were much sought after as potential officers of the state and members

of the clergy. It was they who carried forth the principles of Roman juris-
prudence, which have provided the governing framework of contemporary
civic life (Rashdall [1895] 1936).

Even though a liberal education was closely linked to the cultural needs
of a leisured class which, by dint of its social rank and pecuniary means, was
liberated from the need to obtain employment, in reality, many members
of this class did so (Veblen [1925] 1970). This was certainly the case during
the nineteenth century, when a university education was a vehicle for secur-
ing a position in civil administration or the church. A university education
provided a particular kind of self-formation – in German terms, a *bildung* –
upon which the workings of the church and government were said to be
dependent. In this respect then, though the education involved exhibited
an aversion to working knowledge, its outcomes were assuredly 'instrumental'. In truth though, the instrumentality involved was an indirect one,
more related to the status that attendance at a university conferred on the
individual than the learning that was acquired. For universities were not
places where 'really useful knowledge' was available. Their syllabuses were
for the most part grounded in the classics, which it was believed had the
power to cultivate inner virtue far in excess of more contemporary studies.
This stalled the introduction of such domains as science and technology into
universities until the latter parts of the nineteenth century. The mystique of
liberal education held such a strong attraction that it overwhelmed those
who embarked on its deconstruction (Ashby 1966).

In the post-war period when the university has become more egalitarian
and its demographic profile more diverse, the champions of a liberal approach have had to contend with a variety of enemies. First, there were
those who held that the elements of a liberal education were anachronistic
and were tangential to the needs of the modern world. Nonetheless, its
advocates continued to argue that the elements of a liberal education were
timeless, that they maintained their value in the face of an ever-changing
culture and provided an intellectual grounding transferable to many contexts and types of employment. The outcomes of a liberal education (and
this idea was foreshadowed in Newman's aguments) were portable across
many domains of life, not just work: it was therefore the most suitable form
of vocational preparation and was instrumental precisely because it was so
liberal (Lewis 1994). It was also argued that the subject matter of a liberal
curriculum was more generic than an instrumental one, and that the cognitive and thinking skills involved, such as critical reasoning, were transferable
across a variety of disparate fields, occupations and professions. It therefore
retained its appositeness at a time when other knowledges, particularly of a
more specialized kind, soon lost their utility. Liberal education had a use
value with more shelf-life than more specialized forms of knowledge, and
could survive a bout of unemployment (Filmer 1997). Its staunchest apologists also argued that the values epistomized in a liberal education formed
the bedrock of Western civilization, outlasting more transient and ephemeral
expressions of culture.

A more significant threat to liberal education has been posed by post-structuralists and postmodernists, and has arisen, in part, from the very diversification of the university constituency that occurred in the 'wake' of the upheavals of 1968 and which drew attention to the 'exclusivity' of such education. At the heart of their critique of liberalism is an antagonism towards Western rationality and high culture and its alleged ameliorating powers. For many of the same reasons, they have also challenged the 'universalism' of the university's knowledge base and argued that Mill's 'accumulated treasures' had a rather narrow demographic representation, which overlooked the treasures of many minority voices, principally women, blacks, ethnic minorities and gays (Martin 1993).

In response to the attenuated version of culture offered in the name of liberal education, there has been a general 'de-canonization' of the university curriculum. This has occurred particularly in the humanities and the social sciences where there has been an abandonment of a fixed-state curriculum and the emergence of transdisciplinary fields such as cultural studies.[4] These have challenged the idea that the 'knowledge most worth having' is necessarily that which has stood the test of time; on the contrary, cultural studies has focused on the most timely, on the nature of the most here and now: sport, music, advertising, fashion.[5] It has also led to the development of more inclusive areas of knowledge, which have given representation to the cultures of minority groups in the university. These revampings of the humanities and social sciences to accommodate new areas of interest and new constituencies has also been accompanied by attempts to analyse their 'applied' nature and to demonstrate their use-value, to exemplify the degree to which Discourse 1 had Discourse 2 utility. This was undertaken partly as a riposte to the rampant instrumentalism unleashed by new policies of higher education in the 1980s, which threatened the tenability of the humanities. It has been suggested, for example, that the self-formation associated with the humanities is not empty of utility but provides a range of capacities useful in the public sector where the majority of graduates from the humanities have found employment (Hunter 1991). It has also been argued that the university curriculum, particularly in the humanities and social sciences, has the potential to generate lifestyle changes and 'identity reconstruction' (Brown and Scase 1997). The same authors also aver that the newly constituted workplace, with its less authoritarian organizational ethos, requires a more charismatic personality than that of its predecessors. This is one in which the type of 'cultural capital' associated with the humanities and arts is a dominant element (Brown and Scase 1994).

Knowledge for what it does

The ascendancy of a discourse of instrumentalism (Discourse 2) has much to do with the reformation of higher education that has occurred in the UK, Australia and Canada in the last two decades. The urgency of this reformation has been driven by the need for micro-economic reform, and the recognition that continued national prosperity has become dependent upon producing clever societies through their educational systems. The current 'industrial revolution' (the third in our history, it has been argued) is more dependent on knowledge than previous revolutions that were energy-dependent and relied on muscle rather than brain (Scott 1995). The first industrial revolution left the universities relatively unscathed, whereas the second led to the creation of technologically specialized universities that soon developed Oxbridge aspirations (Lowe 1990). In the third revolution the intellectual ethos of the university is being made to match economic realities and to contribute in a more concerted way to the knowledge economy. This has led governments to insist that educational outcomes are linked to economic productivity and to triumvirates being established between employment, training and education (Birch and Smart 1989) – this in spite of the fact that the efficacy of such has yet to be demonstrated.[6]

Significantly, the policies associated with this trend have called for a more rounded curriculum, drawing on most parts of the knowledge spectrum: from the vocational through to the liberal. They have also emphasized targeting areas of more immediate economic potential such as information technology and trading languages. This has caused universities to change their epistemological orientation, to develop stronger links with business and industry and to integrate their research endeavours with them (see Kemp 1999). Another aspect of their changing ethos is the recognition that universities can assist to regenerate the economic activity of depressed regions, and attract new industry and employment to their communities (Robertson 1999). These imperatives have lessened the hegemony of the Newtonian research paradigm and led to modes of knowing in which there is a more dynamic interplay between discovery, use and application (Gibbons et al. 1994; Turpin and Garrett-Jones 1997).[7] As the pursuit of instrumental knowledge becomes more acceptable in the university, this is leading to educational approaches emphasizing use-value.

The unification of the practical and theoretical parts of the higher education sector has led to the emergence of faculties and fields of knowing formerly outside the ambit of higher education such as catering, nursing, hotel management, health, tourism and leisure studies. The polytechnics and their Australian equivalents, the institutes of technology, which pioneered the epistemological emphases that have emerged in the universities of the nineties, were radical creations in their day, established as alternatives to the universities. They were to be less exclusive institutions, which placed teaching and knowledge in the service of industry and the professions, and which were intended to be more responsive to the economy and social needs of the nation; they were to be places of action rather than contemplation. Moreover, the processes of 'academic creep' which in the past had seen similar types of tertiary institutions become universities were to be prevented (Davies 1989; Pratt 1997). Governments in the 1980s, keen to make education work for the economy, favoured the polytechnic form of higher education far more than they did the university, which in a climate of neo-liberalist parsimony was also perceived to be an expensive enterprise, not offering value for money.[8] As a result, universities were coerced into renouncing their exclusivity and developing a real world focus, in which working knowledge dominated.

The evidence of this move is everywhere to behold. It exists, for example, in awards and degrees with a more utilitarian focus, in the expansion of professional doctorates and masters, in the emergence of work-based degrees with a strong in situ component. Even Sydney's new Bachelor of Liberal Studies, a seemingly incongruous venture in an increasingly vocationalized university sector, is framed in such a way as to accentuate its use-value, promising the communication skills and critical reasoning that are essential in the public service and the knowledge economy. And even before these developments occurred, certain universities prided themselves on the fact that a large proportion of their lecturing staff were part-time, were part of the actual labour force and therefore were in a better position to highlight the practical side of university study. In fact there has been a 'de-liberalization' of universities, and the moratorium on the practical life has been lifted.

Departments, such as classics, which epitomized the 'cultured' university are facing closure, unable to sustain their student numbers in the face of competition from more 'down-to-earth' parts of the academy. For the growth area over the last two decades has been in vocational degrees, in occupationally specific studies, particularly in business and health services. And disciplines such as sociology or history that were once studied in their own right have been assimilated into these applied areas of study, as part, say, of a nursing or leisure studies degree. In fact, the emergence of a more vocationalized university challenges the traditional identity of the academic committed to teaching and research who now competes with the practitioner academic, more committed to her or his profession and the amelioration of its practice than a community of inquiry (Barnett 1997).

The rise of double degrees, which multiply the employment options of students, are another symptom of the spread of vocationalism. In fact these changes to the epistemological profile of the university are at their most manifest in the new nomenclature of undergraduate degrees. The BA and BSc still dominate this nomenclature, especially in the older universities, but it also now encompasses a range of degrees that epitomize the shift to more instrumental patterns of learning. These include a BPopMus (Bachelor of Popular Music) and BExSc (Bachelor of Exercise Science) (from Griffith, a university that seems to specialize in such 'new' degrees) to BRadMedImag (Bachelor of Radiography and Medical Imagery) and BSp&ResRec (Bachelor of Sport and Resource Recreation) (from Monash).

At the same time, the policy articulation associated with higher education has emphasized convergency: the development of outcomes in which the general and the practical are coalesced or that stress more utilitarian outcomes – and that are symptomatic of the shift to working knowlege. The most recent inquiry into Australian higher education (West 1998) provides policy reinforcement for universities pursuing closer alliances with industry and business, as do its counterparts in the UK such as Dearing (1997) and Fryer (1997). The policy discourses are suggestive of the degree to which universities and industries now have interests in common and that arrangements which favour various forms of reciprocity between them, such as training compacts, are to be commended. The Dearing Report, for example, suggests that knowledge will be a crucial driver of the 'new economic order', providing the 'competitive edge of the advanced economies'. The policy ambit of these reports, though broad, is one that in the end is dominated by economic imperatives, and by the idea that in the post-Fordist enterprise, knowledge is an important catalyst of economic growth.

These moves toward a more concerted form of university vocationalism have not been received with unanimous acclamation. It is suggested that it is another reminder of the degree to which the university is a site of commodity production, as a place where the logic of performativity has come to rule almost unimpeded. Such moves, unless contained, will compromise the university ideal as an institution outside the corrupting realm of the economy (Lyotard 1984).

Yet this is an overly romantic view of higher education. It assumes that there was some golden age when universities were totally autonomous, free to do their own thing, without intervention from any state or church authority. This would appear to be a convenient fiction, more ideological than actual, designed to exempt the university from the processes of modernization (Winter 1995). It is also a view that obscures the degree to which universities and colleges were always involved, as was argued earlier, in a certain amount of 'on-the-job' education such as sandwich courses. For example, many faculties, particularly those with strong vocational links such as education and medicine, have always included opportunities for their students to participate in practicums and field work. But aside from these opportunities, a large percentage of students have always combined their studies with work – albeit, in many cases, work of a casual kind, remote from their academic studies; or have been engaged, while in full-time work, in upgrading their qualifications. The idea, then, that university study should or could be insulated from the world of work is difficult to sustain. The genealogy of work-based education, the current jargon for this involvement, is a complex one, with many branches to it. Its most recent manifestation differs from its previous expression only insofar as current policy encourages its realization and the arrangements with participant organizations are subject to increased formalization and scrutiny (Foster and Stephenson 1998).

Knowledge at work

In the context of changing workplaces, the university has become important to the information and knowledge-based industries that are now a hallmark of the post-Fordist economy. In this economy, knowledge is an increasingly valued commodity needed for innovation and production; but it is also one over which universities have ceased to have a monopoly as the numbers of quasi-research organizations and think tanks has grown, fostered by the development of 'contract government' (Dominelli and Hoogvelt 1996). Emerging types of work dependent on symbolic and numeric analysis, on the knowledge acquisition powers of workers, are also symptoms of this trend and have expanded the need for a more educated labour force, more comfortable with processing information than materials (Hague 1991; Reich 1991; Drucker 1993; Burton-Jones 1999). The contraction of manufacturing industry and agriculture has accelerated the need for governments to find ways of diversifying their economic base around knowledge industries. It is significant, too, that corporate culture has embraced the idea that learning is a significant factor in business efficiency and competitiveness (Garwin 1993). The 'wandering scholars' of the modern world are, in fact, the business 'seminarians' who travel the world offering high-priced lectures on improving business management. The culture of training is a feature of the reorganization of capitalism, which has given new meaning to the corporatization of learning and education. However, as more organizations embrace the 'training' ethos, it seems likely that they will want to challenge the monopolies that universities have over credentials and force governments to deregulate the system of educational awards.

In facing this reality, some universities have become more flexible providers. This has meant being able to take their knowledge to the context of the learner, to customize it in such a way that it suits that context, that it meets the ends of the corporate world. To this end, links have been made between some public universities (most notably in the UK and Australia) and corporations, to develop schemes of company-based tertiary education – partnership degrees that are fully work-based. Several examples come to mind: in Australia, the AMP/UTS (Australian Mutual Provident/ University of Technology, Sydney) master's degree in business; in the UK, the MBA (Master of Business Administration) between Brunel and Henley and Ashridge College (a private training organization). Meanwhile, some corporations are circumventing the public institutions altogether, and are beginning to offer their own 'types' of higher education: corporate degrees and awards (British Telecom being one such). Working knowledge, that acquired and elaborated in the workplace, is a central part of the curriculum for such degrees. The former divide, then, between the academy and its surrounding world is being obliterated, another mark of the general dedifferentiation characteristic of much late twentieth-century culture (Edwards 1997).

Such trends have profound ramifications for the accreditation of learning in the university, for they fly in face of conventional pedagogy and the associated processes of assessment. As new institutional arrangements emerge that bridge the gulf between the public and private, and offer new ways of acquiring credentials, knowledge is becoming deregulated, deinstitutionalized – furthering, perhaps, the processes of deschooling that Illich, thirty years ago, thought would be the harbinger of a new age of education. The key to such education was that it would once again permit individuals to learn from the world rather than about the world and release knowledge from oligopolies such as the universities (Illich 1971). This idea is futher explored in Chapter 8.

Work-based learning for a workerless society

Yet it is also true that with the expansion of university education the positional advantages that were once attendant on an undergraduate degree have diminished. Universities have become the finishing schools of the 1990s, grade thirteen, fourteen and fifteen of an increasingly prolonged education system. Diploma inflation has lessened the market value of a university degree which is not, necessarily, a passport to a higher paid job (Marginson 1997). A recent report commissioned by the Department of Education, Employment, Training and Youth Affairs (DEETYA), examining graduate labour trends, provides evidence that degree holders are now turning up in jobs in such areas as retail and the building industry – not traditionally associated with graduate employment (Richardson 1998). Of even more pertinence, though, is the fact that full-time work along with a job for life are in retreat, the dying legacies of the Fordist economy. The twin forces of computerization and corporatization, operating in cohorts with one another, have brought about a mass destruction of jobs that has spared no sector of the labour force, white or blue collar. We now live in a society where work is in short supply: the jobs that do exist are increasingly a travesty of real jobs: short-term, contingent, offering few career opportunities or long-term security. There are simply fewer parts for workers in the new work order and those available are mainly bit parts (Aronowitz and DiFazio 1994). Moreover, the work that there is becoming proletarianized and deskilled, capable of being performed by anyone with keyboard skills. In the digital age of work, it is digits that count.

In this climate the division of labour has increasingly come to define who works and, if at all, for how long. For the profile of the new labour force has three tiers – Hutton's (1996) so-called, because of the percentage of the population in each category, 'thirty, thirty, forty society'. The first comprises the unemployed and the economically inactive who rarely, if ever, secure employment. The second, workers who obtain casual work, who form part of the peripheral labour force; and the third, who form the core of the labour force, are those who enjoy full-time work and who are among the most active in society. The fastest growing area in the job market is in part-time and casual work, mostly in industries and services with the most truncated knowledge base. In this context, the vocationalized university only has any significance for the third tier of the labour force who form, in a context in which work is increasingly being automated, an ever diminishing percentage of the population, some say as low as 20 and falling (Robins and Webster 1999).

Some final remarks

As an institution, the university is not monopolized by a single discourse: nor has it ever been. Indeed, in the current climate of institutional deregulation ushered in by the era of the market, the role of the university is likely to take a multitude of forms and engage in a variety of relationships with the institutions and communities around it. Thus the old idea of university as remote institution, characterized by a relatively homogeneous culture, on the margins of society, a refuge for the 'gifted and talented', a medieval community in the modern age, is now in the process of retreat. Cloisters are giving way to supermarket aisles.

It is not that the other discourses have been usurped by a rampant vocationalism where everything is subsumed to work, for other discourses persist and still have important status in the ongoing polemic about higher education. The discourse universe of the university then is an imbricated one, and vocationalism is but one of a number of discourses that have helped to frame the university. Although it is one that currently seems to be dominant, its existence has to be seen alongside other discourses that provide criteria against which to characterize this trend. They prevent debate about the function of the university falling into a maelstrom of confusion and opacity, points of reference against which to characterize the university's educational endeavour against that of its rivals. In this respect, the university was, and still is, more liberal than further education colleges and more liberal than institutes of technology, where the vocationalism tended to be more overt. But even this has to be qualified, for it has also been argued that in spite of declared aversions towards vocationalism, the university has always provided a grounding for work, either in the professions or the public service. Thus the distinction between a liberal or vocational education is largely a spurious one and one which the latest developments in higher education discourse have only served to accentuate; for all education is vocational and, in the end, it is simply a matter of to what degree.

Notes

1. Much of this circumspection derives from misconceptions about the nature of 'working knowledge', that it does not involve reflexiveness. Yet all work, even the most menial, is knowledge-based. The hostility to more pragmatic approaches to education stems from a more generalized discourse of anti-industrialism, prevalent in the nineteenth century, particularly in England, and whose legacy has been transmitted to the twentieth century. It exists in the work, for example, of liberal thinkers such as Mill and Newman and the 'gothic' socialists John

Ruskin and William Morris, who actively opposed mass production and the mentality with which it was associated (Weiner 1981).

2. It is interesting that these arguments have been most thoroughly aired in connection with schools and rarely ever with universities, though it is of note that Mill's comments, derived from his address to St. Andrew's, where he was the rector, were specifically directed at universities.

3. This tradition is hardly extinct. Its genealogy continues through to the present in the work of such intellectual conservatives as Robert Hutchins and Michael Oakeshott, Allan Bloom and E. D. Hirsch.

4. These trends have not been without their opponents, and theirs have been forthright defences of the traditional curriculum, arguing that departure from its elements risks bringing down the fabric of Western civilization, undermining the moral and ethical sinews of society.

5. A process of re-canonization is occurring here, which is leading to the establishment of a hagiography of popular culture with its own heroes and texts. No doubt this will be studied with the same techniques as the canon of the past, and will have some relevance to the expanding leisure industries, such as popular music and sport.

6. Nations such as Germany and Japan, still prosperous economies, subscribe to the importance of training at work rather than the university which still gives high priority to liberal education (see Hunter 1991).

7. The roots of this tradition originate in the English Enlightenment, with Bacon, Locke and Hobbes, who argued that the inventiveness of the mechanical arts depends on the empirical sciences.

8. The nomenclature here is Australian. For the UK, read polytechnics. The reasons for this divide appear to echo that underpinning the schooling system in the immediate post-war years, which was grounded in the assumptions of the Hadow Report. These held that there were distinctive types of students for whom a distinctive form of schooling is required (Davies 1989).

References

Arcilla, R. N. (1995) *For the Love of Perfection: Richard Rorty and Liberal Education.* New York, NY: Routledge.

Aronowitz, S. and DiFazio, W. (1994) *The Jobless Future: Sci-tech and the Dogma of Work.* Minneapolis, MN: University of Minnesota Press.

Ashby, E. (1966) *Technology and the Academy: An Essay on Universities and the Scientific Revolution.* London: Macmillan.

Ashby, E. (1974) *Adapting Universities to a Technological Society.* San Francisco, CA: Jossey-Bass.

Barnett, R. (1997) *Higher Education: A Critical Business.* Buckingham: SRHE/Open University Press.

Beck, R. (1990) *Polytechnical Education: A Step.* Berkeley, CA: National Center for Research in Vocational Education.

Bengtisson, J. (1993) Labour markets of the future. *European Journal of Education,* 28 (2), 135–58.

Birch, I. and Smart, D. (1989) Economic rationalism and the politics of education in Australia. *Politics of Education Association Yearbook.*

Bourdieu, P. and Passeron, J-C. (1977) *Reproduction in Education, Culture and Society.* London: Sage.

Bowles, S. and Gintis, H. (1976) *Schooling in Capitalist America.* London: Routledge and Kegan Paul.

Braverman, H. S. (1974) *Labor and Monopoly Capital.* New York, NY: Monthly Review Press.

Brown, P. and Scase, R. (1994) *Higher Education and Corporate Realities: Class, Culture and the Decline of Graduate Careers.* London: UCL Press.

Brown, P. and Scase, R. (1997) Universities and employers: rhetoric and reality, in A. Smith and F. Webster (eds) *The Postmodern University? Contested Visions of Higher Education in Society.* Buckingham: SHRE/Open University.

Burton-Jones, P. (1999) *Knowledge Capitalism: Business, Work, and Learning in the New Economy.* Oxford: Oxford University Press.

Castles, S. and Wüstenberg, W. (1979) *The Education of the Future: An Introduction to the Theory and Practice of Socialist Education.* London: Pluto Press.

Davies, S. (1989) *The Martin Committee and the Binary Policy of Higher Education in Australia.* Melbourne: Ashwood House.

Dearing, R. (1997) *Higher Education in a Learning Society: The National Committee into Higher Education.* London: HMSO.

Dewey, J. ([1916] 1966) *Democracy and Education.* New York, NY: Free Pess.

Dewey, J. (1977) On industrial education. *Curriculum Inquiry,* 7 (1), 53–60.

Dominelli, L. and Hoogvelt, A. (1996) Globalisation, contract government and the Taylorisation of intellectual labour in academia. *Studies in Political Economy,* 49: 71–100.

Drucker, J. (1993) The new society of organisations, in R. Howard (ed.) *The Learning Imperative.* Boston, MA: Harvard Business School.

Edwards, R. (1997) *Changing Places? Flexibility, Lifelong Learning and the Learning Society.* London: Routledge.

Filmer, P. (1997) Distinterestedness and the modern university, in A. Smith and F. Webster (eds) *The Postmodern University? Contested Visions of Higher Education in Society.* Buckingham: SHRE/Open University.

Foster, E. and Stephenson, J. (1998) Work-based learning and universities in the UK: a review of current practices and trends. *Higher Education Research and Development,* 17 (2), 155–70.

Fryer, R. H. (1997) *Learning for the 21st Century.* London: HMSO.

Garwin, D. (1993) Building a learning enterprise. *Harvard Business Review,* July–August, 78–91.

Gibbons, M., Limoges, C., Notwotny, H. *et al.* (1994) *The New Production of Knowledge: The Dynamics of Science and Research in Contemporary Societies.* London: Sage.

Hague, Sir Douglas (1991) *Beyond Universities: A New Republic of the Intellect.* London: Institute of Economic Affairs.

Hunter, I. (1991) Personality as a vocation: the political rationality of the humanities, in I. Hunter, D. Meredyth, B. Smith and G. Stokes (eds) *Accounting for the Humanities.* Brisbane: ICPS.

Hutton, W. (1996) *The State We're In.* London: Vintage.

Illich, I. (1971) *Deschooling Society.* Harmondsworth: Penguin.

Kemp, D. (1999) *New Knowledge, New Opportunities. A Discussion Paper on Higher Education Research and Research Training.* Canberra: Department of Education, Employment, Training and Youth Affairs.

Kincheloe, J. L. (1995) *Toil and Trouble: Good Work, Smart Work and the Integration of Academic and Vocational Education.* New York, NY: Peter Lang.

Lewis, T. (1994) Bridging the liberal/vocational divide: an examination of recent British and American versions of an old debate. *Oxford Review of Education,* 20 (2), 199–217.

Lowe, R. (1990) Educating for industry: the historical role of higher education in England, in P. W. G. Wright (ed.) *Industry and Higher Education: Collaboration to Improve Students' Learning and Teaching.* Buckingham: SRHE/Open University Press.

Lyotard, J-F. (1984) *The Postmodern Condition: A Report on Knowledge.* Manchester: Manchester University Press.

Marginson, S. (1997) *Markets in Education.* Sydney: Allen & Unwin.

Martin, J. R. (1993) Curriculum and the mirror of knowledge, in R. Barrow and P. White (eds) *Beyond Liberal Education: Essays in Honour of Paul H. Hirst.* London: Routledge.

Mill, J. S. (1971) Inaugural address at the University of St. Andrews, in F. W. Garforth (ed.) *John Stuart Mill on Education.* New York, NY: Teachers College Press.

Minogue, K. R. (1973) *The Concept of a University.* London: Weidenfeld and Nicolson.

Newman, J. H. C. ([1852] 1947) *The Idea of a University.* New York, NY: Longmans, Green and Co.

Peters, M. (1992) Performance and accountability in 'post-industrial' society: the crisis of British universities. *Studies in Higher Education,* 17 (2), 123–39.

Pratt, J. (1997) *The Polytechnic Experiment 1965–1992.* Buckingham: SHRE/Open University Press.

Rashdall, H. ([1895] 1936) *The Universities of Europe in the Middle Ages, Volume III. English Universities – Student Life.* London: Oxford University Press.

Readings, B. (1996) *The University in Ruins.* Cambridge, MA: Harvard University Press.

Reich, R. B. (1991) *The Work of Nations: Preparing Ourselves for 21st Century Capitalism.* New York, NY: Knopf.

Richardson, J. (1998) More degree-holders take mundane jobs. *The Australian Higher Education,* July 29.

Robertson, D. (1999) Knowledge societies, intellectual capital and economic growth, in H. Gray (ed.) *Universities and the Creation of Wealth.* Buckingham: SHRE/Open University Press.

Robins, K. and Webster, F. (1999) *Times of the Techno-culture. From the Information Society to the Virtual Life.* London: Routledge.

Schultz, T. (1961) Investment in human capital. *American Economic Review,* 51: 1–17.

Scott, P. (1995) *The Meanings of Mass Higher Education.* Buckingham: SHRE/Open University Press.

Silver, H. and Brennan, J. (1988) *A Liberal Vocationalism.* London: Methuen.

Slaughter, S. and Leslie, L. L. (1997) *Academic Capitalism: Politics, Policies and the Enterpreneurial University.* Baltimore, MD: Johns Hopkins University Press.

Smyth, J. (1995) Introduction, in J. Smyth (ed.) *Academic Work: The Changing Labour Process in Higher Education.* Buckingham: SRHE/Open University Press.

Symes, C. (1999) 'Working for your future': the rise of the vocationalised university. *Australian Journal of Education,* 43 (3), 243–258.

Turpin, T. and Garrett-Jones, S. (1997) Innovation networks in Australia and China, in H. Etzkowitz and L. Leydesdorff (eds) *Universities and the Global Knowledge Economy: A Triple Helix of University–Industry–Government Relations.* London: Pintar.

Veblen, T. ([1925] 1970) *The Theory of the Leisure Class.* London: George Allen and Unwin.

West, R. (1998) *Learning for Life: Review of Higher Education Financing and Policy.* Canberra: Australian Government Publishing Service.

Whitehead, A. N. ([1932] 1962) *The Aims of Education.* London: Ernest Benn.

Weiner, M. J. (1981) *English Culture and the Decline of the English Industrial Spirit, 1850–1950.* Cambridge: Cambridge University Press.

Winter, R. (1995) The university of life plc: the 'industrialization' of higher education, in J. Smyth (ed.) *Academic Work: The Changing Labour Process in Higher Education.* Buckingham: SRHE/Open University Press.

Wirth, A. G. (1994) A reconstituted general education: the integration of the vocational and the liberal. *Curriculum Studies,* 26 (6), 593–600.

4

Knowledge that Works: Judgement and the University Curriculum

Paul Hager

... modern society is forming its own views as to what counts as knowledge. Today, it dismisses contemplative knowledge, knowledge which brings personal understanding, even knowledge which offers truth. Now it wants knowledge which is going to have demonstrable effects in the world, which is going to improve economic competitiveness and which is going to enhance personal effectiveness. In the process, our sense of what is to count as knowledge and truth changes; and the university is asked to take these new definitions on board.

(Barnett 1997a: 29)

Introduction

As several chapters in this volume have suggested, work-based learning challenges received notions of academic control and what it is to be an academic. These challenges centre around the notion of knowledge as a major site of contestation in work-based learning. The reason why work-based learning directly confronts common conceptions of knowledge is that academics typically have believed that for something to count as knowledge it needs to be acquired by due academic processes. The due academic processes that have been taken to legitimate knowledge are of two kinds: first, those that specify processes for knowledge production and creation; second, those that specify processes for transmission of knowledge. This chapter argues that our understandings of knowledge are currently skewed and limited precisely because they are unduly shaped by these two kinds of academic control assumptions. Various aspects of these assumptions will be examined and questioned and ways in which they may need to be modified suggested.

The time-honoured academic processes for knowledge production and creation centre upon the objectification of knowledge. This objectification requires freedom to work in ways that issue in the agreed objectivities and which are achieved through the adoption of certain academic protocols.

The time and resources to establish these objectivities, which are examined in more detail in the next chapter, are basic to the idea of a university and the administration of its research culture. The outcome of this objectified process is the production of continually evolving, public, justifiable but revisable bodies of knowledge.

On this account of academic knowledge production, what is taken to be knowledge at any given moment is a 'take' on the state of objectified enquiry in any given field. While this process of knowledge production is portrayed frequently as an inexorable accumulation of truth, it should be clear from the above that the time-honoured academic processes do carry with them the implication that at least some current 'knowledge' is tentative and open to revision. This note of fallibilism will be important to the argument later in this chapter. In the meantime, the 'accumulation of truth' metaphor is powerful. As David Beckett argues in the next chapter, the principle of the objectification of knowledge production and creation by due academic processes has a deep and enduring public significance analogous to the dictum that 'the camera cannot lie'. But just as the camera can lie, since there is a human contribution to image construction, so also with the construction of knowledge. While current trends towards the commodification of knowledge are viewed by many as a distortion of its objectification, this chapter undertakes a reconsideration of the traditional objectification process itself and its inherent distortion of what counts as objectified knowledge. So current trends that question the traditional model may not be so much seeking to replace objectivity by distortion, as one kind of rationally based distortion by another of the same kind.

If the due academic processes for knowledge production and creation are under question, it hardly needs to be added that this raises doubts about processes for transmission of knowledge. However, as will be discussed later in the chapter, this is not the only contemporary source of such doubts. But first the issue of knowledge production needs to be addressed.

Rival knowledge scenarios

A convenient way of approaching current questioning of traditional ideas on knowledge production is to consider Barnett's claim that the university has become the site of contestation between two 'rival versions of what it is to know the world' (Barnett 1997a: 30). Barnett further describes these two forms of knowing as 'rival versions of competence' and characterizes their points of difference in the following lists:

Academic competence	Operational competence
knowing that	knowing how
written communication	oral communication
personal	interpersonal
internal	external

localized capacities	transferability
intellectual	physical
thought	action
problem making	problem solving
knowledge as process	knowledge as product
understanding	information
value-laden	'value-free'
discipline-based	issue-based
concept-based	task-based
pure	applied
proposition-based learning	experiential learning
individualized learning	group-based learning
holistic	unitized
disinterested	pragmatic
intrinsic orientation	instrumental orientation

(Barnett 1997a: 30–1)

While Barnett's binary scheme is a useful start for understanding current questioning of traditional ideas on knowledge production, it also has its own distinct flaws. I will outline what I take to be the main weaknesses of Barnett's scheme as a way of approaching a sounder understanding of the situation. My first concern is that it is very doubtful whether the two lists really represent a contest between 'rival versions of what it is to know *the world*' (my italics). It might be more accurate to view them as ways of understanding two different 'worlds'. While the second list deals with the everyday world of commerce and life activities, the first is directed at a kind of understanding that is in many ways remote from the everyday world. This crucial difference is concealed somewhat by Barnett's initial definition of academic competence as 'the capacity to see *the world* and to engage with it through one or more of the academic disciplines' (Barnett 1997a: 27, italics added). However, that he is, indeed, talking about two different 'worlds' is confirmed by Barnett's later more explicit statement that the dominant focus of the first list is 'the self-production of the academics by the academics' (1997a: 32). Certainly a significant withdrawal from the everyday world is signalled via the cumulative effect of characteristics such as 'personal', 'internal', 'intellectual', 'pure', 'intrinsic', etc. that he attributes to academic competence. This squares with the well-established result that academic performance is a poor predictor of performance outside the academy. Performance in law exams, for example, is only slightly correlated with capacity to practise law successfully. Hence my conclusion that rather than being 'rival versions of what it is to know the world', Barnett's lists describe two different kinds of competence.

While it is possible that either of Barnett's lists might have their proponents as the desirable components for university degrees, I reject both lists. Even if quibbles that I have with some of the contents of each list were resolved, I would agree with Barnett that neither is appropriate for higher education today. However, as will be argued later, neither do I agree with Barnett's proposal to jettison both approaches entirely and replace them with a postmodern alternative. Instead, I favour an approach, rejected by Barnett, that involves reconciling the two lists; only, however, after they have been significantly revised. My reasons for favouring this approach and rejecting Barnett's are developed in the remainder of this chapter. I begin with some further criticisms of Barnett's scheme centred on various weaknesses and oddities that I find in both his lists.

Barnett attributes 'localized capacities' to academic competence while placing 'transferability' as its counterpart in operational competence. I argue that on any realistic assessment of the situation, both attributes should feature prominently in both lists. Indeed, academic institutions often proclaim the generic and the transferable as the main attributes of their graduates. Of course 'localized capacities' and 'transferable capacities' are relative terms anyway. Recognizing this, it is still the case that any academic course that I have ever encountered features many fairly localized capacities and, equally, many fairly transferable capacities. But the same applies to every one of the many workplaces in which I have conducted research. Even assembly line workers require some fairly transferable capacities, such as strategies for coping with boredom, ability to concentrate, a level of self-discipline and the like – strategies that are existential rather than epistemological.

Barnett assigns 'knowledge as process' to academic competence while placing 'knowledge as product' as its counterpart in operational competence. Once again, on any realistic understanding of the situation, both feature significantly in each set of competencies. However, I would go further and argue that in many ways both lists would be more plausible if 'knowledge as process' and 'knowledge as product' were transposed. Certainly the focus of traditional assessment has been overwhelmingly on products (examination papers, essays, laboratory findings, studio work, theses, etc.) rather than on processes. Those seeking to reform university teaching (see Bowden and Marton 1998) typically want to shift attention to the processes of learning. In contrast operational competence is, almost by definition, about processes (operations) rather than products. To the extent that contemporary workplaces are variable and changeable, then the knowledge now needed to function in them is evolving. So being knowledgeable in such workplaces is more the ongoing participation in a process than the acquiring of a product.

Equally puzzling is Barnett's attribution of 'value-laden' to academic competence while dubbing operational competence as 'value-free' (in scare quotes). That both lists are saturated with values should hardly need stating. As Barnett portrays it, the academic competence list might be seen as the home of values, as against their absence in the other list. Nothing could be more misleading. Despite traditional claims to being a source of universal values, the values promoted by the academy have been somewhat more limited. The academy has always favoured some values as basic to its activities such as academic freedom, tolerance of diverse opinions, freedom of speech and the like. However, the performance of the academy in relation to values has not been exemplary. Too often increasing specialization within disciplines has led to tunnel vision with respect to wider values, e.g. conserving the environment. Likewise the idea that science can be 'value-free' and above politics has had some purchase in the academy. As well, the type of 'objectivity' attained by the time-honoured academic processes for knowledge production, as outlined at the start of this chapter, has sometimes been confused with 'value-free' knowledge. Perhaps Barnett's scare quotes around 'value-free' acknowledges that operational competence always reflects some values, even if they are not the same as traditional academic values. If that is so then the supposed difference between the two lists loses its point. The more interesting question is whether the respective values of the two lists are inevitably in conflict. Certainly it has been common to conclude that they are. My proposed reconciliation of the two approaches later in this chapter will argue that such value conflict is far from inevitable.

A further surprising feature of Barnett's scheme is that he portrays academic competence as 'holistic' and operational competence as 'unitized'. In his favour, it can be agreed that academic learning aims to create unified webs of knowledge and to encourage learners to make wider connections across the fabric of knowledge, whereas operational competence might well have a much more modest scope. However, there is at least one clear sense in which the reverse is the case. Operating wisely in the everyday world, whether at work or elsewhere, is more holistic than are typical academic activities. While the former routinely involves the full gamut of human attributes, often in complex combinations such as a range of learned skills, values, and attitudes, the latter deliberately seeks a more restricted range of human activity. The choice of epithets that Barnett uses in his list suggests as much: 'internal', 'intellectual', 'thought', 'concept-based', 'pure', and 'intrinsic orientation'. Thus the argument against Barnett is that academic competence, rather than being holistic, is somewhat narrow and restricted, whereas operational competence is more holistic.

Yet another odd feature of Barnett's scheme is the collocation of 'understanding' with 'knowing that' and 'pure', while 'knowing how' is put with 'information' and 'applied'. This position restricts understanding to an elite who engage in pure contemplation aloof from practice, while the practitioners who actually get things done are left to blunder along with mere information. At best this is a contentious position. There is a body of educational thought that maintains that application of knowledge is necessary for proper understanding: 'It was only in doing it that I really understood it.' This line of thinking would, perhaps, want to move 'information' across to the academic competence list, and replace it with 'understanding' in the operational competence list.

In placing 'understanding' and 'information' where he does, Barnett shows sympathy for one of the worst features of what I will call the 'Academic Knowledge Scenario', viz. its Cartesianism. Cartesianism sharply distinguishes the mind from the body and locates understanding in unitary minds contemplating propositions to distinguish the true from the false and the certain from the less certain. Thus the Cartesian picture of the academic is of a thinking mind cut off from and contemplating the world.

The 'academic knowledge scenario'

This scenario is derived from Cartesianism and has the following main emphases:

- all knowledge resides in individual minds not bodies;
- all knowledge is propositional (true, false; more certain, less certain);
- all knowledge can be expressed verbally and written down in books, etc.;
- the acquisition of knowledge (learning) alters minds not bodies;
- knowledge can be applied via bodies to alter the external world.

Cartesianism is a strong influence in Barnett's academic competence list. This becomes very clear when we remove from his list the characteristics that I have disputed in the above discussion. What is left is a revised list that has strong Cartesian components:

- knowing that
- personal
- intellectual
- problem making
- concept-based
- proposition-based learning
- disinterested
- written communication
- internal
- thought
- discipline-based
- pure
- individualized learning
- intrinsic orientation.

At the beginning of this chapter I suggested that the due academic processes that have been taken to legitimate knowledge are of two kinds: first, those that specify procedures for knowledge production and creation; second, those that specify processes for transmission of knowledge. The time-honoured academic processes for production and objectification of knowledge were outlined briefly at the start of the chapter. The academic knowledge scenario fills in the picture both of the knowledge creators and of the nature of the knowledge that they create.

The due academic processes that have governed transmission of knowledge concern who is selected to learn, what is learnt, how it is learnt, and how learning is demonstrated. The strong influence of Cartesianism on these academic control processes for knowledge acquisition is very evident in the selection mechanisms used in higher education:

- *Selection of students:* admission criteria based overwhelmingly on individual performance in written tests of propositional knowledge, and which, in effect, test the individual's mental capacity.

- *Selection of curriculum*: course content overwhelmingly propositional knowledge logically ordered via disciplines and subjects. Any non-propositional learning, such as laboratory skills, is driven by the propositional, i.e. to gain valid raw data that can be turned into true propositions.
- *Selection of teaching methods*: major focus is on presentation of verbal and written propositions for individual student acquisition and understanding. Hence the use of lectures, tutorials and textbooks.
- *Selection of assessment/progression methods*: learning is demonstrated by individuals reproducing verbal or written propositions in appropriate combinations in response to set questions in examinations and written assignments.

Very clearly, these academic control processes are shaped by a particular understanding of the nature of knowledge, and have not been without their criticisms. These have included: their excessive individualism; their devaluation of non-propositional learning; and their focus on intellectual understanding while neglecting its application.

It is also the case that Cartesianism has not been the only influential theory of knowledge, although the main alternatives have shared many of its features that are reflected in the academic knowledge scenario. For example, a very influential characterization of knowledge has been that it is 'justified true belief' where beliefs are propositions. In some variant theories, propositions are seen as independent existents with which minds can become acquainted. The intractable difficulty for the 'justified true belief' approach has been that attempts to explicate 'justified' seem to be inevitably circular in that they need to assume true propositions or knowledge. Commenting on the failure to develop a consistent and coherent account of knowledge as propositional, Russell (1948: 516) concluded:

> 'Knowledge', as we have seen, is a term incapable of precision. All knowledge is in some degree doubtful, and we cannot say what degree of doubtfulness makes it cease to be knowledge . . .

The fact that propositional knowledge is an imprecise notion serves also to remind us that this applies more to some disciplinary areas such as the humanities than to others (e.g. the sciences). These differences can be very significant in their effects on academic control processes (Bourgeois *et al.* 1999: 105).[1]

The previous section began with the question: What makes something count as knowledge? By now the traditional answer is clear – it needs to meet the standard criteria encapsulated in the due academic processes shaped by the academic knowledge scenario. But there is increasing unease with this answer. It is the belief of a growing number of theorists that our understandings of knowledge are currently skewed and limited precisely because they are unduly shaped by the aforementioned academic control assumptions. The remainder of this chapter will examine and question various aspects of these assumptions and suggest ways in which they may need to be modified as we begin the new millennium.

Challenges to the academic knowledge scenario

The previous section on the academic knowledge scenario arose from a critique of Barnett's first list of the elements of academic competence. Some aspects of Barnett's second list, the one that purported to describe operational competence, were also rejected. In order to arrive at a knowledge scenario that I argue is appropriate for post-twentieth-century universities, we need to consider more closely some of the main forces for change that are now impacting on them. I identify five of these:

1. a pronounced shift to mass higher education;
2. the emergence of a knowledge society;
3. advances in technology leading to rapid change in workplaces;
4. globalization leading to a 'corporate model of higher education';
5. moves to alternative and flexible modes of delivery.

1. A pronounced shift to mass higher education

The high levels of literacy and education required to support post-industrialism have led to the move from elite to mass higher education (Scott 1995, 1997; Robertson 1997). It is a trend that has attracted criticism. For instance, it has intensified various access and equity issues. Trowler (1998: 16) questions whether a situation that is a long way from equal representation of all relevant groups can really be classed as mass higher education. However, the current shift in the higher education population has been sufficient to place pressure on our academic conceptions of knowledge. The rise of the mass university has seen its growing incorporation of more practice-based areas such as nursing, podiatry, and acupuncture. Thus universities are increasingly dealing with a type of knowledge, know-how, that was traditionally learnt largely by engaging in occupational practice. As well, the admission to higher degrees in various fields of practitioners who were originally trained in the vocational and training sector, has pressured universities to recognize forms of learning other than traditional academic ones. All this can be seen as a part of a gradual trend, illustrated further in 2–5 below, of universities losing their exclusive power to define and privilege knowledge.[2]

2. The emergence of a knowledge society

The term 'knowledge society' has gained wide currency to describe a society in which new sites of knowledge production spring up in all kinds of places (Gibbons *et al.* 1994; Coffield and Williamson 1997: 18). This replaces a society in which knowledge is thought of as being produced in and disseminated from a small number of designated locations such as universities and research organizations. According to Scott (1997: 41) there is a 'standard, but perhaps superficial, account' of the knowledge society based on 'an economy in which codified knowledge is becoming a primary resource'. This kind of society would be 'likely to enhance the role and prestige of knowledge institutions, among which universities are arguably pre-eminent'. However, Scott goes on to note an 'alternative, and perhaps more subtle, account' of a knowledge society based on two phenomena much more problematic for the future of universities:

> The first is the emergence of new kinds of 'knowledge' institutions, that are not characterized by the same patterns of academic and pro-fessional socialization as the universities and which apparently offer a rival model. The second is that 'knowledge', conceptually and opera-tionally, has become a much more capacious category; it has spread far beyond academic and/or scientific definitions.
>
> (1997: 42)

This second account of a knowledge society is subtler because, unlike the universities, it does not privilege the disciplines as the foundation of all credible knowledge. On the other hand it does privilege the workplace as a site of knowledge creation and significant learning. The development of work-based learning awards and degrees reflects the emergence of the know-ledge society. Difficulties experienced in implementing these degrees can be seen to be in part due to learning in the workplace not squaring with traditional assumptions about the nature of knowledge and its acquisition by individuals. The challenge for universities is how to recognize different legitimate forms of knowledge, without allowing anything to qualify. For example, mere information should not usually be privileged as knowledge (Marshall 1998).

3. Advances in technology leading to rapid change in workplaces

Although it is something of a cliché that the current era is characterized by an historically unprecedented change, the impact of this change on work and on vocational preparation cannot be ignored. Certainly it is a very signific-ant factor in the current debate about the nature of workplace practice and ways to improve it. One clear effect of the rapid change of the current era has been to place pressure on the front-end approach to occupational education. This is reflected, for instance, in growing dissatisfaction with courses for professions (Hager 1996). More and more, a formal two-, three- or four-year course at the start of a career is seen merely as the necessary foundation for the early years of practice, rather than as the sufficient basis for a lifetime of practice. Hence the increasing interest in lifelong learning as a guiding principle for occupational education. Of course, it is a plaus-ible view that some work-based learning has always been necessary for pro-ficient practice. If so, the new era of change merely increases this need. In so doing it points to the crucial role of types of knowledge acquired via non-traditional, non-formal learning. This questions several of the academic knowledge scenario assumptions. Thus, it seems doubtful that the traditional front-end model of occupational preparation, based on the academic knowledge scenario, will survive unscathed in an era of rapid change.

4. Globalization leading to a corporate model of higher education

Globalization refers to a restructuring of the world order represented by such trends and movements as internationalization of economies, reduction in the size of the public sector, deregulation of markets to enhance privatization, greater efficiency and accountability in expenditure of resources and growing managerial control of higher education. In this climate many predict:

> . . . the end of the traditional, nationally-based, 'bricks-and-mortar' university, and the rise of the globalised, networked and 'virtual' university.
>
> (Flew 1998: 7)

This new type of university, with reduced public funding, is likely to become more student-centred as 'the kinds of courses which the global consumer is demanding are flexible, adaptable, portable and interactive' (Mason 1998: 7). These trends have increased pressure for the recognition of new kinds of knowledge via what is efficient and effective rather than what meets traditional criteria. This privileging of efficiency, value-for-money and accountability has been sharply criticized as an abandonment of the broader aims of higher education in favour of internal management processes (Barnett 1990: 26).

5. Moves to alternative and flexible modes of delivery

This trend to alternative and flexible delivery modes is partly fuelled, of course, by the compound effects of 1–4. However, the prime factor behind flexible delivery is advances in information and communication technologies (ICT) that have led to the 'virtualization' scenario. Of course mass education always has been significantly shaped by technologies (chalk, readers, biros), but broadbanded ICT represents a change of an entirely different order, particularly in its capacity to diminish distance and time. A combination of databases, electronic journals, synchronous and asynchronous conferencing, and multimedia course packages that feature interactivity on-line is, in effect, a virtual university. Clearly if the teaching and learning functions can be mounted satisfactorily, such a virtual university (whose inadequacies are identified by Beckett in the next chapter) has the potential to provide more access for more people to more educational resources than ever before.

Overall these changes are leading to valuations of knowledge that reject the various academic knowledge scenario assumptions. Instead they demand flexibility in who learns, what is learnt, how it is learnt, and how learning is assessed. This adds up to a drastically changing set of relationships between universities, knowledge and society. Thus a different sort of knowledge scenario needs to be developed, one that recognizes and incorporates some of the key ideas discussed so far in this chapter.

Barnett's proposed scenario

Barnett argues that while the two rival versions of competence that he critiqued earlier are not entirely contradictory, neither are they reconcilable into a 'judicious mix' (1997a: 39). Thus Barnett sees a need to abandon the earlier scenarios completely and replace them with something novel. He gives two reasons for rejecting attempts to reconcile the two rival versions of competence. His first reason is that the two rival lists are 'marked by schisms'. He illustrates these with instances such as the supposed centrality of understanding to one version and its neglect by the other. However, it has been shown earlier in this chapter that on a number of such issues the two lists are not really as disparate as Barnett suggests. Barnett's second reason for rejecting attempts to reconcile the two rival versions of competence points to their different and incompatible 'fundamental purposes', i.e. 'disciplinary engagement' versus 'economic competitiveness'. A simple response would be that it is fallacious reasoning to infer that a purpose that belongs to a collection of items thereby belongs to each of the individual items taken singly. That being so there is no reason why selected items from the two lists could not be combined into a third list which would have a quite different overall purpose. An example of this kind will be provided in the next section. Thus, I find that neither of Barnett's reasons for rejecting attempts to reconcile the two rival versions of competence are convincing. Nor does his proposed 'fresh start' fare any better.

Barnett's proposal centres on the key idea that the 'world is unknowable'. By this he means that 'there are *no* supreme frameworks for yielding a firm grip on the world' (Barnett 1997b: 176). He expands further on this by pointing to four senses in which he takes the world to be unknowable. First, because what we take to be the meaning of knowledge is not fixed. That is, knowledge is 'socially reflexive in that humans continually modify their understandings'. Meanwhile 'the world is always moving on in advance of our efforts to understand it'. Second, no one knowledge framework has all the answers. So we have to rely on various frameworks, some of which are incompatible. Third, there are 'few, if any, secure knowledge claims', while even technologies linked to the hard sciences 'are forever coming unstuck'.

Fourth, knowledge has failed to deliver the promised control of nature as shown by the ecological crisis.

From this Barnett concludes that we need:

> . . . to do nothing short of jettisoning the whole way we have construed higher education for one thousand years and, instead, work out a new conception of education which starts from the understanding that the world is unknowable in any serious sense.
>
> (Barnett 1997a: 43)

Barnett's suggested 'new conception of education' he calls the 'life-world becoming scenario'. According to this scenario, 'higher education for an unknowable world' has the following features:

Epistemology: Reflective knowing
Situations: Open definition (with use of multiple approaches)
Focus: Dialogue and argument as such
Transferability: Meta-critique
Learning: Meta-learning
Communication: Dialogical
Evaluation: Consensus
Value orientation: The 'common good' (defined consensually)
Boundary conditions: Practicalities of discourse
Critique: For better practical understanding

While there is much in this proposed scenario that would gain wide support, there are a number of clear problems with Barnett's conception, problems about its basic assumptions which, if valid, destroy the rationale on which his conception rests.

First, his 'world which is unknowable' is too strong an assertion. All that seems to follow from the arguments that he presents is fallibilism, i.e. the view that no piece of knowledge is immune from revision; that knowledge claims that were taken once to be true may be understood subsequently as false. But fallibilism has been a commonplace for most of the twentieth century (e.g. Russell, Dewey and Popper) without unnerving consequences. In some ways Barnett's 'third' scenario is very Deweyan:

> . . . the only means of effective survival is for us collectively to go on reviewing the world we are in and refashioning it and ourselves in the process. The refashioning, of course, will include considerations of what it is to know and live effectively in the world.
>
> (Barnett 1997a: 42)

Second, the weak basis of the 'world which is unknowable' claim can be seen from an example of its implications. For instance, it would appear to be indisputable that there has been a growth in human capacity to build bridges. This growth in capacity seems to be somewhat independent of debates about whether the meaning of 'knowledge' is or is not fixed or the extent of its social reflexivity. This growth in capacity also seems to be perfectly consistent with the possibility that humans may need to revise their theoretical understandings of bridge building as better theories come along. While better theories may result in some changes to our bridge-building practices, they are unlikely to require that we demolish present structures and start again. Thus, at least in respect of bridge building, it does not seem to be the case that 'the world is always moving on in advance of our efforts to understand it'. Nor does this human capacity rely on there being a single knowledge framework that has all the answers about bridge building. So while it is possible that our bridge-building technology might yet come unstuck, all that seems to follow from this example is that our bridge-building knowledge is fallible. Certainly, in respect of our need to cross over rivers and gorges conveniently, the world is definitely not unknowable.

Third, Barnett takes the 'world as unknowable' thesis to be established on the basis of recent philosophical arguments about the nature of language. Yet the arguments for this position are open to challenge in just the same way as are all philosophical arguments. A century ago, many thinkers found convincing the philosophical arguments for the view that, despite appearances to the contrary, 'all is mind'. The history of philosophy is littered with once fashionable arguments that no longer convince anyone. The current fashion for discursivism has been created by the perceived failure of science-inspired methods in the humanities and social sciences. The 'world as unknowable' thesis can be viewed as the ultimate rejection of science. However, as a more critical stance comes to displace the recent tendency to treat Foucault, Derrida and Baudrillard as holy writ, gaps in their arguments become apparent, as do the dubious interpretations of some of their more enthusiastic followers (Hager 1999).

Earlier the unfortunate influence of Cartesianism on the academic knowledge scenario was outlined. Barnett's postmodern scenario, centred as it is on language and discourse, foreshadows a new Cartesianism that, instead of favouring mind over body, elevates cognitive meaning making over all other practices. For postmodernists languaging or discursive practice is the only ontological category since it constitutes everything else. Thus meaning making becomes the significant mode of cognition. In effect, though postmodern writings claim to engage with practice, what they mean by 'practice' is 'discursive practice' that boils down to a species of theoretical cognition. An unintended consequence of this move is that it serves to reinforce the traditional contempt for the vocational in educational thought. Though postmodern writers claim to be centred on practices, including vocational ones, once practical involvement is construed simply as meaning making the focus shifts to the theoretical and the cerebral, thereby creating a 'remoteness from practice' problem.

It is also of note that at the same time as proclaiming the need to jettison the way we have construed higher education, Barnett is using the traditional academic paper argued in the time-honoured way. Thus he proposes two opposing models, arguing both inadequate, proposing a third, relying on the distinct categories of epistemological, social, etc., quoting writers in support, and so on. It seems that developing a new knowledge scenario may not require a complete break with the past after all!

The 'knowledge as judgement scenario'

As an alternative this chapter proposes a scenario that I have developed in conjunction with Beckett (Hager and Beckett 1998; Hager 2000; Beckett and Hager 2000). We call this the 'knowledge as judgement scenario'. This scenario involves some reconciliation of Barnett's two rival versions of competence, a reconciliation that he rejected. The following discussion will aim to show why such reconciliation is both feasible and desirable. There is no claim that the knowledge as judgement scenario is entirely original. With its holistic conception of knowledge and its overall focus of successful action in the world, it owes obvious debts to thinkers such as Dewey and Whitehead. However, what Beckett and I do claim is that the significance of the work of these earlier thinkers for the issues discussed in this volume has largely gone unnoticed.

Our study of the performance of work in a range of occupations has pointed to the importance of judgements in the work performance of teams and individuals (Beckett and Hager 2000). We hypothesize that making better judgements represents a paradigmatic aim of work-based learning, and that therefore growth in such learning is represented by a growing capacity to make appropriate judgements in the changing, and often unique, circumstances that occur in many current workplaces. This scenario values not just the disciplinary knowledge that is central to the academic knowledge scenario, but includes also the diverse professional knowledge that is acquired from work performance. On this view, the category knowledge includes many sorts of components that are characteristically integrated and synthesized in judgements. For the purposes of this work, we understand judgement as deciding what to believe or do, taking into account a variety of relevant factors and then acting accordingly. More generally and technically, according to Lipman '[t]o judge is to judge relationships, either by discovering relationships or inventing them' (1991: 16).

Of course, the extent to which workers make judgements during the course of their work depends, among other things, on the way that the work is structured and organized. An assembly line is organized in such a way that workers will exercise minimal judgement, which means there will be little or no workplace learning. The much discussed learning organization maximizes the exercise of judgement and, hence, learning. Most jobs fall somewhere between these two extremes. In theorizing work-based learning in terms of people learning to make judgements, we can then take account of the effects of the many variables that influence such learning via their influence on the judgements. It turns out that the many variables that influence work-based learning are just the kinds of factors that are taken into account when judgements are made.

The knowledge as judgement scenario, which is proposed as a replacement for the Cartesian-inspired academic knowledge scenario, has the following main emphases:

- knowledge, as integrated in judgements, is a capacity for successful acting in and on the world;
- the choice of how to act in and on the world comes from the exercise of judgement;
- knowledge resides in individuals, teams and organizations;
- knowledge includes not just propositional understanding, but cognitive, connative and affective capacities as well as other abilities and learned capacities such as bodily know-how, skills of all kinds, and so on. All of these are components conceivably involved in making and acting upon judgements;
- not all knowledge can be or has been expressed verbally and written down;
- acquisition of knowledge alters both the learner and the world (since the learner is part of the world).

These features of the knowledge as judgement scenario can be further clarified by expounding the general thinking on which the scenario is based. The holistic, integrative emphasis aims to avoid dualisms such as mind/ body, theory/practice, thought/action, pure/applied, education/training, intrinsic/instrumental, internal/external, learner/world, knowing that/knowing how, process/product, and so on. The argument is that judgements, as both reasoning and acting, incorporate both sides of these ubiquitous dualisms. Thus, this account does not reject as such any pole of these dualisms. For instance, there is no rejection of propositional knowledge. Rather, propositions are viewed as important sub-components of the mix that underpins judgements – though the range of such propositions extends well beyond the boundaries of disciplinary knowledge. What is rejected is the view that propositions are timeless, independent existents that are the epitome of knowledge. By bringing together the propositional with the doing, the knowledge as judgement scenario continually judges propositions according to their contribution to the making of judgements. Because the judger is immersed in the world, so are propositions. So they lose their classical transcendental status.

Formal education has generally focused on propositions, skills and attitudes but has neglected judgement (Lipman 1991), which is precisely where the capacity to apply the learned propositions, skills and attitudes becomes important. However, according to the knowledge as judgement scenario, learning the propositions, skills and attitudes is only the start of learning. This is so because applying the propositions, skills and attitudes, far from being unproblematic, as the academic knowledge scenario had assumed, actually requires significant further learning. The making of sound judgements requires not just further knowledge, skills and attitudes, but also the capacity to deploy and combine selections from all of this learning in judgements that are sensitive to the needs and characteristics of the particular situation. Thus the framing of appropriate judgements is far from being routine or educationally uninteresting. Yet its neglect by, and exclusion from, the academic knowledge scenario is tantamount to assuming just this.

It is the holistic, integrative character of the knowledge as judgement scenario that ensures that it includes elements from both the earlier Barnett rival versions of competence, including those elements such as values that, contra Barnett, were argued to be crucial to both versions. The holistic, integrative character of the knowledge as judgement scenario also means that it does not take the jaundiced view of competence approaches that is typical of those under the sway of the academic knowledge scenario. The Cartesian assumptions of the latter scenario guarantee that a narrow approach to competence is seen as inevitable. Competence statements become atomistic, true propositions that can be written out explicitly with individuals assessed directly against them. (Compare this with the similar emphasis on explicit written propositions in the academic knowledge scenario.) However the knowledge as judgement scenario is not linked in any way to such propositional atomism. Rather, this scenario favours integrated competency standards that are based on the inescapability of holistic judgement. This approach avoids all the usual educational criticisms of the notion of competence since, almost invariably, such criticisms stem from assumptions about education deriving from the academic knowledge scenario, assumptions which do not apply to integrated competency standards (Hager 1994; Hager and Beckett 1995).

Some important broad features of the judgements that are central to the knowledge as judgement scenario are:

1. Judgements denote, i.e. they have '*direct* existential import' (Dewey [1938] 1991: 123). While a lot of ink has been spilt in recent times about the supposed futility of connecting language to the non-linguistic, Dewey would reject this way of posing the problem as a form of 'intellectualism'. Rather than starting from abstract theorization about the nature of language, Dewey takes the fundamental human situation of doing and being done by as his starting point. Judgements are central to this doing and being done by in that they make a difference to these basic existential conditions. Thus, judgements denote that they are about acting in the world rather than about contemplating it. It also follows from this that judgement is learned and refined from experience of acting in the world rather than from contemplating it. Thus practical experience is necessary for the acquisition of judgement. Of course, it does not follow that all practical experience is equally effective to achieve this end. This remains a matter for investigation.

2. Judgements often involve a series of intermediate judgements prior to the final or culminating judgement. Dewey ([1938] 1991: 124–5) calls these intermediate judgements 'adjustments'. For example, the final or culminating judgement might be a doctor's diagnosis of a patient's condition.

In arriving at the diagnosis many intermediate judgements will have been made, such as the significance of the patient's reports of symptoms, connections if any of this case to previous cases, tests that needed to be carried out, and so on.

3. In line with the fallibility of all knowledge claims, discussed earlier, judgements need to be recognized as defeasible. This is because judgements often concern what is most satisfactory or most effective in a particular context, rather than what is true or false. But notions such as satisfactoriness or effectiveness are relative. So judgements about them are defeasible because further understanding or information might require a change of judgement. The contextual sensitivity of workplace practical judgements ensures that more understanding or information is always a possibility.

4. Although judgements involve much more than disciplinary knowledge, they are not independent of it. Because mainstream education has focused on disciplinary knowledge at the expense of more contextual knowledge, such as that gained by informal workplace learning, proponents of judgement sometimes talk as though there is no connection between the two. This is a mistake. For instance, the doctor arriving at a diagnosis might well make considerable use of disciplinary knowledge. Certainly such things as interpreting the patient's test results presuppose a great deal of such knowledge. Likewise doctors called on to justify their judgements in a legal context appeal to significant amounts of disciplinary knowledge as underpinning and reinforcing their judgements.

Since in the knowledge as judgement scenario the knowledge that counts is that expressed by actions and outcomes, this scenario clearly requires somewhat different approaches to curriculum, teaching methods and assessment in higher education. For example, it is typical of real-life practice in the workplace that ready-made problems do not simply present themselves to the practitioner. Thus, a major role of good practitioners is to identify what the problems are in a given set of circumstances. Nor do these problems always have a clear-cut solution. So higher education courses need to prepare students for judging what the problem is in particular cases. This is a consideration that is often ignored as students are given a steady diet of pre-packaged problems to solve, problems that usually have unambiguous solutions. Many of the innovative teaching methods and initiatives of recent higher education, such as problem-based learning and work-based learning, appear to exemplify in various ways the different approaches required by the knowledge as judgement scenario. The extent to which this is so is the subject of ongoing research by the author.

Back to the camera metaphor

At the start of this chapter it was observed that just as the camera can lie, since there is a human contribution to the image construction, so also with the construction of knowledge. The claims to objectivity of the traditional knowledge production process have been questioned in this chapter. Its inherent distortion of what counted as objectified knowledge and the need for a different take on knowledge suited to the present era have been argued. Rather than replacing objectivity by distortion, what will happen is the displacement of one kind of rationally based distortion by another. One kind of camera lens is being replaced by another kind of lens. This newer knowledge lens is focused on the capacity for making novel changes in the world. It integrates a series of conceptions that were perceived as opposites in the older knowledge lens, such as the practical and the theoretical, process and content, the particular and the universal, the cognitive domain and other domains such as the affective and the social, and the formal and the informal. It is in overcoming traditional binary opposites such as these that learning theory can give a fairer place to judgement in the university curriculum.

Acknowledgements

This chapter has benefited from audience comments on an earlier version that was presented as a seminar at the University of Technology, Sydney. Assistance from reading some of Liz Devonshire's unpublished work on related topics is also acknowledged.

Notes

1. However, Barnett (1997a: 32) argues that such differences between discipline areas are not sufficient to overturn his academic competence list.
2. Another different effect of the move to mass higher education is increasing attention to the needs of graduates once they leave the university. Whereas it was arguable that the major preoccupation of elite higher education was the production of future academics, this outcome receives less priority in a mass higher eduation system.

References

Barnett, R. (1990) *The Idea of Higher Education*. Buckingham: SRHE/Open University Press.
Barnett, R. (1997a) Beyond competence, in F. Coffield and B. Williamson (eds) *Repositioning Higher Education*. Buckingham: SRHE/Open University Press.
Barnett, R. (1997b) A knowledge strategy for universities, in R. Barnett and A. Griffin (eds) *The End of Knowledge in Higher Education*. London: Cassell.
Beckett, D. and Hager, P. (2000) Making judgments as the basis for workplace learning: towards an epistemology of practice. *International Journal of Lifelong Education*, 19 (in press).

Bourgeois, E., Duke, C., Guyot, J-L. and Merrill, B. (1999) *The Adult University.* Buckingham: SRHE/Open University Press.

Bowden, J. and Marton, F. (1998) *The University of Learning: Beyond Quality and Competence.* London: Kogan Page.

Coffield, F. and Williamson, B. (1997) Introduction, in F. Coffield and B. Williamson (eds) *Repositioning Higher Education.* Buckingham: SRHE/Open University Press.

Dewey, J. ([1938] 1991) *Logic: The Theory of Inquiry. Volume 12 of John Dewey: The Later Works, 1925–1953,* edited by J. A. Boydston. Carbondale: Southern Illinois University Press.

Flew, T. (1998) New media and borderless education. *Australian Universities' Review,* 41 (1), 7–9.

Gibbons, M., Limoges, C., Nowotny, H. *et al.* (1994) *The New Production of Knowledge: The Dynamics of Science and Research in Contemporary Societies.* London: Sage.

Hager, P. (1994) Is there a cogent philosophical argument against competency standards? *Australian Journal of Education,* 38 (1), 3–18.

Hager, P. (1996) Professional practice in education: research and issues. *Australian Journal of Education,* 40 (3), 235–47.

Hager, P. (1999) Robin Usher on experience. *Educational Philosophy and Theory,* 31 (1), 63–75.

Hager, P. (2000) Know-how and workplace practical judgement. *Journal of Philosophy of Education,* 34 (in press).

Hager, P. and Beckett, D. (1995) Philosophical underpinnings of the integrated conception of competence. *Educational Philosophy and Theory,* 27 (1), 1–24.

Hager, P. and Beckett, D. (1998) What would lifelong education look like in a workplace setting?, in J. Holford, C. Griffin and P. Jarvis (eds) *International Perspectives on Lifelong Learning.* London: Kogan Page.

Lipman, M. (1991) *Thinking in Education.* Cambridge: Cambridge University Press.

Marshall, J. (1998) Information on information: recent curriculum reform. *Studies in Philosophy and Education,* 17 (4), 313–21.

Mason, R. (1998) *Globalising Education: Trends and Applications.* London: Routledge.

Robertson, D. (1997) Social justice in a learning market, in F. Coffield and B. Williamson (eds) *Repositioning Higher Education.* Buckingham: SRHE/Open University Press.

Russell, B. (1948) *Human Knowledge: Its Scope and Limits.* London: Allen & Unwin.

Scott, P. (1995) *The Meanings of Mass Higher Education.* Buckingham: SRHE/Open University Press.

Scott, P. (1997) The postmodern university?, in A. Smith and F. Webster (eds) *The Postmodern University? Contested Visions of Higher Education in Society.* Buckingham: SRHE/Open University Press.

Trowler, P. R. (1998) *Academics Responding to Change: New Higher Education Frameworks and Academic Cultures.* Buckingham: SRHE/Open University Press.

5

Eros and the Virtual: Enframing Working Knowledge through Technology

David Beckett

On the first walk Chloe and I head toward a multitude of long zoom lenses that go nuts when we approach. Under the TV floodlights models glide by each other, each foot swinging effortlessly around the other. Chloe's hips are swaying, her ass is twisting, a perfect pirouette at the runway's end, both our stares unflinching, full of just the right kind of attitude.

(Ellis 1998: 121)

Introduction: bringing the body back in

Dazzling and yet degraded, the main characters in Bret Easton Ellis's novel *Glamorama* (1998) live in a world of jet-setting celebrity and designer consumption. Their bodies drip with Calvin Klein, Cartier, Krug and each other. Amidst all this Ellis tells, quite brilliantly, a story 'full of just the right kind of attitude' – a story of visual style, and of visceral, amoral brutality. This chapter is not about the glamour and the drama of the high life, but is about a similar tension between embodiment and consumption, particularly insofar as this involves the educational implications of new technology. Western society is fascinated by embodiment. The cult of youthful image making, the possibilities of cosmetic surgery, and the effects of disease and ageing are just three prominent manifestations of this fascination which Ellis, and many other writers and artists, articulate so well. Yet it seems to me curious that new educational technologies, which have culminated in the notion of a 'virtual' university, require the denial of that embodiment. New technologies in education, like the world of celebrity, glitter enticingly and their acolytes abound, but they play upon the coloured surfaces: they shimmer, without materiality, and they have a shadowy aspect. The non-material (that is to say, disembodied) learning which I believe flows from these new technologies relies upon a prior conversion of knowledge into information, which thus presents learning as a consumption of marketed 'education' packages. Universities are at the forefront of this, which is surely one of the great ironies of our times, given their historic provenance in substantial and material learning. Yet, in the corporate world, newfound interest in individuals' self-directed (even lifelong) learning, in groups' teamwork, and what some call broadly post-Fordist 'knowledge production' fleshes out humanist adult learning principles that virtual technologies cannot exemplify.

This chapter explores the tensions between the embodied and the disembodied, across university and corporate worlds. Let me expand on this and problematize it. Now, immediately, some will assert that the corporate world is marketing anything educational as fervently as any university can – and they are correct to assert that. But corporations primarily exist for other reasons.

Corporations grow, dig, drill, manufacture, retail, import, export, and add value to everything required in twenty-first century globalized economies. Some of these activities are educational. Indeed, universities are increasingly corporations whose business is education with a capital E, so the boundaries are inevitably blurred. Given that blurring it is accurate to claim that, in general, within most of these activities in any sort of corporation is a new requirement of the workforce to learn better at, and for, their work. In this volume Garrick and Clegg have taken up the details of this, so suffice it to list some examples. Coaching, mentoring, appraisals, professional development programmes, job rotation, project management, off-site and on-site training and so on are all implicitly or explicitly learning opportunities. They assume an embodied worker, and assume humanist (rather than behaviourist) adult learning principles. People are expected to develop an enthusiasm for their own learning in the particular socio-cultural context of their workplace. Of course there are new material technologies which are deployed in these workplace-based activities – computer-assisted learning, email, the web, and on-line courses and training packages with self-paced elements. But basically the contention in this chapter is that the corporate usage of new technologies stays closer to a more natural materiality (the 'embodied') worker than do the universities' rampant enthusiasm for new technologies. This enthusiasm, paradoxically and unnaturally, 'disembodies' the learner.

It will be argued that this represents a fundamental misinterpretation of the role of technology in human life on the part of universities, which is an ontological claim (about what sorts of beings humans are) with epistemological consequences for work-based learning. The materiality of learning – the embodiment of it, if you will – is increasingly found outside universities.

'Informatization' and learning: it's immaterial

How do universities compromise the materiality of learning? An obvious start on an answer is to acknowledge that new technology is undoubtedly transforming learning, and it does so by converting language to data, or information. Virtual technologies, now in increasing usage in tertiary education, are automata which replace natural languages and, in so doing, provide streams of information, which flow across course and subject design, content, pedagogy and assessment, submerging and converting traditional material forms of these (print-based; humanly embodied) into electronic, or virtual forms.

Peters and Roberts (1998: 18–21), in making this general point, draw on Lyotard. Lyotard claims that science, technology and the economy are now converging and being recentred in daily life, partly caused by 'the multiplication of commodities with integrated automata and, more generally, with an integrated language (the logical language of microprocessors) used in both production and consumption' (1993: 16). Peters and Roberts identify a tension that this 'informatization' has generated, which they see as increasing

> . . . the concentration of the means of production of knowledge while allowing for its decentralisation; it brings 'technological unemployment' into being and devalues productive labour; and it disperses the horizons of everyday life by transforming the relationship to wealth, encouraging the individual initiative of the user. Perhaps most importantly, and rekindling the inspiration of Heidegger, Lyotard asserts that by *informatising language, the new technologies informatise the social bond, transforming our (inter) subjectivities.*
>
> (1998: 21, italics added)

So, on the one hand, there is a growing concentration of knowledge-as-informatized-language, since there is technological convergence in the ways computers link to each other; but, on the other hand, the new technologies tend to democratize this knowledge production because that same convergence allows more people to use initiative to construct their own learning.

Indeed, Larry Wall, the creator of Perl, which he calls 'the first postmodern computer language', states almost exactly that, starting with what amounts to an attack on Enlightenment meta-narratives:

> You've all heard the saying: If all you have is a hammer, everything starts to look like a nail . . . Modernism itself was a kind of hammer, and it made everything look like something to be hammered . . . Modernism oversimplifies . . . [it] puts the focus squarely on the hammer and the nail.
>
> In contrast, postmodernism puts the focus back onto the carpenter. You'll note that carpenters are allowed to choose whether or not to use hammers. They can use saws and tape measures if they choose, too. They have some amount of free will in the matter. They're allowed to be creative . . .
>
> [O]ne of the characteristics of a postmodern computer language is that it puts the focus not so much onto the problem to be solved, but

rather onto the person trying to solve the problem. I claim that Perl does that, and I also claim that . . . it was the first computer language to do that.

(1999: 6)

Despite the support for democratized initiative in this example, there is one glaring difficulty for Wall. Carpentry, in being (literally) constructivist, requires appropriate technology for nailing to occur at all, and no sane carpenter is going to expect a saw or a tape measure to achieve the penetration of timber by a nail. Modernism, for all its universalist pretensions, has generated a staggering diversity of forms of work specializations, embedded in discourses, practices and technologies, such that a spade is a spade – and a nail is a nail. One does not expect much convergence of those two. Digging and hammering are what spades and hammers, respectively, are best used for.

But Wall's claim about computer languages is right. Natural languages, like money, are becoming streams of data. This informatization confronts what Peters and Roberts (1998) call the 'social bond' in the particular manifestation of that bond known as the university. The term 'university' itself smacks of modernism. In a material sense, a university is a universal institution: it is the hammer that, after graduation, equips the working carpenter to nail everything in sight. You go to university, and your learning experiences (both the educational and the extra-curricular kinds) are embodied in you. Informatizing these experiences reduces their materiality. A virtual version of this informatization replaces that materiality completely. What is at stake for learning and scholarship in universities?

From Grand Hotel to shopping mall

Peter Scott, writing about ten years ago on the postmodern challenge to universities, uses this metaphor:

Modernists see culture science and perhaps society itself as a Grand Hotel, linked enterprises organised according to a commanding theme. Postmodernists see them as a shopping mall, an infrastructure that supports disparate enterprises without any common authoritative thread.

(1991: 15)

Education everywhere, including that within universities, is subject to market forces which through individuals' choices (like Wall's 'carpenters', exercising Peters and Roberts's 'initiatives') are expected to determine not only the prospects for successful learning for those individuals, but also which educational structures best engage those prospects. In an increasingly user-pays educational world, where is Scott's 'common authoritative thread'? The pessimism implied by this question comes about in the following way:

1. Starting out optimistically, the informatization of knowledge proceeding rapaciously via computer languages such as Perl offers the prospect of the ultimate democratization of learning – but seems to surrender epistemic authority.
2. Institutional survival has an impact: the virtual university – an epistemic shopping mall – could be said to have traded its identity in a Faustian bargain with market forces. Informatized knowledge has become a commodity, available to the crowded mall, but on an individualistic basis, with its price dictated by what the market will bear, not by the authority of its claim to be knowledge at all.
3. Finally, the 'social bonds' between the producers of this knowledge and between its producers and its consumers, and among the consumers themselves, will have been fractured by the reliance on technology-driven market forces.

But this is not what the techno-evangelists conclude. Their missionaries have returned and they have seen the future. Nothing less than the complete transformation of the 'learning industry' is supposedly required (Norris and Dolence 1996). If this is so, universities will have been colonized – 'informatized' we may say – by the new technology. I want now to critique what this means for the existence of teaching and the quality of learning.

Real time, real space: just being there

Let us grant this colonization. Let us grant, even, that such globalized colonization is a *desirable* future. What, however, are the consequences of access to 'delivery' of learning, where a major part of that access is now technologically unbound by real time and real space? In real time and real space, learners appear as embodied beings, in what Berge (1995) has called 'synchronous interaction'. However, in 'asynchronous' time and space, learners' embodiments are educationally irrelevant. They need not appear in learning at all. We know they are out there, but their interactions are mediated through technologized time and space. This must affect the quality of learning and, as I will argue below, a phenomenon crucial to high-quality learning is, due to flexible delivery, endangered.

Classroom dynamics and management have been a close focus of education research for at least three decades, perhaps since the realization in the late 1960s that Western society was becoming more diverse and that, in schooling, one shoe no longer fitted all feet. Class sizes, gender- and ethnicity-related learning styles, teacher behaviours, activity-based and experiential pedagogies, assessment variables, and so on, have all been ingredients in debates about how just being there in a classroom as an individual learner-in-a-group improves one's education (or perhaps impedes it). Diversity has emerged locally, classroom by classroom, as a fact of teachers' and learners' lives. Rather late in all this, new information technology has arrived promising individualized (or self-directable) ownership of learning.

Now we can arrange learning environments through new technology which removes the need 'just to be there' – that is, in the room. At once, you may say, we have eradicated the pathology of the classroom: learners will no longer feel their very presence has generated an inscription on their bodies by others. Fat, thin, shy, squeaky-voiced, slow, boisterous, late, sleepy, hairy – the whole Seven Dwarfs roll-call – will be irrelevant in the new virtual learning environment. Learners can log on and off in their time, arranging their learning programme without regard for appearances in real time or real space. And isn't this a great advance?

Undoubtedly so. Yet at the same time as diversity and technology are engaging, our culture is coming to terms with a new emphasis on visual literacy. Perhaps the greatest cultural change we are facing is the shift from the primacy of the printed word to the primacy of the visual image. We live in an image-driven age. *Glamorama* draws out the literal iconography of that when Ellis splatters his text with designer brand-names, but he also splatters gore and viscerality in his powerful descriptions of sado-terrorism. We see just those two aspects of contemporary culture in the mass media most nights. People expect to be entertained in cinematic as well as literary versions of all this. The visual and the virtual are intimately connected.

Looking at visual literacy

But to what extent does the virtual, in educational settings, engage this new visual literacy? On-line courses can look very pretty, but to get any-where with them the learner-as-viewer requires fairly high print literacy, not just a visual literacy. Understanding the icons and images is not as helpful as being able to read the print instructions and then following the protocols. Moreover, in the absence of a real-time, real-space classroom, learners require (virtually, that is) all the instructions in great detail lest, in their real time, they lose their way. On-line subject material is, in this sense, ambiguous. With its visual appeal and immediacy (which persuades learners that they can get along well with visual literacy), it *invites* learning, but to *achieve* learning, print literacy is essential. This is not merely an informational point, but an epistemological one. Hypertext links, which must be read as print and are presented as information, can leave a wide variety of sequenced, and randomized, pathways open to the learner. In terms of self-direction, this is exceptionally liberating. Smart minds can turn information into self-education, given half a chance. But in terms of socio-culturally significant learning (that is to say, information structured into knowledge claims) even the smartest minds need to know, eventually, what their peers think, and even what the teacher thinks, about the information they have cut and pasted into their own 'take' on the world. Furthermore, everyone expecting to learn 'on-line' needs a distillation of the previous attempts to establish, structure and overturn what counts as worthwhile knowledge. The information-presenting function of on-line

courses (as an example of flexible delivery) is unquestioned. But as know-
ledge-presenting functions, such delivery is ambiguous. Like the huge shopping mall, the technology in itself invites the learner to buy, but only to
satisfy mindless consumption. We learn because we have a social curiosity.
We want to learn because we know our own limitations, our own ignorance.
Self-direction, especially in front of the worldwide web, looks increasingly
capricious. In the face of this, virtual learning needs, at the very point of
learner experience, to be heavily structured. This is almost paradoxical.
The paradox is compounded when we notice that the more divergent from
printed text such on-line courses appear (the more they engage the visually
literate, perhaps), the greater they rely on traditional print literacy for
navigation.

Of course, new technologies permit flexible delivery, and require feed-
back. All manner of group-based networking, with and without the teacher,
is possible, and assessment tasks can key in to these. This is true – and it is
essential. But the more essential point remains: the informationalized (even
'virtual') university offers an excessively individualistic educational ideology
which, to avoid eccentric and idiosyncratic knowledge-claims emerging, structures masses of teacher input, in printed text format. It is, in brief, lonely
and disembodied learning.

The workplace and 'the eros of learning'

In contrast, lonely and disembodied learning is not what most workplaces provide. Work for most of us occurs in the here and now, in real
time, and in real space, with real bodies present. I will now outline what
it is about workplaces (including offices, factories, classrooms, training
rooms, meeting rooms, conference halls and so on) that tends to generate
high-quality learning, by concentrating on a phenomenon ignored by the
rush to the new technologies. Some in education call this 'the eros of
learning'.

The eros of learning is not the pursuit of the erotic-as-sexuality (although
that may well be present). Instead it is the recognition of the wider notion
of the erotic-as-pleasure, and it is to be found in the work of the best
practitioners (trainers, teachers, managers, mentors – anyone in a leadership role for learning at work). This occurs when they energize learners
(including students, protégés, colleagues, subordinates and so on) with a
love for the content, and a love for learning in itself. This is a professionally
responsible characterization of the *enthusiasmos* which inspires learners to
learn more. It typically happens in the real time in real work sites of real
embodied people. McWilliam and Palmer (1996: 164) write:

> In describing teachers and students as 'bodies' we are conscious that
> the reader may regard this descriptor as impoverished or demeaning of
> persons engaged in pedagogical work. However . . . this descriptor . . .
> is being reclaimed in a new area of social theorising called *embodiment*

theory... [where] authors speak of a 'lived body'... or a 'mindful body'
... in ways that constitute a departure from the traditional Western
'mind/body' distinction. The 'self' is understood to be an integrated
being in which capability is not ascribed to a decorporatised mind
but in a body as a lived structure ... and locus of experience ... This is
an important shift for understanding how new forms of pedagogy
are being experienced or 'lived out' when they demand the absence,
removal, or semi-disappearance of the fleshly bodies of teachers and
students from the university seminar room or staff room.

McWilliam and Palmer nail home the point well. There is a strong and
inevitably visual element in this environment: workplaces can tap our emerging visual culture – say, as performance – the way 'asynchronous' interaction could not even identify. Humour, anecdote, negotiation and spontaneity
are hallmarks of this kind of learning, and of this sort of teaching. Putting
out spotfires, seizing the moment, catching the nuance and making something unique out of human sensibilities as they are inevitably revealed are
all part of this, too. You have to be there! This usefully practical body is
what Wittgenstein draws to our attention throughout his writings on philosophical psychology (see 'on raising one's arm'; Beckett 1992). This is
recently interpreted anew by Schatzki (1996: 69), who states: 'In sum the
expressive body, on this systematising interpretation of Wittgenstein, is a
socially moulded and naturally expressive entity whose activities manifest,
signify, and effect conditions of life.'

In programme terms, what is going on is not the delivery of content by
actions that are facilitated by a teacher or trainer, and chosen by self-
directed learners. Instead, what is going on is the construction of content
by processes that are negotiated during that construction. The workplace
leader has broad aims which she or he works towards with the group or the
individual, but the energy generated on the way through is formative. There
are detours, backtracks, byways, brick walls and many fallings-short. The
point is that cues from all those who are bodily present are central to all
that. These cues will be behavioural in the richer sense that involves the
inference of meanings from 'body language', especially the visual – eye
contact (and therefore the oral and the aural). These inferences actively
transform the content and the processes in reflexive fashion, on the spot,
to arrive at a unique programme.

This is the 'hot action' of the workplace (Beckett 1996). It is, if you like,
the erotification of learning in the sense that the dynamics of such classrooms play out the intentions presented in planned and accredited documents. Competency-based training, on a behavioristic reading of such
documents, minimizes the chances of this occurring. On a more humanistic
reading, in which the ascription of competence acknowledges the performativity of the competence, and hence its construction in real time and real
space on a daily and fluid basis (Mulcahy 1998), the chances of the erotification of learning are maximized.

Notwithstanding this richer, humanistic reading of workplace activities, the point remains that 'informatized' programmes, delivered (rather than constructed) through new virtualized technologies, reduce the learner to disembodiment. And that, dear reader (not viewer!), reinstates the 'ghost in the machine': all mind plus mechanistic body (Ryle 1949; Schön 1987). This has been the picture of elite education of all kinds, for centuries, in grammar schools and Oxbridge, and, yes, among senior secondary credentials like the International Baccalauréate, and its equivalents around Western schooling (the academic mind reigns supreme). The effect of all this contributes to keeping workplace-based learning in its lowly place – as mechanistic, behaviouristic, and therefore unthinking.

An ontology of practice

Let me swing the whole debate around and come at it from the other side. In dramatic contrast to the Cartesianism implicit in universities' enthusiasm for new technologies, the corporate workplace, wherever it is found in the Western world, is rightly serious about bodies and what they can do, and identifying this with thinking.

I want to argue, now, that one of the most desirable forms of knowledge – in fact, one that is now emerging as a top priority in the corporate world – is what is least likely to be produced by a virtual university. Let us remind ourselves that learning in a virtual university is constructed primarily through electronic journals and databases, synchronous and asynchronous conferencing and forums, and a variety of multimedia course packages, all mainly glued together 'on-line'. What sort of learner is being constructed in the resort to and reliance upon these new technologies? In other words, what are the ontological implications of this transformation?

A prior comment to set the scene for an answer to this question. It is fairly clear that the corporate world is quite serious about 'knowledge production' – and this means there is a diversity of sites of knowledge, some in competition with traditional universities, and some in partnership. A prominent example of this wider pursuit of knowledge production is a recent collection of essays entitled *Rethinking the Future* (Gibson 1997). Its modest subtitle, 'Rethinking business principles, competition, control and complexity, leadership, markets and the world', is symptomatic of its ambitions! The big names of the corporate world are present: Handy, Bennis, Covey, Hammer, Kotter and Senge are some of the contributors, and in their writing one senses a breathtaking reassessment of the construction and ownership of knowledge. As an anonymous rhetorician put it: 'There is more engineering knowledge in Silicon Valley than in the Engineering Faculty at Stanford.'

Handy (1997), for example, makes the first contribution, 'Finding sense in uncertainty', and seizes the postmodern mood of doubt and instability. He develops, almost evangelically, a crusade for constructivist (rather than traditional, inherited) values, at work, in education, at home and in the community at large. Now that capitalism is triumphant, Handy believes the enemy is within:

> Communism had a cause – which was, ideally, a sense of equality and prosperity for all, that all people were and could be equal – but it didn't have an appropriate mechanism to deliver that cause. Whereas capitalism is a mechanism, but it seems to me that it lacks a cause. Is it all just to make us rich, or is there more to life than that?
>
> (1997: 27)

This raises the values previously the preserve of the university-based Left – those sceptics of capitalism as an economic 'system' – and reapplies them within the 'system', as a critique of the values of the corporate Right. Handy goes on to show this crossover when he states:

> The first stage in rethinking capitalism is to be absolutely clear about what it's all for and *who* it's for. I don't think the answer that it's for the financiers – i.e. the shareholders – is a very adequate answer at all, either practically, or morally. We have, for instance, to realise that the new source of wealth is intelligence. It's not land, or money, or raw materials or technology. It's the brains and skills of people . . .
>
> But, in the age of intellectual capital, who owns the capital? It's not the shareholders. It can't be in any real sense. *The people who own the capital are the core workers of the company. In other words, it's the assets who own the assets* . . . So a model that says that the company is owned by the people who finance it – and that the people in it are just instruments of those owners – is no longer pertinent in this day and age, and it certainly won't be appropriate in the future. It just isn't the right sort of concept.
>
> (1997: 30, italics added)

Given Handy's assumptions about ownership, then, mapping the virtual university's epistemological territory requires some boundary crossing. Asking, as does Handy, what is the meaningfulness of capitalist enterprise, and answering that question with educationally resonant concepts (intelligence, skills and the like) redraws the old territorial imperatives: universities are about knowledge; corporations are about business. Instead, universities are about business (advanced by their enthusiasm for virtual i.e. informatized learning), and the corporate world is about knowledge.

And in the corporate world, the knowledge productivity of the workers is their greatest asset. Witness this dramatic and messianic claim on the university's future, from the first issue of the *Virtual University Journal*:

> The scholarly business must be re-thought. Tomorrow's business cannot be seen with yesterday's eyes. It is time to separate what the parties do from what they are, and to be again what they are. What they do and have done is no longer appropriate as the driving impetus (sic) of

the business. Universities, libraries and publishers must find new things to do which reflect more accurately what they are and need to be.

(Peters et al. 1998: 2)

This quotation seems to run together the business and educational realities of universities, but relies on virtual technologies to cement these realities together. Clearly new learning and new work practices are entailed by this evangelism, within universities and beyond. The ontological map is being redrawn, whatever we make think of the evangelism itself.

In this spirit, we have now identified a new ontology of practice. Workers are integrated thinking and doing beings who exercise all manner of judgements during the working day – these are their practices. Following from these states of being, there are new, powerful and experientially authentic knowledge claims made of workers and of work which challenge the formality of traditional university-based education (see the previous chapter). For example, managers' 'know-how' connects readily with the Aristotelian notion of *phronesis* – practical wisdom (Beckett 1999).

In bridging the ontological to the epistemological I want, briefly, to return to the big picture. It is important to remember that the experientially authentic working knowledge espoused within corporate workplaces – via strategies such as mentoring, appraisals, project management and so on – seems to fly in the face of the movement within universities. This is leading towards a virtual mode of existence, where the pursuit of practical wisdom as a pedagogical and academic purpose looks precarious.

Practical workplace learning across the corporate world assumes and expects the dissolution of the traditional (that is to say, modernist) mind/body Cartesian world, and its privileging of the pure mind. Even computer languages (such as Perl, as we noted) throw the initiative back to the worker-as-carpenter to construct their work from a variety of tools and strategies. It is the person, not merely the mind, which is significant, and persons are inevitably embodied. In the light of this postmodern conceptual shift, the new material technologies in education, of which on-line delivery is the most prominent, look arcane. More ominously, to the extent that these new technologies discount teaching in favour of the delivery of learning, they impart an instrumentalism that enshrines the old Cartesian dualism between mental labour (thinking) and manual labour (doing).

Thus the irony: just as contemporary Western society is exploring what can be meant by 'writing on the body' (in the arts, for example: see Peter Greenaway's film, *The Pillow Book*, although it must be emphasized that mainstream cinema continues to exploit stereotypes), in the new educational technologies we are 'writing off the body'. If bodies are written off (or rather out of) learning, vast and crucial experiences, and possibilities of experiences, will be denied us. Disembodied learning, in my view, will be a poor substitute for the materiality of real-time/real-place learning. Such disembodied learning will, however, be very widely available, but will not have the practicality now required in most workplaces, where an ontology of practice is emerging. We return to this point after considering the knowledge claims such an ontology generates.

An epistemology of practice

What are the epistemological implications of this new embodied worker? In the *Nichomachean Ethics*, Aristotle writes extensively of various forms of knowledge, of which practical wisdom, or *phronesis*, is the 'true and reasoned state of capacity to act with regard to the things that are good or bad for man' (1941: 1025). Virtuous actions, those with ends beyond the mere doing of something, transform that doing into practical wisdom. It is this sort of practice to which professions aspire, and therefore which award courses in universities have mainly been about: professional preparation and induction into practice.

But Aristotle has a separate category of knowledge for *productivity*:

> . . . the reasoned state of capacity to act is different from the reasoned state of capacity to make . . . *art* is identical with a state of capacity to make, involving a true course of reasoning. All art is concerned with coming into being, i.e. with contriving and considering how something may come into being which is capable of either being or not being, and whose origin is in the maker and not in the thing made.
>
> (1941: 1026)

Art is essentially about making, or productivity, but of course we need to acknowledge that there are myriad human activities which are not necessarily artistic: we can make love, a mess, a fuss, amends, and so on. What is crucial is the creativity, or contrivance (in Aristotle's terms), whereby something is brought into being due to the actions of the creator, or producer. The entity or state exists due to the work (that is, the labour) of that person. There is a significant role for skill in this. Aristotle, and Plato before him, even more fully, recognize the *techne* all artists and all 'makers' possess. But we do not exhaust 'making' by dealing only in skill-attribution. Skill, or *techne*, contributes to (w)holistic construction of what is regarded as a creative action. Aristotle's term for this form of knowledge is *poiesis*. *Poiesis* differs primarily from *phronesis* in its pursuit of beauty, whereas *phronesis* is the pursuit of what is right.

It is therefore entirely congruent with Aristotelian theories of knowledge to embed, within corporate knowledge productivity, an integrative and creative propensity for artistry. Schön (1983, 1987) has already claimed as much for the reflective practitioner. Schön's legitimate disdain for the traditional technical–instrumentalist conception of practice is well taken, but we have advanced the analysis somewhat by emphasizing the breadth of the value-ladenness of knowledge productivity. If we take productivity in the Aristotelian sense as outlined above, we are able to generate a development of 'know-how' or *phronesis*. Bear this in mind, because the virtual university has almost nothing to contribute to the formation of productive 'know-how'. But the corporate world is moving along – and their universities (the Motorolas, Disneys, Siemens and so on) have 'scholarship' intimately tied to an epistemology of practice.

An Aristotelian epistemology is itself enriched by Dewey, who brought to our understanding of working and thinking the significance of technology in his 'philosophy of enquiry' – true vocational education. Hickman (1990), taking as central Dewey's breadth of interest in technology (beyond the material, to include *techne* – productive skill, in the ancient Greek sense), writes:

> Active productive skill . . . took its place in Dewey's thought as a means by which he could, in his role as opponent of unresolved dualisms of all sorts, place human experience *in medias res*. Active productive skill offered Dewey a key to understanding the place of human beings within and at the cutting edge of the activities of nature . . . Nowhere is Dewey's treatment of technology more insightful than in his radical reconstruction of traditional theories of knowledge and his replacement of them with a theory of enquiry.
>
> (1990: 19)

Here, amid the epistemological reconstruction, we note an underpinning ontological claim: active productive skill is a natural phenomenon, in that it displays the sort of beings we are. Dewey's main ontological project was the dissolution of the traditional (that is to say, 'modernist') mind/body Cartesian world, with its privileging of the 'pure' mind. For Dewey, and drawing on Aristotle, we can claim that the very being of humans is shaped by active productive skill, with thinking (judgements, wisdom, values) central in this activity.

Can we connect this ontology of practice with the epistemology of practice even more tightly?

Ontology and epistemology: being and knowing

There are two themes to be combined. First, as we discussed earlier, some educational theorists (McWilliam and Palmer 1996) want to bring the body back in to learning experiences, by emphasizing the eros of learning. This is an ontological claim, relating to the kind of beings we are – ones who have erotic desires that can be excited in the classroom. It does however have epistemological implications because it avers that we learn best from more vivid (sensationally complex) experiences. Second, we have just determined that Dewey (underpinned by Aristotle) wants to bring active skilled work back in to learning experiences. This is initially an epistemological claim, about the kinds of knowledge we should value. It does however have ontological implications because it avers that we are beings that define ourselves by what we do.

Taking this first, ontological, theme together with the second, epistemological, theme, we may conclude now that it is the working body that learns – in (mainly) social activity, some of which is mental, some of which is physical. Through this activity mental and physical aspects are intertwined. The educational significance for us when we are conceptualizing working knowledge is that these activities are experienced holistically, by people in daily life, in social interrelationships, and often through the leadership of work-based colleagues, who track through these inevitably embodied experiences with the learners. In this sense, *learning is written on the body*, rather than ascribed to the ghost in the machine.

We can assert, now, that new technologies in education, of which the virtual university is the ultimate manifestation, start to glitter rather less. In fact, they look increasingly arcane! A virtual university enshrines an epistemological instrumentalism that assumes the old Cartesian ontology – a dualism of mental labour (thinking) and manual labour (doing). A digital world is disembodied, and leaves embodied learning to others.

By contrast, and outside universities, the corporate world, as we have seen, has moved quickly and with more innovation into humanistic adult learning possibilities – and requires an embodied (i.e. real-time, physically present) worker for the working out of *phronesis* through productivity of various kinds. There is something more truly human about that, and something less than truly human about the virtual version: after all, 'virtual' is a 'not-quite-the-real-thing' claim. I have established that its less-than-real status is explicable (but not justifiable) because it denies the materiality of the learner. It disembodies the individual, and it does so mainly because new technologies have 'informatized' knowledge and 'disembodied' it by reducing it to data.

Practical wisdom and productive knowledge

Yet is this pessimism justified? Let me unpack the work of a university just a little. Scholarship – the traditional work of academics – relies upon certain canons and traditions that provide the basis for the objectification of knowledge. Furthermore, this objectification requires freedom to work towards the production of agreed objectivities. It is these that are the 'common authoritative thread' of academic work as manifested in a number of practices typically associated with scholarship and research. These include valid and reliable experiments and the development of linear arguments. This often involves the use of selected original documents to establish a 'paper trail' with authenticated provenance, impeccably resourced secondary references, and so on. The time and space to establish these objectivities is at the heart of the idea of a university, and the outcome of this objectified knowledge is the issue of public, contentious, justifiable bodies of knowledge, always and endemically in flux. What we take to be knowledge at any given moment is a 'take' on the state of objectified enquiry in any given field. Postmodern scholarship itself is a worthy and substantial contributor to these enquiries.

I want to argue that this authority-laden epistemological claim has a deep and enduring public significance analogous to the dictum that 'the camera cannot lie'. There is a standard of truth for knowledge objectified in the work practices of universities, which is recognized at large as veridical with the force that photography carries: the camera is used to 'take' a picture of reality, and the image that results is commonly taken as honest and faithful. But of course this analogy is not so straightforward.

In one way we want (as when we use a camera) to preserve the traditional university 'take' on knowledge – if *that* sort of objectification cannot establish truth for us, there are very few other places to look for it. However, in another way, the objectification of knowledge just outlined is a form of lying. Just as we now know the camera *can* lie and, therefore, that a reconsideration of human responsibility for the construction of image making is urgent (Mitchell 1992), so is some reconsideration of our responsibility for the construction of knowledge, similarly, an urgent matter. And it is the very informatization of knowledge by virtual technologies which is provoking that reconsideration of its objectification.

When a university is seduced into the informatization of knowledge, it loses out on two fronts. On the one hand, it compromises the presentation and re-presentation of knowledge which traditional scholarship has objectified (cameras define reality so long as we are aware of their propensity to lie!). On the other hand, the innovative practical judgements now being emphasized in the (embodied) corporate world owe little to virtual technologies. Instead they owe much to human creativity and risk taking in the enactment of *phronesis* in everyday working life (much like the actions and enactions of painting a picture: a 'making', not a 'doing'). A university that uses new technologies to enhance the objectification of knowledge is going to do comparatively well. If it can use these technologies in partnerships with workers in the corporate world, it will enhance the subjectification of knowledge (or, rather, of knowing), and it should do superlatively well.

Conclusion: transforming our (inter) subjectivities

Recall that Peters and Roberts draw on Lyotard to assert that 'the new technologies informatise the social bond, transforming our (inter) subjectivities' (1998: 21). In his landmark 1953 essay, *The Question Concerning Technology* ([1953] 1977), Heidegger also emphasizes this melding of the epistemological and the ontological. First, he sets out the epistemological claim, and it is worth noting that Heidegger, drawing upon Aristotle, explictly moves us beyond the instrumental, or the merely technical, the *techne* (elsewhere he connects technology with the artful making of *poiesis*):

But where have we strayed to? We are questioning concerning (sic) technology, and we have arrived at *aletheia*, revealing. What has the essence of technology to do with revealing? The answer: everything. For every bringing forth is grounded in revealing ... Instrumentality is considered to be the fundamental characteristic of technology. If we enquire step by step into what technology, represented as means, actually is, then we shall arrive at revealing ... Technology is therefore no mere means. Technology is a way of revealing. If we give heed to this, then another whole realm ... will open itself up to us. It is the realm of revealing, i.e. truth.

([1953] 1977: 318)

What is revealed, according to Heidegger? Simply put, and without Heidegger's metaphysical accretions, he, and we, can agree that humans come to know ourselves and our world through technology, not as a means, but as an end:

Wherever man opens his eyes and ears, unlocks his heart, and gives himself over to meditating and striving, shaping and working, entreating and thanking, he finds himself everywhere already brought into the unconcealed.

(Heidegger [1953] 1977: 324)

This is redolent of the world of daily experiences that are the bases of adults' learning, particularly the self-discovery experiences (the *eros* of the workplace) which thoughtful workplace activities (c.f. Dewey) over time construct as practical wisdom (c.f. Aristotle's *phronesis*).

In this crucial sense, then, technology embodies us: our human purposes are revealed to us in the relationship we have to technology. Heidegger's famous term for this is 'enframing', which 'gathers man with a view to ordering the self-revealing'. It is the argument of this chapter that in the workplace, rather than in the 'virtualized' university, we are more likely to encounter enframing experiences. This is because the workplace is an embodiment of knowledge. As Mary Kennedy wrote almost 20 years ago, in relation to a very specific setting, that of school managers:

Working knowledge is the organised body of knowledge that administrators and policy-makers use spontaneously and routinely in the context of their work. It includes the entire array of beliefs, assumptions, interest, and experiences that influence the behaviour of individuals at work.

(1983: 193)

Scepticism towards new technologies in education is essential. On present indications, the corporate world looks much closer to developing working knowledge, though a much more selective approach to technology, than universities are displaying. However, while the contrast has mainly been between such a virtual university and the corporate worlds I do not want to leave the impression that all innovation is going on out in real-time corporate learning environments populated by enthusiastic workers inspired by a recent love of Aristotelian *phronesis*. This contrast is instead intended to emphasize that knowledge creation anywhere is the job of the creative, embodied individuals, and that new technology, in universities as much as anywhere else, is not more likely to advance creativity. In fact I have hinted that even the artistry of work, wherever it is done, is not much advanced by such technology, so we would be unwise (strictly, deficient in practical wisdom) if we looked to decontextualized, ephemeral and internationally marketed educational activities for sustained and systematic creativity. Rather, isn't that creativity what working (the) knowledge is all about?

References

Aristotle (1941) *Basic Works,* edited by Richard McKeon. New York, NY: Random House.

Beckett, D. (1992) Straining training: the epistemology of workplace learning. *Studies in Continuing Education,* 14 (2), 130–42.

Beckett, D. (1996) Critical judgement and professional practice. *Educational Theory,* 46 (2), 135–50.

Beckett, D. (1999) Past the guru and up the garden path: the new organic management learning, in D. Boud and J. Garrick (eds) *Understanding Learning at Work.* London: Routledge.

Berge, Z. (1995) Facilitating computer conferencing: recommendations from the field. *Educational Technology,* Jan–Feb., 22–30.

Ellis, B. (1998) *Glamorama.* London: Picador.

Gibson, R. (ed.) (1997) *Rethinking the Future.* London: Nicholas Brealey.

Handy, C. (1997) Finding sense in uncertainty, in R. Gibson, (ed.) *Rethinking the Future.* London: Nicholas Brealey.

Heidegger, M. ([1953] 1977) The question concerning technology, in D. Krell (ed.) *Martin Heidegger: Basic Writings.* San Francisco, CA: Harper.

Hickman, L. (1990) *John Dewey's Pragmatic Technology.* Bloomington, IN: Indiana University Press.

Kennedy, M. (1983) Working knowledge. *Knowledge: Creation, Diffusion, Utilization,* 5 (2), 193–211.

Lyotard, J-F. (1993) New technologies, in J-F. Lyotard, *Political Writings,* translated by B. Readings and K. Geiman. Minneapolis, MN: University of Minnesota.

McWilliam, E. and Palmer, P. (1996) Pedagogues, tech(no)bods: reinventing postgraduate pedagogy, in E. McWilliam and P. Taylor (eds) *Pedagogy, Technology, and the Body.* New York, NY: Peter Lang.

Mitchell, W. (1992) *The Reconfigured Eye: Visual Truth in the Post-Photographic Era.* Cambridge, MA: MIT Press.

Mulcahy, D. (1998) Designing the user/using the design: the shifting relations of a curriculum technology change. *Social Studies of Science,* 28 (1), 5–37.

Norris, D. and Dolence, M. (1996) IT leadership is key to transformation. *Cause/ Effect,* 19 (11), 11–20.

Peters, J., Wills, G. and Sanderlands, E. (1998) Footsteps in the sand: a reflection on past and futures in our institutions of scholarship. *Virtual University Journal,* 1 (1). http://www.openhouse.org.uk/virtual-university-press/vuj

Peters, M. and Roberts, P. (1998) Introduction: the question concerning virtual technology and tertiary education – the shift from knowledge to information, in M. Peters and P. Roberts (eds) *Virtual Technologies and Tertiary Education.* Palmerston North, New Zealand: Dunmore Press.

Ryle, G. (1949) *The Concept of Mind.* London: Hutchinson.

Schatzki, T. (1996) Practiced bodies: subject, gender, and minds, in T. Schatzki and W. Natter (eds) *The Social and Political Body.* London: Guildford Press.

Schön, D. (1983) *The Reflective Practitioner.* New York, NY: Basic Books.

Schön, D. (1987) *Educating the Reflective Practitioner: Toward a New Design for Teaching and Learning in the Professions.* San Francisco, CA: Jossey-Bass.

Scott, P. (1991) *The Postmodern Challenge.* Stoke-on Trent: Trentham Books.

Wall, L. (1999) *Perl: The First Postmodern Computer Language.* http: www.wall.org/ -larry/pm.html

6

The Policy Environment of Work-based Learning: Globalization, Institutions and Workplaces

John McIntyre and Nicky Solomon

Education policy is something that affects all Australians either directly or through its long-term contribution to the quality of life. The Government has a commitment to a knowledge-based society.

(Editorial 1999)

Introduction

Work-based learning has a provenance. It is a development that springs from a political context that needs to be rendered visible and analysed. This can be done from a number of perspectives. In this chapter our interest is with the policy environment that surrounds post-compulsory education and which has fostered the idea that the workplace can be a significant site of learning. For some, though, the proposition that there is a 'policy environment' that has coerced institutions into work-based learning is an overstatement that magnifies the influence and significance of governments. It might be readily argued that work-based learning simply extends the principle of cooperative education or work placement, the result of individual companies approaching universities and colleges. As a development, it does not have to appear as being driven by the policies of restructuring that have been imposed on higher and further education systems in the last two decades by a variety of Australian governments, Labour and Coalition, federal and state. As the epigraph to this chapter suggests, this restructuring aims at bettering the quality of life through a commitment to a knowledge-based society.

The view developed in this chapter is not a refusal of the politics of work-based learning, for such learning is primarily a policy solution, in its own terms and in terms of policy at large, to a range of problems that have emerged for both employers and institutions. Moreover, it is an expression of the response of institutions to other more macro developments outside the nation-state, in particular the forces of globalization, which are impacting on national economies, their politics and their social institutions.

While it is true that the development of work-based learning represents an organic accommodation of educational institutions to the new times and new external pressures, it is also important to ask how this development is posed as a solution to other pressures on educational institutions. Among these are the pressures to be more relevant and to customize their courses to suit the needs of clients and stakeholders. It is essential to inquire into the nature of the environment that has endorsed work-based learning as a worthwhile development, as an answer to perceived problems. We argue that the educational policy environment has been decisive in creating an institutional environment that is conducive to work-based learning.

We highlight educational policy in this environment because it is policy that has sought the reform of educational institutions and encouraged them to be more flexible and adaptive, in the interests of national economic competitiveness. Policy has been one of the factors that has encouraged universities and colleges to 'behave' in a more entrepreneurial and outward-looking way. In this sense, we will argue that it is policy intervention in post-compulsory education that has been the major catalyst of work-based learning.

In suggesting that policy has engineered the shift to work-based learning, we suggest also that the policy involved has been conditioned by globalization processes. As others have argued (Yeatman 1991; Marginson 1993), the rationales of policy intervention in education derive primarily from the challenges that nation-states now face from the globalized economy. However, this is only one of a number of changes that are serving to reshape institutions. In this chapter we outline various narratives of globalization that have provided rationales for national governments, including those of Australia, to reform their education and training systems in line with the current economic pressures.

At the same time, suggesting that policy has catalysed work-based learning is not to suggest that it mandates such an innovation. But it has provided touchstones such as flexibility, recognition of prior learning and responsiveness that has obligated educational institutions to seek educational alliances with industry and business. How this is done is another story, but here it is remarkable how publicly funded institutions have been remaking themselves without much intervention by government beyond, say, funding stringencies. This leads us to explore the way in which work-based learning ushers in new modes of governmentality, dependent on self-regulating professionals who negotiate the new arrangements and determine the parameters of acceptable institutional performance.

Globalization and educational policy

State policy interventions that have encouraged greater institutional responsiveness are conditioned by broader economic and social rationales for action.

The policy environment can be seen as rewriting various narratives drawn from the 'epic' of globalization, where nation-states are depicted as faced by imperatives to adapt to the new times if they are to remain economically prosperous and socially stable. However, as Brown (1999) notes, globalization has been deployed in a highly uncritical way in analysing educational contexts. Yet its narratives continue to dominate the formation of state educational policy and provide powerful accounts of the imperative to restructure institutions. As Waters (1995) suggests, the global underlines the significance of the local, for the forces of globalization are expressed in local communities, shaping people's experiences in new and profound ways. The local is increasingly an extension of the global. As Giddens (1990: 64) has suggested:

> Globalisation can . . . be defined as the intensification of worldwide social relations which link distant localities in such a way that local happenings are shaped by events many miles away and vice versa . . . Local transformation is as much a part of globalisation as the lateral extension of social connections across time and space.

Work-based learning is an educational example of such a 'local happening'. For globalization creates varying conditions that act on corporations, institutions, governments and learners alike to promote work-based learning as a policy solution in the new economy. In this way, work-based learning is a key location of change in post-compulsory education, converging around many lines of influence. Thus policy provides a vantage point for analysing work-based learning in its globalized context.

Policy has been rediscovered by educationalists as a consequence of the intervention by the state into their work (Dale 1989; Ball 1990, 1994). In Australia, reform of the historically centralized administration of education has provoked analogous analysis (Yeatman 1991, 1994; Marginson 1993, 1997; Taylor *et al.* 1997). The term 'policy intervention' needs comment, since public education has been a defining feature of state activity for over a century. The very notion that the reform of education and training is needed, and that policy is a way of achieving such reform, implies that political agendas have disrupted what professional educators have come to regard as their territory.

The literature suggests that policy intervention has occurred because economic rationalism has disrupted the post-war policy settlement. This had assumed that increasing growth and Keynesian public sector expenditure along with professional control over educational decision making would never cease. Faced with the unravelling of this settlement, educationalists have turned to theorizing the politics of educational reform, theorizing the state and its policy processes, and the way these processes merge to reshape and refract educational contexts (Taylor *et al.* 1997).

Though modern states differ historically in the extent to which they made state education serve as an instrument of national policy (Green 1990), all nation-states are now subjected to the imperative of making their education and training systems responsive to the needs of economic globalization. It leads national governments to make education policy more strategic in character but, in doing so, they work with policy understandings that are themselves more international in character.

Accounting for globalization

The concept of globalization (Brown 1999) is a complex one. Waters (1995) suggests that globalization emerges as early as the sixteenth century, then develops through European imperialism and colonialism and becomes in our time an important feature of modernization that has facilitated the spread of transnational capitalism.

Economic globalization is associated with the intensification of economic competition that is open and deregulated. It is also associated with the rise of multinational corporations, the decentralization of financial markets and the mobility of capital, and the deregulation of labour. The latter is also associated with the technologization of work and the consequent reduction in the power of organized labour. Under the dynamic of so-called 'fast capitalism' the relation between 'automated' and 'informated' systems is a critical one (Zuboff 1984; Castells 1996). New information technologies, by increasing inter-connectedness, provide a technological basis for global capitalism, knowledge work and the information society. Changes to the patterns of work, especially the recognition that knowledge is an important dimension of the culture of work, have had an impact on educational institutions and increased the demand that they be vocationally relevant (Kenway and Langmead 1999).

Political globalization has been hastened by these economic trends, threatening the authority and power of sovereign states, which are now more constrained in their ability to govern their populations. This has led to the contraction of the welfare state and the wane of social democratic politics in the West (Yeatman 1991). It has also been suggested that globalization is characterized by the growth of international government and non-government agencies such as the United Nations (UN), the Organisation for Economic Co-operation and Development (OECD), aid, peace and law enforcement agencies, as well as religious, professional and labour organizations (Waters 1995). Globalization thus can undermine 'customary' definitions of citizenship based on racial exclusiveness. Many nation-states have had to reshape their institutions to accommodate the diversity that immigration and diasporization has engendered (Yeatman 1994: 104).

A key aspect of political globalization is that of global policy hegemony. Bodies such as the OECD have internationalized the processes of policy formation, which are now integral parts of policy formation at the local level of the nation-state. Economic theories dominate educational policy, dictating the reform of education and training systems in such a way that they contribute to the goal of generating competitive and efficient economies.

In this way, human capital has become a global policy discourse that justi-fies the restructuring of public education to promote individual choice but requiring individuals to contribute to its costs (Marginson 1993). At the same time, human capital theory is also the rationale for recognizing learn-ing in the workplace, promoting the 'learning organization' and giving industry bodies and employers more control over vocational education and training. In the new vocationalism concepts such as productivity have gained ethical weight – nowhere more significantly than in warranting the virtues of work-based learning.

Cultural globalization refers to tendencies for the local to be at once obliterated and accentuated (Waters 1995). Local identity and ethnicity are undermined by the spread of consumer materialism and 'privatized consumption', yet at the same time, fundamentalist religious movements and regionality are fuelled by this breakdown. Cultural globalization brings transculturation – the increased movement of people beyond national fron-tiers and the crossing of cultural boundaries creates changing and 'hybrid' cultural identities through migration, creating ethnically diverse national populations in settler societies (Rizvi and Walsh 1999). Cultural globalization is accelerated by new technologies enabling better transport and commun-ications, and information exchange. A narrative of global inter-connectedness emphasizes the ways new technologies have made possible better transport and communications, and information exchange. It emphasizes the crossing of national and cultural boundaries enabled by the virtual relationships of computer-mediated communications that have changed the significance of space and time, compressing them, causing the instantaneous experience of events (Harvey 1989). These new technologies at the same time could undermine the hegemony of cultural elites exercised through the higher education system by democratizing access to knowledge.

The changing university

These globalization processes are reshaping further and higher education, as they are reshaping the workplace and the interactions between it and the academy. However, there are important questions about how these processes are mediated to educational institutions, and how the policies of institu-tions mediate the very desirability of change to those who are participating in innovations such as work-based learning. Working with the idea of policy as discourse (Fulcher 1989; Ball 1990), we are suggesting that policy acts as a mediating device between the meanings of globalization and the imperat-ives of institutional adaptation and change. Policy discourse defines what is problematic and where action is imperative, and suggests new directions for change and rational solutions. These are manifested at an institutional level in an ethos of change management and adaptation.

It is important to recognize that this meaning of policy extends beyond that of a 'state control perspective' to acknowledge the negotiated and contingent character of policy processes worked out at the institutional level. As Ball (1994: 10–11) has argued:

> Policy . . . is an 'economy of power', a set of technologies and practices which are realised and struggled over in local settings. Policy is both text and action, words and deeds, it is what is enacted as well as what is intended . . . Policies are always incomplete insofar as they relate to or map on to the 'wild profusion' of local practice. Policies are crude and simple. Practice is sophisticated, contingent, complex and unstable. Policy *as* practice is created in a trialectic of dominance, resistance and chaos/freedom. Thus, policy is no simple asymmetry of power.

Policy, for example, is not merely texts, in the sense that the state regulates vocational education and training through its financial powers. Contemporary social theory has unlocked the vital role policy plays in structuring institutional activity and reality. Policy mediates in the presentation of change as a semiotic form in the symbolic economy of institutions. It mediates new representations of the contemporary workplace and its education and training requirements, just as it does new representations of the adaptive academy and the kinds of relationships that ought to obtain between education and the economy.

Policy also embraces the ways institutions themselves have taken on forms of governmentality in which enacting institutional policies, setting strategic directions and monitoring outcomes has become central to their work. In this, it is not only the state that has demanded outcomes, but the institution itself has become 'performative' in understanding its work in this way. Policy signifies a new form of governmentality in public education, which is evident in the pervasive and persuasive ways policy processes feature in the new management cultures of the corporate university. It is policy that sets the parameters of the performative university. These assist to position the university competitively in a globalizing environment and, at the local level, to its academic workers (Kenway and Langmead 1999). Therefore, it is useful to identify the particular policy discourses – five in all – that are mediating the impacts of globalization on the learning and work environment of the university.

The first is corporatization, which refers to the transformation of traditional models of state bureaucratic control of the public sector practices by the adoption of business management models. This shift to the concept of public sector management and its consequences is best known in Australia through the analysis of Yeatman (1991: 13–32). She suggests that the corporatization of public institutions has been a key focus of the intervention of the state in public education, since in itself it is a rationalization that is required to bring about other kinds of change. A neglected aspect of corporatization is the remodelling of public policy as business policy. Policy becomes more strategic in character, and targets outcomes and resources through programmes with measurable outcomes – that focus institutional practices around performance outcomes. Policy as discourse facilitates this transformation to the performative institution. Universities and Technical and Further Education (TAFE) institutions may well have very different histories and traditions, but corporatization subjects them to similar regimes of quality and performance, and sets up styles of educational management that do not differ much from sector to sector. Furthermore, they are increasingly portable across public and private enterprises.

The second discourse is that of commercialization, and involves the application of market economics to educational provision. It represents the leading edge of economic rationalism as applied to public forms of education. As Marginson's work (1993, 1997) demonstrates, there are many aspects to the way economic theories, particularly neo-liberalist ones, have 'colonized' all areas of public policy. Neo-liberalism prescribes economic life as the basis of social value and extends economistic methodologies to the allotment of public goods such as health, welfare and education. In this context, the market is a key set of discourses which legitimate measures to privatize and commercialize educational activity, including establishing quasi-markets through competitive tendering for service delivery. Clearly, the commercialization of education also legitimates new forms of commodified knowledge, as the curriculum is adapted to meet client demands, particularly those of the workplace. The point here is not that knowledge was not 'commodified' before the advent of workplace learning, but that this process has been consolidated and has now taken on new manifestations.

The third discourse is that of knowledge commodification which arises out of the marketization of courses. It has various aspects such as those in relation to the codification or packaging of knowledge, about which we will have more to say in another chapter in this volume. It is also associated with knowledge work and intellectual capital, the challenge to disciplined knowledge and so on. These have emerged through a more concerted engagement of learning with the world of work and professional practice. (These processes of knowledge codification are described in our next chapter.)

The fourth discourse is that of internationalization. It is where the impact of globalization is most keenly felt, as it not only accelerates the exchange of ideas through communication but creates new possibilities of trade in educational products, including the internationalization of the curriculum (Rizvi and Walsh 1999). The globalized economy requires transcultural workers at its highest levels and this becomes a new form of human capital, which is embodied in transcultural professionals – the new 'citizens of the world'. The reconstituted workplace and its acknowledgement of 'productive diversity' and new valuations of cultural knowledge has produced these professionals.

The final discourse is that of performativity. This has created new parameters through which to judge the efficiency and outcomes of higher education and which are related to the strategic directions of universities. This highlights the role of 'policy discourse' as we use it here, to refer to a way of governing our thinking about educational work. Again, these changes are occurring across universities and TAFE colleges, subverting the stratification and relative privilege of higher learning and giving reasons for greater cooperation and collaboration across the various sectors of education and the private, community and public domains.

The changing workplace

In this section the changes within the contemporary workplace, understood as a set of parallel yet related responses to the various narratives of globalization, are examined. We will argue that work-based learning initiatives are produced from the convergence of governing and policy discourses. We will suggest that this convergence has more of an impact because it has become natural to see higher education as an industry, as a commercial enterprise. Thus when talking about contemporary workplaces and their practices we, as academics, are no longer talking about the 'other'. Indeed, we suggest that the binary of the academy and the workplace is problematic and difficult to sustain. The following view of the workplace utilizes the lens of governmentality, a concept derived from Foucault in which the state:

> . . . is viewed as an ensemble of institutions, procedures, tactics, calculations, knowledges and technologies, which together comprise the particular direction that government has taken; the residue or outcome of governing.
>
> (Johnson 1993: 140)

At the macro level the objective of governmentality is to increase the capacity of the population through the technique of consent. Our interest here is how this is realized at the micro level and in particular how 'subjects' self-regulate – not in a compliant sense but as active subjects who have the freedom to act. Foucault argues that power is only power when it is addressed to individuals who are free to act one way or another. We take the view that self-regulation is not about compliance. Compliance suggests passivity, coercion and imposition – but our interest is in varied self-regulatory practices that embody multiple subject positions, including resistant ones.

There is little argument about the fact that management and work practices in the contemporary workplace have changed significantly over the last decade. Our observations, and indeed our experiences, reveal a considerable transformation. Not only are managers and employees 'doing more for less', but work is managed and organized in quite different ways as conventional authority and responsibilities are dispersed and as managing uncertainty penetrates the work of all. Some of the familiar characteristics of the new work order are as follows:

- all employees are responsible for quality control;
- work is organized around fluid teams rather than static departments;
- flexibility is central to all operations, processes and employee understandings of their work;

- employees are appraised and evaluated as job descriptions have given way to performance management agreements;
- most employees have knowledge of work outside their own domain including the current state of production levels and accounts;
- organizational decisions are made in cross-functional meetings as well as within management ranks;
- and finally (for the purposes of this listing) there is increased communication (both spoken and written) as employees are informed and inform.

This list of characteristics (as limited as it is) demonstrates the way workplaces have been reinvented. This reinvention is connected to the changing economic imperatives and relationships in the local and global market place as well as to the emergence of information and communication technologies. Both conventional and radical understandings of policy suggest that these transformations are policy driven – policies embedded in discourses around productivity and competition. However, at the same time the economic policies that drive the reorganization of work are not just a consequence of government nor do they in themselves prescribe particular ways of being – either as an organization or as an employee. For example, there are no direct state policies on the management and organization of work that say that work is to be organized around teams and within flatter hierarchies. It would be difficult if not inaccurate to see the construction of and participation in teamwork, flattened hierarchies and learning as a top-down, one-way notion of state policy and power relations.

We argue that such changes to the organization of work are not a consequence of government per se, but rather a consequence of governmentality. The reorganization of work requires self-regulation to be effective, that is, self-regulation of both organizations and their employees. Here we see a manifestation of technologies of power and technologies of the self where power shapes knowledge of the self and where technologies shape human conduct. This, we argue, is how governmentality works at the micro level, where diverse forces and mechanisms shape the conduct of both organizations and employees. This is in line with Ball's argument (1994) cited above which views policy as discourse rather than text.

The discourses of the workplace

We will now attempt to characterize the contemporary workplace in terms of a number of interrelated discourses. We suggest that these discourses, as described below, are constructing work practices, employees and managers in particular ways, that are both the cause and effect of certain conditions. These relate to understanding the workplace as a site of knowledge and as a site of learning. These discourses are also part of the construction of the conditions for the new relationships between workplaces and the academy as manifested in work-based learning awards. They are discourses that relate to corporate language, if not corporate policy, that is constructed through employers' reading of and response to the global environment and the new regimes of truth that link productivity and competition with particular work practices.

The multiplicity of these discourses is important to our argument. Each discourse does not have its own predetermined trajectory with predictable paths and outcomes. Rather the trajectory of discourses is contingent and always in a state of becoming as they intersect and interact, resulting in new discursive practices and new subject positions. The intersections themselves create conditions for critique and intervention. Such a view suggests that policy cannot be experienced as a monolithic force, but as something that is open to counter-moves and counter-positions.

The focus on discourse and discursive practices draws attention to the central role of language in government and in governing. Rose (1990) uses the term 'intellectual technology' to capture the significance of language – not language as a neutral or innocent medium that transmits information but language as a technology for producing social realities, for creating a domain of thought and action. Language, according to Rose, provides 'a mechanism for rendering reality amenable to certain kinds of action' (1990: 81). This understanding underpins the following analysis of a number of discursive practices.

* *Humanization of the workplace.* The humanizing of the workforce is often understood as a consequence of the replacement of manual work by sophisticated technologies. Within this understanding the technologization of work draws attention to employees as human beings, rather than as operatives or 'hands' working in a factory. This explanation, though, needs to be accompanied by an understanding of the significance of this focus on humans in terms of the management of people. In accord with Rose (1990, 1996) and du Gay (1996) we suggest that the humanization of the workplace is a technology for managing people and constructing particular kinds of worker subjectivities. These technologies of the self are engendered through a focus on the interpersonal and through the language of motivation, job satisfaction and the entrepreneurial self. As personnel departments give way to human resource units, humanization provides a mechanism for structuring the way employees think, make decisions and act in alignment with organizational norms, attitudes and values. The organization of work through human technologies is an interesting way of understanding the social nature of work. The emphasis on self and the touching of human desire and self-fulfilment is a way of maximizing capacities in the workplace. This happens not through coercion or force but through freedom of choice. The active subject is a productive subject and to be a productive subject one has to be permitted to be an active one and to think of oneself and others in this way.

- *Valorization of knowledge.* Contemporary work is named as 'knowledge work' and contemporary employees as 'knowledge workers' – critical members of the society mentioned in the epigraph. This naming of 'knowledge' as classifying work and worker operates at a number of levels. It describes the work of employees working with symbols, such as concepts, theories, numbers, symbols, models, data and computer-mediated communication. It also complements the focus on performance and signals the importance of locating performances within understandings of the complexity and diversity of organizational products and processes. In such understandings, knowledge functions as an important tool in ameliorating and improving manufacturing and service operations – indeed knowing about the organization and its current status is a key mechanism for self-regulation. Further, it captures the way knowledge goods now sit alongside material commodities, while it also describes (as it encourages) the emergence of knowledge industries, particularly those organizations which are now in competition with the academy in this area.

- *The learning organization.* Integral to the construction of knowledge work, the focus on 'flexibility' and the emphasis on people is a recognition that the capacity of an organization depends on the learning potential of its workforce. Learning in the context of the rapidly changing nature of work has process and product dimensions. Employees need to learn about the new ways of working, they need specific and generic skills to participate in the new decision-making processes, they need more knowledge to work flexibly and so on. Learning at work can no longer be understood as a discrete activity limited to a few, nor as an activity that occurs only at occasional moments in one's career. Learning is a productive part of everyday work, embedded in structures, relationships and processes of the workplaces. Learning embedded within practice presents an interesting entry point for work-based learning partnerships. The design and indeed content of each set of work-based awards is individualized. It is an individual partnership between the organization and the academy, and its parameters are negotiated so that they link directly into the strategic directions of a particular organization. Furthermore, the learning programmes are individualized and thus able to penetrate into the very heart of the structures and processes of worker–learners' productive work.

- *Consultancy, expertise and outsourcing.* At the same time as employees develop their generic capacities, specialist knowledge is needed. But the nature of specialist knowledge varies considerably and the most efficient source of this knowledge is considered to be outside the organization. Thus outsourcing and the use of consultants are mechanisms for bringing in particular kinds of expertise, which are assumed to contain specialized 'truths'. These truths are linked to particular projects and are seen to be untainted and neutral, and thus more able to be incorporated into the desires and needs of the organization. Expertise can be understood as one of the many strands within the ensemble of technologies that are part of the process and outcome of governing (Johnson 1993). After the experts have completed their projects their expertise is woven into the structural arrangements that have come together in the contemporary construction of knowledge. The chapter by Chappell *et al.* in this volume provides an account of such trends. As academic expertise is brought into the workplace, so industry expertise is brought into the academy. Here there is an important argument about the changes in contemporary knowledge production that ties together the academy and the corporate workplace in yet another way.

Convergence of the academy and the workplace

Thus there is a convergence between the academy and the corporate workplace that has facilitated the rise of work-based learning. Intensified relationships between the academy and the workplace are becoming an everyday lived experience for many academics as globalization has its impact both in the academy's construction of new discourses of corporatism and commercialization and the emerging discourses of the humanization of the workplace. Yet the pressures we speak of are also catalysing a merging of the discourses of education, learning and training. These are coalescing in a common frame of reference for workplaces and the academy. Flexible learning, lifelong learning and the vocationalizing of education are all signalling the de-differentiation of the boundaries between academic learning, working knowledge and learning through or at work. Work-based learning initiatives are just one of the manifestations of this de-differentiation and the emergence of new conditions of possibility for the relation of education and work. The appeal of work-based learning is multiple and indeed work-based learning awards are simultaneously seductive for employers and employees, academics and students.

As Boud and Symes point out in their chapter, students are asking for more relevant learning and increased choice in delivery modes, while they are seeking more qualifications in order to enhance their employment options when they have little time to participate in conventional forms of study. Employers are understanding the importance of supporting learning environments at work in order to enhance their organizational capability and productivity at a time of ongoing change and uncertainty, and they are seeking to 'professionalize' their workforce in order to be more competitive and to retain their 'cleverest' employees. Universities, financially stressed by the results of neo-liberalist policies, are searching for new educational markets to generate income. Such trends are causing academics to reorient the focus of their educational practices from teaching to learning.

Some concluding caveats

While work-based learning may be a strategic policy within an institution, its practices are varied, and it would be a mistake to suggest that academics are wholeheartedly embracing an approach that might involve yet more professional reconstruction. Though the processes of educational reform have targeted the definition and regulation of academic work and helped to bring about the 'performative university' (Usher and Solomon 1999), academic work offers scope for resistance. This can take multiple forms. Here it may be useful to name just a few of the management, pedagogic and identity issues through which academics articulate their resistance.

The first issues are pedagogical. To the extent that work-based learning programmes are instrumentally-driven, questions arise about the place of theory and critical reflection in such programmes. Related to this are questions about the maintenance of academic standards and the future of the university in a context where the majority of students pursue work-based learning. But even for its avid enthusiasts, there are daunting conceptual and practical complexities involved in converting work into learning.

The second issues relate to academic work practices. Academics engaging in work-based learning are faced by transformations of their identity as they engage in not just corporatizing the academy but also with the corporate world. Here the limits of their competence are stretched, for not only must academics manage the design, delivery and assessment of individual programmes, but these normally exacting processes are complicated by the multiple kinds of negotiation required with the organization, its employees and their workplace supervisors. The corporate press of decision making itself reduces the time to discuss the emerging curriculum issues and there is a lack of professional development resources that are needed to acquire expertise in these areas. There is a lack of educational resources to support the pedagogical shift to work-based learning, which is very dissimilar from other workplace-oriented practices, such as sandwich courses, cooperative education arrangements, work placements and even workplace learning subjects or assignments.

Finally there are the managerial issues raised by work-based learning. Already, senior managers have begun to question the appropriateness of work-based learning awards. Their reservations may be financial, insofar as work-based learning awards have not, contrary to expectation, proven any cheaper (read more profitable) than conventional awards. This is partly due to the key problem of 'converting work into learning' to which reference has already been made, and where assessing individual learning outcomes requires substantial one-to-one supervision. This makes it potentially more expensive than more conventional forms of university study.

Such difficulties deserve more analysis than is possible within this chapter, and we are particularly aware of the tendency to emphasize the determined nature of the new discourses of academy and workplace. Work-based learning partnerships are being negotiated, and at times resisted as much as embraced by academics. Symptomatic of these co-existing practices is the emergence of work-based learning partnerships within any university that are very different in shape and design. While the policy says one thing the practices reveal complex and diverse outcomes. Indeed work-based learning exemplifies the way policy is never monolithic but is subject to multiple readings and forms of implementation. That it is so fluid means that it can make a signficant 'contribution to the quality of life'.

References

Ball, S. J. (1990) *Politics and Policy Making in Education: Explorations in Policy Sociology.* London: Routledge.

Ball, S. J. (1994) *Education Reform: A Critical and Post-structural Approach.* Buckingham: Open University Press.

Brown, T. (1999) Challenging globalisation as discourse and phenomenon. *International Journal of Lifelong Education,* 18 (1), 3–17.

Castells, M. (1996) *The Information Age: Economy, Society and Culture. Volume I: The Rise of the Network Society.* Oxford: Blackwell.

Dale, R. (1989) *The State and Educational Policy.* Milton Keynes: Open University Press.

Du Gay, P. (1996) *Consumption and Identity at Work.* London: Sage.

Editorial (1999) Education is a matter of knowledge. *The Australian,* December 29.

Fulcher, G. (1989) *Disabling Policies? A Comparative Approach to Education Policy and Disability.* London: Falmer Press.

Giddens, A. (1990) *The Consequences of Modernity.* Cambridge: Polity.

Green, A. (1990) *Education and State Formation.* London: Macmillan.

Harvey, D. (1989) *The Condition of Postmodernity.* Oxford: Blackwell.

Johnson, T. (1993) Expertise and the state, in M. Gane and T. Johnson (eds) *Foucault's New Domains.* London: Routledge.

Kenway, J. and Langmead, D. (1999) Governmentality, the 'now' university and the future of knowledge work. *Australian Universities' Review,* 41 (2), 28–32.

Marginson, S. (1993) *Education and Public Policy in Australia.* Cambridge: Cambridge University Press.

Marginson, S. (1997) *Markets in Education.* Sydney: Allen & Unwin.

Rizvi, F. and Walsh, L. (1999) Difference, globalisation and the internationalisation of curriculum. *Australian Universities' Review,* 41 (2), 7–11.

Rose, N. (1990) *Governing the Soul: The Shaping of the Private Self.* London: Routledge.

Rose, N. (1996) Identity, genealogy, history, in S. Hall and P. du Gay (eds) *Questions of Cultural Identity.* London: Sage.

Taylor, S., Rizvi, F., Lingard, B. and Henry, M. (1997) *Educational Policy and the Politics of Change.* London: Routledge.

Usher, R. and Solomon, N. (1999) Experiential learning and the shaping of subjectivity in the workplace. *Studies in the Education of Adults,* 31 (2), 155–63.

Waters, M. (1995) *Globalization.* London: Routledge.

Yeatman, A. (1991) *Bureaucrats, Femocrats, Technocrats: Essays on the Contemporary Australian State.* Sydney: Allen & Unwin.

Yeatman, A. (1994) *Postmodern Revisionings of the Political.* London: Routledge.

Zuboff, S. (1984) *In the Age of the Smart Machine: The Future of Work and Power.* New York, NY: Basic Books.

7

Imposing Structure, Enabling Play: New Knowledge Production and the 'Real World' University

Robin Usher

... knowledge has succeeded energy as the basic resource

(Scott 1995: 101)

Introduction

The position that I am developing in this chapter is essentially conceptual but with a critical undertone. My hope is that it will help in providing a means of understanding current theorizations of the place of 'working knowledge' in the contemporary university. I'm highlighting this because I feel that there is a danger in current trends that certain lines of argument based on unexamined binary assumptions are beginning to be too readily accepted. I see part of my task as being that of introducing a problematizing element with the hope that we don't fall back into arguing with rigid dichotomies because the frameworks of understanding we have at the moment over-simplify a very complex situation.

What I want to do therefore is to argue that the recognition of the 'knowledge of work' and 'knowledge at work' has created a paradoxical situation for universities and that this accounts for at least some of the current difficulties which all universities are experiencing in coping with apparently new types of knowledge and 'new modes of knowledge production'. By the latter, and deliberately using their language, I'm referring to the position put forward by Gibbons *et al.* (1994) in a book significantly entitled *The New Production of Knowledge*. They argue that there are now two separate and distinct modes of knowledge production – Mode 1 and Mode 2 – with each linked to different kinds of knowledge: culturally concentrated knowledge in the case of Mode 1, socially distributed knowledge in the case of Mode 2.

The new production of knowledge

Mode 1 is defined as conducted by disciplinary communities and results in those intellectual products produced and consumed inside traditional research-oriented universities. On the other hand, although Mode 2 is not exactly a new way of producing knowledge, it is according to Gibbons *et al.* becoming increasingly prevalent and is taking its place in significance alongside the traditional and hitherto dominant Mode 1. Mode 2 is described as a new form of knowledge production and one that is opposed to the long-standing Mode 1 form:

> The new mode operates within a context of application in that problems are not set within a disciplinary framework. It is transdisciplinary rather than mono- or multi-disciplinary. It is carried out in non-hierarchical, heterogeneously organised forms which are essentially transient. It is not being institutionalised primarily within university structures. Mode 2 involves the close interaction of many actors throughout the process of knowledge production and this means that knowledge production is becoming more socially accountable. One consequence of these changes is that Mode 2 makes use of a wider range of criteria in judging quality control. Overall, the process of knowledge production is becoming more reflexive and affects at the deepest levels what shall count as 'good science'.
>
> (Gibbons *et al.* 1994: vii)

As Luke (1996: 7) indicates, Mode 2 knowledge is increasingly produced and consumed outside traditional university settings, in a context of application rather than reflection. It is 'performative' in nature, reflecting a contemporary situation where the sources of supply and demand for different forms of specialized knowledge are diverse and in which market processes define the contexts of application. Furthermore it is heterogeneous in terms of the skills deployed, transdisciplinary in the sense that it cuts across conventional disciplinary structures, and is located in a multiplicity and diversity of sites.

Socially distributed knowledge has, as it were, found its moment within the folds of globalization. Globalization and flexible capital accumulation seem to depend upon the ability to reconfigure knowledge even while new modes of knowledge production can also be seen as a consequence of globalization and the reconfiguration of capital. Lash and Urry (1994) have referred to contemporary socio-economic processes as a 'reflexive accumulation' where knowledge production, flexibility and symbol processing skills are key components of these processes. In this contemporary economic environment, technological innovation becomes the means of keeping ahead – and technological innovation requires the generation and deployment not only of new and specialized knowledge but of a knowledge geared to problem solving in work contexts and one that lends itself to computer-mediated communication. As Luke (1996) also indicates, the capacity to generate and process this kind of knowledge is increasingly seen as the source of productivity and economic growth, particularly at a time when notions of the knowledge economy are gaining in popularity and impact (see other contributors to this volume). Given this therefore it is perhaps hardly surprising that the place and status of socially distributed knowledge has become a key factor in the foregrounding of knowledge and learning in the workplace – itself now seen as a site of Mode 2 knowledge production.

The characteristics of Mode 2 knowledge production and socially distributed knowledge have certain implications and raise a number of important issues in thinking about the place and significance of new types of work-based knowledge and the response of universities to these developments. First, the global growth of higher education with consequent increases in the output of graduates has enlarged that percentage of the population familiar with and competent in knowledge production. Although there remain important hierarchies in the production, reading and evaluation of knowledge, these are less exclusive and are no longer the preserve of a select group of academics. With the parallel growth of knowledge and knowledge-based industries many now work in ways which incorporate a research dimension but where the worksite is no longer the university. Thus knowledge production is increasingly recognized as something that goes on outside the disciplinary communities of the academy and in sites other than the university – although whether this research would be considered 'competent' in Mode 1 terms is still a critically contested matter within university communities of practice. Partly, this is because Mode 2 knowledge is output-driven rather than discipline-driven. While it is still validated its validation lies in its use-value or performativity. It therefore answers to pragmatic rather than to disciplinary 'truth'. We also think there is a danger in disparaging such knowledge, and not recognizing the degree to which it often enriches life and ameliorates its conditions.

Second, there has been an expansion in the demand for work-based Mode 2 knowledge but this knowledge is costly to produce – thus this has now become a critical factor in determining an organization's comparative advantage. Given that no organization can afford to 'go it alone', the consequence is that many organizations are increasingly involved in a complex array of collaborative arrangements to produce the knowledge they need. Many of the collaborations involved are with universities, that is, when it is perceived some mutual benefit might result. This might entail organizations seeking certain kinds of expertise from universities and universities seeking certain kinds of knowledge from organizations.

Mode 2 knowledge has therefore assumed a contemporary significance beyond its status – certainly this is the argument Gibbons *et al.* are putting forward. It is not answerable to 'truth' in the sense that the regimes of truth of disciplinary communities define truth (although, as I have noted, it is answerable to a kind of performative truth). Most significant, however, it is not answerable to academic research paradigms and traditions in terms of the process by which it is produced and hence validated. It is output-driven, not motivated simply by the spirit of curiosity and free enquiry and, given that the focus is on application rather than contemplation, there is no ambition to discover the deep truths and underlying laws of the natural and social world. Mode 2 type knowledge is specific and transient and in Mode 1 terms much of this Mode 2 knowledge is automatically suspect as partisan, non-objective, undisciplined, ad hoc, unsupported or unreliable (Luke 1996: 9).

The impact of Mode 2 knowledge production has caused friction and conflict within the academy. On the one hand, cuts in state funding of higher education and demands from policy makers and governments for universities to work more closely with industry have meant that the academy can no longer refuse to recognize forms of knowledge sourced from outside its walls. On the other hand, as Luke (1996) points out, there is now a strongly held view that the culturally concentrated knowledge structures found in universities are mostly ill-adapted to producing the socially distributed knowledge needs of individuals as lifelong learners and organizations as learning organizations.

Unhelpful binaries

While it is undoubtedly the case that universities now have to work in a new situation, the arguments about the nature of this new situation tend to be cast in terms of unhelpful binaries. The question I want to ask is in what sense is this situation new? Furthermore, in what sense has the onset of working knowledge been a prime factor in bringing this about? After all, for universities knowledge has always been 'at work' and in an important sense knowledge, even in the confines of the ivory tower, has always been 'working' knowledge. Looked at this way, the liberal university (which is described in the chapter by Symes) is not significantly different from the 'vocational' university. Of course, I would not want to suggest that there is no difference but I would suggest that the difference lies in what the knowledge *is* and *for whom it is working* and, most importantly perhaps, how its role and status is *articulated* and *understood.*

The liberal university certainly understood itself as 'vocational'. It educated individuals for the vocations, trained minds for entry into the public service, to the mainstream professions and for the academy itself, and in this sense of vocational, believed itself to be providing an education for the 'real world'. Furthermore, the distinction between pure and applied forms of knowledge, now projected as a significant differentiating feature, was not so prevalent as it is conventionally believed to be. For example, the 'fundamental' or apparently 'pure' orientation of university research has historically been favoured and indeed sometimes demanded by industry. Equally, as Foucault's work has very clearly demonstrated, the development of disciplinary knowledge production in the human sciences is linked to its application in the governance of populations (1979) – there was, in other words, a coming together of theory and practice, thought and action. Thus the pure/applied distinction was perhaps never as complete as sometimes thought. However, despite the historical inaccuracy the distinction or binary was nonetheless 'real' in its effects and certainly was and continues to be powerful in constructing hierarchies of knowledge. Furthermore, and important for my argument here, it is its power as a binary that has helped to define the 'real world' in a particular way. What is significant therefore is that the 'real world' which the university understood itself to be located in was constructed *differently* to the 'real world' of the contemporary moment. What was 'real' then would not be considered quite so 'real' now.

One conclusion which can be drawn from this is that to highlight the difference between the traditional liberal and the new vocational university in a dichotomized way in terms of 'relevance' and location in the 'real world', and from this implicitly to privilege either one over the other, is undoubtedly to point to a historical fact but is not helpful in understanding the problems surrounding 'working knowledge' in the contemporary university. Both types of university have been and are 'vocational'; the difference lies in the different conceptions at work of what constitutes 'vocational'.

There is another important point here too. Referring back to the characteristics of the so-called new mode of knowledge production (Mode 2), it is not difficult to see that in key respects this is neither new nor dichotomously opposed to Mode 1, as Gibbons *et al.* seem to be arguing. This is certainly the case if we consider the types of knowledge they identify. The 'socially distributed' type has certainly been around for a long time; it is not in the least bit new although there is an important set of new factors here that have given it its current profile. There is, on the one hand, the post-Fordist organization of work and on the other, the impact of information technologies and computer-mediated communication. Both of these have helped transform the impact and significance of Mode 2 knowledge production.

However, to dismiss the argument of Gibbons *et al.* that there is now a new mode of knowledge production on the grounds of its historical accuracy alone is in an important sense to miss its significance. One key point here is that Mode 2 type knowledge has hitherto not been *named* as such, nor attributed the significance now accorded to it. Another is the very use of the term 'mode' to characterize knowledge production, implying that there are different kinds of knowledge all produced through particular kinds of social practice and within specific socio-cultural contexts. Finally, because the thesis points to more than one mode, this suggests that there is now a diversity of ways in which knowledge can be produced and a consequent fluidity and boundary permeability in the landscape of knowledge production.

Another criticism that has been made, with more justification in my view, is that Mode 1 and Mode 2 cannot be dichotomously opposed to one another. Research has always (and not only in Mode 2) been constantly shifting between the fundamental and the applied. As Godin points out, Mode 1 has never actually existed – rather it 'corresponds perfectly to scientists' conception of their own identity, their desiderata, and to their efforts to distance themselves from applied research' (1998: 469). Mode 1 knowledge is in effect an ideal type, abstracted from what scientists would like to think they were doing rather than what they were actually doing. Furthermore, because Mode 2 is not as recent as is suggested, Godin argues that its current manifestation is a 'desiderata put forward by the social and political spheres . . . an ideology presented (by Gibbons *et al.*) as a reality'. In conclusion he suggests that 'the distinction between Mode 1 and Mode 2 may not be as sharp as (Gibbons *et al.*) believe' (Godin 1998: 471). Thus it could be argued that the notion of Mode 2 knowledge production is an artefact purely of discourse and contemporary forms of governmentality.

Thus the binary opposition which structures the argument and presents Mode 2 knowledge production as a radical new departure, and which implicitly valorizes it in relation to traditional and 'irrelevant' Mode 1 knowledge production, is both flawed and unhelpful. What perhaps then is more helpful is to see Mode 1 and Mode 2 as always interlinked and inter-relational, always existing in tension with and yet necessary to one another and changing in their relative valorization through processes located in the larger socio-economic and cultural context. Indeed, Godin (1998: 478) is inclined to the view that 'there are probably not two modes of research but a single one – Mode 2 – with a varying degree of heterogeneity over time'.

When these problematic elements in their argument are highlighted in this way, it does raise the question of why the proponents of the 'new knowledge production' thesis could not figure this out for themselves. Clearly, there is a failure of reflexivity here that once recognized points to another possible way of reading their work. The model of new modes of knowledge production that they present is in effect a performative discourse. In arguing for the reality of a new mode of knowledge production they are, in effect, actually participating in its realization – to put it simply, they are doing by saying or writing in this case. As Godin suggests, they are doing two things in one – both explaining what they take to be a new organization of knowledge *and* at the same time helping to realize it – and maybe, for the reasons noted earlier, it is the latter that is most significant.

It is undoubtedly the case that *The New Production of Knowledge* is a key text of contemporary globalization. Most obviously it reports significant new trends in knowledge production even while the newness and uniqueness of these trends is, as we have seen, open to debate. Most significantly, it foregrounds the performative dimension of knowledge production – of which the text is both a celebration and an instance. Thus the work is performative, assisting to create that of which it speaks. It is a participant in the creation of what Foucault (1972) would call a 'discursive domain' which constitutes a realm of thought and action. Moreover, this is a discursive domain which foregrounds the diversity and fluidity of the globalized moment, and from which universities have not been able to remain immune.

The workplace as discursive domain

My argument is that the workplace is now being constituted as such a discursive domain – where it is understood and articulated as a site of learning, knowledge and knowledge production outside traditional sites of knowledge production. In other words, the workplace is no longer seen simply as a site to be researched but as a site where research or knowledge production itself takes place. It is here that the 'new production of knowledge' book assumes a significance beyond its existence as an academic text. In foregrounding what is called Mode 2 knowledge production and defining it in terms of a production of knowledge that is socially distributed, the book contributes to the articulation of the workplace as a discursive domain where learning and knowledge production legitimately take place. At the discursive level, it is the very articulation of 'socially distributed knowledge' as a significant and alternative form of contemporary knowledge, and its defining in contrast to the 'culturally concentrated knowledge' of discipline-bound universities, that marks it as part of a new discourse foregrounding the workplace as a site of knowledge production. There is then through this discourse a valorizing of this particular articulation of the 'real world'.

Thus, as I have noted, Gibbons *et al.* are not only describing a new mode of knowledge production located in the workplace but also through the text itself contributing to the realization of that mode. The notion of knowledge produced in the workplace becomes therefore, in an important sense, an artefact of contemporary discourses of human resource management and the forms of governmentality of which the former is a part. What Gibbons *et al.* articulate then as Mode 2 is more than just a way of producing knowledge; rather, it is perhaps more usefully seen as an aspect of a social technology, a means for bringing together technologies of the self and technologies of power in the contemporary workplace.

Structure and play

The significance accorded working knowledge and the problems it is posing for universities is not so much a matter then of epistemology – in terms of the *legitimacy* or otherwise of such knowledge – because, as I have just argued, the production of Mode 2 knowledge has always occurred. Moreover, an orientation to the work environment outside the walls of the academy is also a familiar one. Nor for that matter is it the case that Mode 1 knowledge is or has been absent from the workplace.

Nevertheless it is clear that the increased significance of working knowledge is causing problems for universities at conceptual, policy and practical levels, so perhaps we need to look elsewhere for the location of these problems. This of course is not to say that there are no epistemological issues at stake, as we shall see in a moment. But at this stage, I'm going to argue that the problems are not primarily epistemological but are perhaps best understood as located in a paradoxical situation that has emerged out of the significance accorded working knowledge in the contemporary practices of universities. The paradox I want to point to is that, on the one hand, working knowledge enables the possibility of play – a 'play' in the system as it were, while on the other, imposing a new and different structure. It is this combination of structure and play that is 'new' in the context in which all universities currently find themselves. Universities are now in a position where they have to work with the paradox and manage the resulting tension. It is with exploring the tension between structure and play – both necessary while opposed yet mutually interactive – that the remainder of this chapter is concerned.

Universities at play

What universities have experienced is a gradual loss of their status as primary producers of a particular kind of knowledge and, correspondingly, their monopoly position as certifiers of competence in knowledge production. Something which is both a cause and a consequence of this is that the parallel expansion in the number of potential knowledge producers on the supply side and the expansion in demand for specialized knowledge has multiplied the number of those in the knowledge production business and the sites where knowledge is produced (in this sense Gibbons *et al.* are right). At the same time, knowledge is being produced through universities forging collaborative research partnerships with organizations in the public and private sectors. These collaborations have forced the academy to question the traditionally sanctioned ways of doing research. In broad terms, universities, because of the sheer explosion in the amount of knowledge and the speed of its dissemination and globalization, are now less able to control the production and exchange of knowledge. This also extends to the varieties of access that the technology of the web has facilitated.

There are then internal features at play but what I am talking about here is not a purely internal matter. As the previous chapter suggested, we have to look wider than that. The paradox and its resulting tension is linked to the wider contexts in which universities find themselves. These include the impact of globalization, the spread of computer-mediated communication and the commodification of knowledge symptomatic of the postmodern condition. Stronach and MacLure (1997) talk in this context about an 'unruliness' of knowledge. This can be understood as another way of referring to the decentredness of knowledge and the de-differentiation or breakdown of fixed and bounded rules about what constitutes knowledge and knowledge production, the greater permeability and fluidity of hitherto tightly defined disciplinary communities. 'Unruliness' is manifested in the epistemological and methodological questioning which is such a pronounced feature of postmodernity.

Of course, this is a complex picture. On the one hand, the contemporary emphasis on performativity has played a part in reorienting research to the 'applied' and to tangible outcomes, in the process subverting the very notion of knowledge as something that has to be validated by a 'scientific' epistemology. Generally speaking, this has contributed to the undermining of traditional ways of doing research and of the power of disciplinary communities. As Gibbons *et al.* point out:

> Knowledge can no longer be regarded as discrete and coherent, its production defined by clear rules and governed by settled routines. Instead it has become a mixture of theory and practice, abstraction and aggregation, ideas and data. The boundaries between the intellectual world and its environment have become blurred . . .
>
> (1994: 81)

Anything, anywhere is now potentially researchable by a wide variety of knowledge producers no longer accountable solely to the gatekeepers and epistemological policing of disciplinary communities. In a specific sense, this relates to such things as the multiple sources of funding now available for research, the increasing dependence of universities on 'soft' money, the push to collaborative relationships with industry and the consequent multiple purposes to which research is oriented. These purposes are not so much oriented, as they were in the past, to the discovery of disciplinary truth. The current emphasis on the practice of research is also significant here. This is manifested in the focus on the process and effects of doing research and the general foregrounding of research training that is now no longer seen as simply an induction into an academic way of life and a socialization into traditional research paradigms. Thus, while it would be simplistic to argue as Stronach and MacLure (1997) seem to do that there are now more 'playful' options in the sense of transgressive research, there is nonetheless a 'play' in the system that mirrors the 'unruliness' of knowledge which is so obvious a characteristic of the contemporary moment.

This then is what I am characterizing as the situation of play which I am arguing is a prominent feature of all universities whatever their provenance and type. Like all situations of 'play' it provides uncertainties and discomforts as well as pleasures and possibilities. It marks a 'freeing-up' of university workers, a de-differentiation or breaking down of boundaries, particularly at the disciplinary level. It presents new and productive opportunities for multidisciplinary and transdisciplinary work, for new partnerships and collaborations in different kinds of research and curricula and for more flexible modes of delivery. It enables 'new' technological universities to narrow the gap somewhat in terms of their research standing vis-à-vis more long-standing traditional universities. At the same time however it also increases the possibilities for the loss of cherished roles that are clearly defined and 'safe', and a fear of not being able to 'keep up with the play'. All this is productive of a situation of uncertainty and discomfort – a situation that often results in epistemological angst.

This new 'play' in the system is, moreover, only one aspect of the current picture. There is also a need to recognize the other side to playfulness, which is that of the new structures that are being forged. In universities, the movement is not simply from disciplinary-focused structures to an absence of structure or structures. Some might argue this view for example in relation to such developments as work-based learning programmes and flexible modes of delivery, given that these developments mark a learning that is located in sites other than that of the university and a pedagogy and curriculum not exclusively under institutional control. My argument, however, is that this does not mean that structures are absent or not operative. While it is the case that the disciplinary and organizational structures that have hitherto segmented the university into faculties and departments based on these are no longer so prevalent or potent, other and different structures are coming into play. Work-based learning programmes are a good example of what I am arguing for here because while they could be seen as contributing to 'freeing up' the system, they certainly require structures, albeit ones that transcend the traditional disciplinary and organizational structures of universities.

The whole point about work-based learning programmes is that the learning opportunities they afford are not structured in terms of the university curriculum but through work. Knowledge in the work-based learning curriculum is mainly of the socially distributed type; it is specific, applied, pragmatic, neither generated by, nor responsible to, the academic community. With these programmes, the role of the university becomes more that of providing an enabling framework and a credentialling mechanism. It is not possible simply to drop a body of disciplinary knowledge into a workplace and expect to sustain the same boundaries and structures. Thus the curriculum sourced in work becomes a challenge to the academy's view of appropriate boundaries and conventional structures as the need becomes clear for new and different structures to accommodate these programmes.

The contractual and practical dimensions emerging from work-based learning programmes, with the consequent layers of politics and power relations, both necessitate and generate new discursive practices centred on the co-production of knowledge. Not surprisingly, this way of working means a blurring of the conventional boundaries between theory and practice, between disciplinary and working knowledge, between one discipline and another, between being a learner and a worker, and even between working and learning itself. With this blurring, the boundaries themselves become a site of contestation. This is another manifestation of 'play' in the system, yet again it is a 'play' which is intrinsic to the development of structure. It is of course a disturbing play in that it presents an unprecedented challenge to dominant conceptions of what a university education is and what a curriculum and 'legitimate' knowledge should be. At the same time, the very notion of the workplace as a site of knowledge generation is a new and difficult one with which the academy has to engage.

Furthermore, there are structural problems difficult to overcome in practice. For example, while work-based learning awards deploy socially distributed knowledge, the validation of this knowledge is now being carried out in sites which have had very different standards and conceptions of what constitutes legitimate knowledge. Work-based learning then raises questions about the role of universities and the identity of academics within them – issues that are explored in later chapters in this volume. Academics confront challenges to their identity which arise through their having simultaneously to tackle changes, as Solomon and McIntyre suggest in the next chapter, in curriculum ownership, power and control. They are trying to find answers to questions about the relationship of work performance outcomes and learning outcomes. They are wondering about the place of critical thinking and the theorization of practice particularly in courses of learning where learning outcomes are linked to pay packets. Thus the obverse side of the new and perhaps liberating play in the system is the fear that work-based learning might ultimately be simply a means whereby the very reason for the existence of academics and the academy is removed.

A key feature of a work-based learning programme is its 'flexibility'. Indeed flexibility in both process and content is an important part of its appeal for both the organization and the learner/employee, even though universities have been somewhat less enthusiastic in embracing this notion. While boundaries are inevitably becoming blurred it is also in the interest of universities to reconstruct boundaries and to attenuate the more disturbing and disruptive effects of the new 'flexibility'. Adapting to the demands of this new 'real world' is seen as necessary, yet this adaptation is also seen as one that needs to be mediated within a structure, albeit reconfigured, of traditional continuities. Hence the attempt to develop structures that accommodate the new reality yet also maintain academic standards. This is manifested in the generation of new textual practices such as the development of a Capability Framework designed to maintain these standards while at the same time providing some definition and shape to the notion of socially distributed knowledge. The purpose of the Framework is in effect to provide boundaries, in the form of descriptions of cross- and trans-disciplinary learning outcomes that can frame educational decisions about the nature and quality of learning. It is a textual practice that can be seen as an attempt to make explicit the educational parameters within which work-based learning programmes are negotiated, organized and assessed, given that they are constituted by learning which does not fit within conventional curriculum boundaries. Thus, whilst existing boundaries are being dismantled, new and different kinds of boundaries are forming. These have the effect of framing the work-based learning curriculum and the identity of the learner. But as earlier chapters in this volume have suggested, it also amounts to a search for new codifications and curriculum representations of knowledge.

The academic valuing of the 'curriculum in the workplace', which involves socially distributed knowledge, is a complex process that requires institutional resources and structures supporting this kind of teaching, learning and assessment. The partnership at a course level between the organization, the university and the learner, and the accompanying relationship of work and learning, between being a worker and a learner, between the educational institution and the workplace, is under constant negotiation. This directs attention to the organization of learning and its assessment, which requires a very particular set of boundaries in relation to structures, resources and processes. While these need to be located within the framework of conventional university-based courses, they also require a different slant and a different shaping. This leads to different structures, resources and processes that more appropriately capture the different kind of learning, the different kinds of assessment and the different layers of negotiation that are needed between the three partners. In a sense, it is possible to see the work-based learning programme with its capability frameworks, quality guidelines and accreditation bodies *as* the structure. So I would argue that work-based learning programmes do not lead to boundaries disappearing, without any framing. Rather the framing is different, certainly more local and specific and certainly more complex, contested and fluid but nonetheless very present.

Back to the 'real world'

What I am suggesting therefore is that in the contemporary situation it is not a matter of recognizing or failing to recognize the 'real world'. I would argue instead that there is no such thing as a preconstituted and given 'real world'. There are things happening – phenomena, events, processes, trends – but it is how these are *articulated* and therefore understood and acted upon that is critical – and it is this articulation which defines what is to be taken as the 'real world'. The question that needs to be asked therefore is how 'relevance' is discursively constituted in relation to how the 'real world' is now differently articulated.

I argued earlier that it was not that the 'old' or traditional universities did not have any notion of relevance or that they failed to connect with the 'real world'. It was more that they were located in a different discursive domain or frame of governmentality. This constituted the 'real world' differently and had different criteria for what was relevant. In other words, the 'real world' has literally changed and is changing, its reality no longer what it used to be. It is this 'different' real in which universities now find themselves located and within which they have to operate.

I have argued that the prime challenge for universities in this different world is the management of the tension between structure and play, and which has emerged from the way the 'real world' is now being articulated. When linked to the pluralization of roles that is such a distinctive feature of the contemporary academy, the interaction of structure and play affords some the opportunities for 'play', while inhibiting the 'play' of others.

Marketization is a case in point: it provides new scope for the new breed of academic entrepreneur while placing serious limitations on the play of traditional academic values. Thus academic life is marked by contradictions exhibiting both more and less autonomy simultaneously, the tension of co-implicated limitations and possibilities, structure and play.

I have taken work-based learning programmes as a prime example of this tension. It must be emphasized that this is not an argument for seeing structure and play as binary opposites and for valorizing either one at the expense of the other. Both are present, they are mutually interactive; for universities the need is to manage both in harness. Again, work-based learning programmes illustrate this very clearly. I have also argued that this condition is not simply internal to universities. Universities are responding to play and 'unruliness' by creating new rules and new structures, developing and positioning themselves in different articulations and discourses. Without these they simply could not handle the larger trends and processes occurring in the wider context. The same tension or paradox between imposing structure and enabling play is manifested in the wider context of the 'real world' as currently articulated in the political, economic and cultural spheres. Thus what is being 'played out' in the micro level of the universities are the processes operating at the macro level of the globalized moment.

References

Foucault, M. (1972) *The Archaeology of Knowledge*. New York, NY: Harper Colophon.
Foucault, M. (1979) *Discipline and Punish*. New York, NY: Vintage Books.
Gibbons, M., Limoges, C., Nowotny, H. *et al.* (1994) *The New Production of Knowledge: The Dynamics of Science and Research in Contemporary Societies*. London: Sage.
Godin, B. (1998) Writing performative history: the new *New Atlantis*. *Social Studies of Science*, 28 (3), 465–83.
Lash, S. and Urry, J. (1994) *Economies of Signs and Space*. London: Sage.
Luke, T. W. (1996) The Politics of Cyberschooling at the Virtual University. Paper presented at the International Conference on *The Virtual University*, University of Melbourne, Australia.
Scott, P. (1995) *The Meanings of Mass Higher Education*. Buckingham: SHRE/Open University press.
Stronach, I. and MacLure, M. (1997) *Educational Research Undone: The Postmodern Embrace*. Buckingham: Open University Press.

8

Deschooling Vocational Knowledge: Work-based Learning and the Politics of the Curriculum

Nicky Solomon and John McIntyre

... most people acquire most of their knowledge outside school
(Illich 1973: 20)

Introduction

In a previous chapter, we suggested some reasons for the increasing vocationalization of knowledge represented by developments such as work-based learning. We argued that a policy environment of deregulation, corporatization, globalization, marketization and fiscal stringency has given impetus to higher education institutions to engage more with government, industry and enterprises. This has been catalysed by the state's policy interventions aimed at reforming education through reshaping institutions and their management of vocational knowledge. This is supposed to make them more responsive to the imperatives of labour, which have been shaped by new pressures of post-Fordism and neo-Fordism (Marginson 1993; Peters and Marshall 1996; Taylor *et al.* 1997; Robins and Webster 1999).

At the same time, we argued that this policy environment encouraging work-based learning and a new order of vocational knowledge is also a response to and a reflection of broader changes in society. Traditionally, there have been the strongest of boundaries between working and learning, so our assumption is that other disruptive tendencies must be in play. We thus argue that the increasing emphasis on professional and vocational practice manifest in work-based learning is apparent in the changing knowledge production practices at large. The fact that these changes are in part mediated by the new workplace has had an impact on our understandings of vocational learning. These changes call into question the way universities are managing their knowledge economies and their associated pedagogic systems. In short, academic curricula are incompatible with the transformations occurring in the knowledge economy and workplaces.

In this chapter, therefore, we want to explore the idea that work-based learning represents a deinstitutionalization of vocational knowledge. We argue that the organizing principle of the curriculum of work is both a continuation of a vocationalizing tendency in higher education and a radical break with 'knowledge codes' that have prevailed in higher education. We say that work-based learning amounts to a 'deschooling' of vocational knowledge and as such it threatens existing power–knowledge relations in higher education. Thus it is important to understand how such a change can be understood as generating a new politics of the curriculum. This order of change involves a struggle for control over the meaning and direction of the curriculum. Not only is there a disestablishment of the formal vocational curriculum (through negotiated pathways of learning), but there is also an extension and institutionalizing of new areas of vocational experience.

Work-based learning: a new curriculum code

The emergence of initiatives in work-based learning can be understood as a manifestation of the intersection of a number of social and political trends and discursive practices. These trends and practices have already challenged the distinctions between working and learning. The boundary between these has already been disturbed through the vocationalization of higher education and its increasing emphasis on professional practice and promotion of partnerships between universities and business, particularly corporate business. Symes and Hager in this volume deal in a more concerted way with this development, which is located within a discourse about lifelong learning and related to a number of pedagogical policies and practices, such as flexible learning, which increasingly support work and the workplace as a 'legitimate' site of learning. In addition to these trends, the commodification of knowledge along with the marketization of education means that work-based learning is becoming part of the search by universities for new sources of students and revenue.

In work-based learning (WBL) awards each worker/learner designs a learning programme around their work responsibilities (frequently as defined in performance management agreements) and each student identifies and names the areas of learning. As described by Boud and Symes in their chapter, students undertake study for a degree or diploma through activities conducted primarily in their workplace and in topic areas in which there may be no immediate equivalence with university subjects. The learning opportunities found in work-based learning programmes are not contrived for study purposes, but arise from normal work. The role of the university is to equip and qualify people already in employment to develop lifelong learning skills, not through engagement with existing disciplines or bodies of knowledge and a programme defined by university teachers, but through a curriculum which is unique for each student. The organizations in which students work benefit directly through projects which advance the enterprise as well as contributing to student learning. Some examples of such curriculum projects are:

- an employee in an informational technology section of an organization in the financial industry designs a data warehouse for a Distribution and Remuneration Business Programme;
- a principal in a secondary school focuses on the design of a quality assurance system within their school.

This kind of curriculum is indeed a challenge to the place of disciplinary knowledge in the university and to the role of academics (oft-times, more myth than actuality) in seeing themselves as producers of knowledge. In the WBL curriculum we cannot simply transfer a body of knowledge into a workplace and sustain the boundaries that surround it in the academy. The knowledge in such a curriculum is specific and pragmatic and certainly not solely responsible to the academic community. Rather, in a WBL curriculum, representatives from the workplace and the university in conjunction with the individual student participate in the 'tri-production' of specific and non-disciplinary knowledge.

Work-based learning is both a natural next step and a radical approach to the notion of a university education. It is natural in the sense that many of the new universities have used 'professional practice and the workplace as both a site of learning and as a source for making their current curriculum more relevant' (UTS 1998). This often involves workplace action learning projects and learning contracts. In other words, work-based learning represents not a first challenge to traditional discipline-based knowledge but the culmination of a long development of alternative knowledge formations arising from an increased emphasis on professional and vocational practice. Boundaries around disciplines and around work and university study have already been breaking down as theoretical knowledge is increasingly accompanied by problem-based know-how. Indeed, at UTS (University of Technology, Sydney), educational provision increasingly falls into a category of provision that has been named 'work-integrated learning'. In work-integrated learning the curriculum is derived from a combination of a disciplinary area, professional practice and workplace requirements in which both the university and the workplace are treated as sites of legitimate learning. This differs from the more conventional curriculum where the primary source is a disciplinary area and where the university is the main site of learning (physically and/or virtually) (UTS 1999).

However, these developments are also radical in that what is significant in the new approaches to work-based learning is that work is not a discrete and limited element of study, as is the case in sandwich courses and cooperative education. Neither are issues arising from problems encountered in work used merely as subjects of assignments, as is common in many forms of flexible provision which use learning contracts. In WBL degrees, work is the foundation of the curriculum. In other words, the learning opportunities found in such degrees are not contrived for study purposes but arise from normal work.

The learning arrangement in work-based learning is a three-way partnership between the organization, the learner and the university, where the individual's learning programme is linked to the strategic goals of the workplace, while assessment and accreditation are the responsibility of the university. This contractual partnership sets up additional layers of politics and power relations that are manifested in new discursive practices around the co-production of knowledge. The boundaries between theory and practice, between one discipline and another, between being a learner and a worker, between working and learning have become blurred and, not surprisingly, have become objects of contestation. We would argue that while these particular boundaries are being dismantled there are now new and different kinds of boundaries and frames around the work-based curriculum. In other words, the work-based learning curriculum is not unbounded or deregulated, but rather it is bounded and regulated in different ways. For example, the knowledge involved is locally specific, more complex, more contested and more fluid.

It is for this reason that such learning presents an unparalleled challenge to the dominant codes through which a university education is provided and to existing conceptions of knowledge. Precisely because it radically rewrites the authority for the academic curriculum, academics are struggling with the conceptual and practical shifts it presents. Work-based learning raises questions about the role of universities and the role of academics within them. It has the potential to transform these roles and could, in the most radical of scenarios, provide a vehicle for rationalizing them out of existence. In this context, academics are confronting threats to curriculum proprietorship and to the control over the content and form of the curriculum. They are trying to find answers to questions about the relationship of work performance outcomes and learning outcomes. They are wondering about the place of critical thinking and the theorization of practice particularly in courses of learning where learning outcomes are linked to pay packets and performance awards. Work-based learning creates a politics of 'curriculum' precisely because it raises myriad epistemological, conceptual and practical quandaries.

Curriculum codes and vocationalized knowledge

The emergence of work-based learning is intensifying debate around knowledge and its relationship to the curriculum. Work-based learning is a site of considerable tension and contestation in the academy because it challenges in a fundamental way the strong classifications surrounding disciplinary knowledge (Bernstein 1975). In Bernstein's terms, work-based learning represents a shift towards an 'integrated code', which disturbs the existing authority structures surrounding the distribution and classification of knowledge.

We assume curriculum to have the broad meaning that it has for Bernstein (1975), who suggests it encompasses syllabus knowledge and the pedagogic practices associated with the transmission of knowledge. The curriculum comprises those social practices that are realized through educational activities. In Bernstein's terms, work-based learning challenges:

- curriculum knowledge categories, particularly what kind of work counts as the curriculum and what does not, and how this is constituted;
- pedagogical relationships, or the nature of the transactions which mediate work-based learning;
- assessment, or the problem of representing and validating learning;
- location, or the question of the site of educational activity.

Bernstein also sees disciplinary knowledge not as inherent in types of knowledge but as something defined and maintained through the range of social practices associated with education (Bernstein 1975; Atkinson 1985). Curriculum knowledge is about boundary maintenance, separating out what counts as knowledge and what does not. Thus work-based learning creates a crisis of boundary maintenance for universities which are institutions historically defined by the rigidity of their 'knowledge codes' and their regulation of access to them.

Work-based learning frustrates institutional control over the selection and privileging of knowledge, and both the creation of discrete knowledge categories and the strict policing of knowledge boundaries. However, it also frustrates (to use Bernstein's phrasing) the 'tight framing' of particular experiences as knowledge through pedagogy. In the curriculum of work, while there may be much that is learnable, there may be no particular experiences that are teachable in a disciplinary or institutional sense. This problem is exemplified, if not amplified, in work-based learning pedagogical relationships where the role relationships of teacher/learner are weakened and redefined in terms of workplace categories such as the mentor and the mentored.

This area of work-based pedagogy illustrates how the politics of curriculum is also a politics of representation (Yeatman 1994). Opponents of work-based learning will contest this weakening of teaching and learning as they contest the lack of clearly classified curriculum knowledge (or the tenuous relationship of learning at work to defined bodies of knowledge). It is difficult to resolve the problem of pedagogical relationship without anticipating in what place or by what means an educational exchange will occur. To say this presupposes that learning is mediated by some kind of relationship, which need not be constituted as such by participants (as in the mentor–mentored relationship). Possibly a good deal of the transaction of work-based learning is to be understood as the learner's interaction and processing of the experiences of work in ways yet to be identified and defined. All the more reason why the meaning of pedagogy in work-based learning will mean struggles around what can count as an adequate pedagogical relationship. These struggles will probably call on discourses (models) of clinical supervision, problem-based methodology, work placement, internship, induction and the like as a basis for defining such relationships and resolving tensions around the 'invisibility of pedagogy' (to borrow another of Bernstein's trenchant phrases).

Another area of contestation is assessment. This centres on the problem of validation – the identification of what signifies learning at work, which relates to what counts as knowledge in the curriculum of work. This too is likely to be a key area for struggle over the representation of work-based learning. Its difficulties go back to the very ambiguities of distinguishing pedagogical relationships at work, the difficulties of saying what counts as learning and what counts as work, or at least, how the one might be found in the other. Here what constitutes knowledge in the curriculum of work is operationalized in what is taken to be outcomes. Defining products or outcomes presupposes some agreement on these categories for assessment purposes. However, the pragmatics of doing work-based learning are likely to make this an early site of struggle, because of pressures to objectify if not codify assessment procedures. There will be arguments about how learning is to be represented, which may be the place where knowledge issues are resolved, as it were, in practice. Knowledge issues in principle are more difficult and likely to be deferred in the face of pressures to define and legitimate assessment.

It is also worth noting in what sense there is a problem of location in work-based learning. Where exactly will learning exchanges occur? Is it possible to define these locations more precisely than a generic workplace? The meaning of a site of learning at work will be contested, we suggest, because of the press of the other areas of struggle already discussed. There will be a press to say at what time and in what place and manner learning is occurring (and to what extent it occurs off-site or after hours). The problem of location exemplifies physically the question of boundary definition in a curriculum of work. We would predict that how the location of learning is represented to various parties, will be apparent in other aspects of struggle over the meaning of work-based learning.

Struggle over location is more than merely contestation of the site of learning. The shift of location symbolizes the challenge to the locus of control over the educational process that was once unquestionably located within the boundaries of academics units such as a university or college. The politics of representation relates to this loss of unquestioned control, a ceding of authority to determine the curriculum to other and more powerful interests beyond these educational institutions.

The implications of this deschooling of knowledge amounts to a radical challenge to the authority relationships that exist between university and business. Such challenges would not be tolerated if there were not far-reaching changes to be met in the way knowledge production is operating in the new contexts of alliances between business and the academy. Thus, the strong codifications of knowledge inherent in the traditional university curriculum are out of step with knowledge-production practices in the professions and corporate world where more 'integrated codes' prevail.

Culturally concentrated versus socially distributed knowledge

Clearly there are problems with using Bernstein's curriculum framework, which takes for granted the authority of disciplinary knowledge and the hegemony of a certain form of 'cultural capital' (Bourdieu 1986). Work-based learning brings into the spotlight the interrelationships between the categories 'curriculum' and 'pedagogy', 'knowledge' and 'experience'. Though these interrelationships have always existed in the traditional university curriculum where learning is mediated and relational, their significance has suddenly been noticed because work-based learning undermines the significance of these interrelationships for analysing educational experiences. Furthermore, the complexities around pedagogical relationships in particular are intensified in work-based learning. For example, such learning brings into sharp focus the nature of what is learnt and how it is learnt, which can be contested by both corporations and universities, as well as the learners themselves. One outcome of these contestations is that they lead to a degree of 'unmanageability' or 'unruliness' in educational institutions (Stronach and MacLure 1997). The power and control over the new modes of vocational learning are more diffuse, therefore less visible or transparent and thus less easily described, represented or managed by all concerned, including academics, workplace supervisors and learners themselves.

These developments also need to be understood in terms of a shift in the nature of knowledge production in the contemporary moment. We refer to this challenge to vocational knowledge as a shift from 'culturally concentrated knowledge' to 'socially distributed knowledge', which Gibbons *et al.* (1994) have described at length in their account of new modes of knowledge production. They distinguish between Mode 1 and Mode 2 forms of knowledge, where Mode 1 is related to 'the social and cognitive norms which must be followed in the production, legitimation and diffusion of knowledge' (1994: 2), whereas Mode 2 is produced in the context of application. It is useful knowledge produced in negotiation with all the various actors seeking more differentiated and applicable forms of specialist knowledge. 'Such knowledge is non-traditional in form: that is, it is applied, heterogeneous, non-hierarchical, transient, commodifiable and specific knowledge, which may not be widely disseminated or openly published' (1994: 2–3). Accordingly, Mode 2 knowledge is challenging the long dominance of the Newtonian model of knowledge production in science which has been extended, with varying degrees of success, to other fields of inquiry such as the humanities and social sciences.

Mode 2 knowledge is produced across institutions and organizations such as universities, corporations, public sector organizations and industry. New knowledge is not received but created around problem solving in a business context, born not of management science but in the real-time application of theory to corporate life, where problem solving calls on economics, finance, organizational theory or whatever knowledge bases can assist in generating new understandings. It thus constitutes perspectives that are 'transdisciplinary' and, according to Gibbons *et al.* (1994), this knowledge cannot be reduced to disciplinary components. Importantly, the diffusion of Mode 2 knowledge takes place through the communication networks in which it is produced rather than scholarly channels. Its production is sustained by information technology and communication networks which cross institutional boundaries and represent a 'socially-distributed knowledge production system' (1994: 10). In no sense can there be a reduction of this knowledge to the 'purely' academic disciplinary base if it is to remain relevant. Thus Mode 2 knowledge is a powerful element of what Castells (1996) has called the 'network society', in which individuals often feel more affiliation with their network colleagues than those with the organization which employs them.

We emphasize the key point that 'deschooled knowledge' is only possible through the weakening of (disciplinary) boundaries that characterize the old academic knowledge codes – it is enabled by the crossing over of academic and corporate contexts. Hence, there is potential for conflict in judging the worthwhileness of the Mode 2 knowledge produced, since the criteria must satisfy more than scholarly interests and involve more than a peer review process. Thus it can be argued that WBL participates in and reflects the rise of new knowledge-production modes, and that it is these which are pressing radical changes on how we need to think about not only university curricula but their relation to research activities. It is manifestly clear that Mode 2 knowledge, for example, is being generated through state-sponsored and industry-collaborative research that feeds directly through into professional practice.

Work-based learning and the new unruliness

It is not difficult to see the work-based learning curriculum as an exemplification of socially distributed knowledge in terms of the production of useful locally specific knowledge. The instrumentality and relevance of work-based learning awards ensures that both for the organization and its employees what is learned can 'add value'. In these terms legitimate knowledge is that which is constituted by performance agreements rather than constituted by disciplines. Through this, the organization can control not only the content but also the learning process. Thus, with work as the content of curriculum knowledge and learning defined in terms of performance-related outcomes, it is not difficult to see the replacement of disciplinary boundaries by the boundaries of work. However, it is not so straightforward. It is simplistic to see organizations as the sole controller and regulator of a work-based learning curriculum. The partnership of organizations, the worker/learner and higher education institutions make this a complex and contested form of surveillance and regulation.

Educational institutions are significant sites of regulation in the contemporary social formation, and are notable exemplars of the audit society (Power 1997), where many activities are the targets of verification and accountability. University academics are no strangers to the audit society in action, which has now been extended to the workplace. As Usher and Solomon (1999) suggest, the role of universities in assessing and accrediting learning in work-based learning awards in conjunction with the role of performance management agreements in the workplace means that both the university and the workplace are intersecting sites of surveillance (and thus knowledge production). Both the university and the workplace 'speak' in terms of power–knowledge discourses that in the context of the practices of work-based learning are sometimes congruent but often are not. Hence the shaping of subjectivity is a fraught and tension-filled process for the 'subjects' of the new vocational learning.

Furthermore the third participant in these partnerships, the learner, provides another layer of complexity. Learners want their learning in the workplace to have the same unequivocal status as a university-based degree in order to enhance their job prospects and career development. At the same time they want their learning to enhance their performance and thus their pay. This ambivalence neatly illustrates the problems of identity and subjectivity which the worker/learner confronts continually. Learners for example are subject to multiple layers of surveillance – from management in relation to performance agreements and learning programmes and from academics in their role as assessors of learning.

At the same time the worker/learner has to struggle with the complexities involved in being given 'responsibility' for designing a learning programme that has no 'natural' subject boundaries, no timeline, no 'teachers' and no set readings. It would be easy to interpret this as an exemplification of the undisciplined (with several meanings) nature of work-based learning. However, in the contemporary workplace discipline is not absent but reconfigured and re-represented, and in the process less transparent but with more complex power relations and increased responsibility for the worker/learner.

One example from the experience of the work-based curriculum shows something of its local and fluid nature. Faculties within the same university have different conceptualizations of the work-based curriculum, even when working within the same organization and using the same accreditation documents. Faculty X conceptualizes work-based learning in terms of a mode of delivery, where the workplace as a site of learning is the critical factor. On the other hand, Faculty Y sees work-based learning as intricately fused with course content, in other words work is the curriculum. These differences are exemplified in their nomenclature – in Faculty X, the work-based learning award has the same name as a university-based award, while in Faculty Y, the award has a different name and includes the words 'professional practice'.

Implications

There are a number of implications of this analysis of the contemporary vocational curriculum. The first of these is that we should insist on an analysis of knowledge and critique the tendency to conflate 'vocational knowledge' and 'vocational learning'. The emphasis on challenges to codified knowledge in traditional curricula does not mean that analysis of these curricula ought to be abandoned. It is clear that huge resources continue to be poured into institutionalized processes to the benefit of those individuals who thereby acquire the cultural capital associated with traditional curricula. In no sense are we suggesting that Illich's 'deschooled society' is about to dawn and the information age will necessarily put an end to inequalities created through formal education. If anything, the challenge is to explore the ways in which elite social groups are adapting and accommodating to the contemporary challenges to the near-monopoly their institutions have exercised over the social distribution of (high-status) knowledge. Recent evidence from the UK suggests that elite institutions are consolidating their grip on high-status occupations through privileging new forms of cultural capital that are allied to the values associated with post-Fordism (see Brown and Skase 1994).

Work-based learning requires disciplinary knowledge in order to constitute itself, and it is only when set against the monopolization of professional and technical knowledge by formal institutions that innovations such as work-based learning appear radical in form and intent. But just as they appear to threaten the established forms of disciplined knowledge they are also an accommodation to the new modes of knowledge production. Therefore, there is a need to consider which groups are standing to benefit from such innovations and how they are to be understood as a reconfiguration of the ways by which cultural capital is acquired by professionals and managers.

Another implication, therefore, is that it is important to contest human capital theory from the perspective of social and cultural theories of knowledge. The 'commodification' of academic knowledge may be understood as one element of the marketization of education, but it also needs to be understood in terms of the institutionalization of knowledge, its codification, regulation and so on. Work-based learning is a particular commodification of knowledge, a type of representation of curriculum knowledge that has currency at the moment. Commodification is usually spoken about pejoratively – in respect of economic rationalist prescriptions for the marketization of courses. Yet educational knowledge has always been packaged and marketed – with disciplinary knowledge being badged in particular ways and acquired by particular social and economic interests. Again, the point of work-based learning is to ask what this commodification of vocational knowledge entails and how this particular commodification is allowing some groups to position themselves more advantageously than others in order to gain access to such knowledge.

Perhaps one way of responding to this challenge to conventional codifications of knowledge is to understand how the discursive practices in the new partnership arrangements in the co-production of new knowledges in work-based learning unsettle a number of conventional binaries. These include organizational learning/individual learning; informal learning/formal learning; performance outcomes/learning outcomes; performance/knowledge; and working knowledge/disciplinary knowledge. As the partnerships work together we in the academy need to resist the temptation to reprivilege the status of academic knowledge. Rather we need to talk through the intersections in the culture of the academy, which will enable academics to work more effectively within the processes now associated with legitimatizing and communicating new knowledges.

There are many other aspects of the deschooling of vocationalized learning which deserve comment. We have tried to suggest some ways to theorize the challenges to institutions and their knowledge formation practices, and to show that developments such as work-based learning entail a politics of curriculum. Among other important issues, such a politics would raise questions about the social distribution of knowledge which ought to be debated and critiqued more than it is at present.

References

Atkinson, P. (1985) *Language, Structure and Reproduction. An Introduction to the Sociology of Basil Bernstein.* London: Methuen.

Bernstein, B. (1975) *On the Classification and Framing of Educational Knowledge, Class, Codes and Control. Volume 3: Towards a Theory of Educational Transmissions.* London: Routledge and Kegan Paul.

Bourdieu, P. (1986) *Distinction. A Social Critique of the Judgement of Taste.* London: Routledge.

Brown, P. and Scase, R. (1994) *Higher Education and Corporate Realities: Class, Culture and the Decline of Graduate Careers.* London: UCL Press.

Castells, M. (1996) *The Information Age: Economy, Society and Culture. Volume I: The Rise of the Network Society.* Oxford: Blackwell.

Gibbons, M., Limoges, C., Nowotny, H. *et al.* (1994) *The New Production of Knowledge: The Dynamics of Science and Research in Contemporary Societies.* London: Sage.

Illich, I. (1973) *Deschooling Society.* Harmondsworth: Penguin.

Marginson, S. (1993) *Education and Public Policy in Australia.* Cambridge: Cambridge University Press.

Peters, M. and Marshall, J. (1996) *Individualism and Community: Education and Social Policy in the Postmodern Condition.* London: Falmer Press.

Power, M. (1997) *The Audit Society: Rituals of Verification.* Oxford: Oxford University Press.

Robins, K. and Webster, F. (1999) *Times of the Techno-culture: From the Information Society to the Virtual Life.* London: Routledge.

Stronach, I. and MacLure, M. (1997) *Educational Research Undone: The Postmodern Embrace.* Buckingham: Open University Press.

Taylor, S., Rivzi, F., Lingard, B. and Henry, M. (1997) *Educational Policy and the Politics of Change.* London: Routledge.

Usher, R. and Solomon, N. (1999) Experiential learning and the shaping of subjectivity in the workplace. *Studies in the Education of Adults,* 31 (2), 155–63.

UTS (University of Technology, Sydney) (1998) *Work-based Learning at UTS,* Fact sheet. Sydney: University of Technology, Sydney.

UTS (University of Technology, Sydney) (1999) *Integration of Work and Professional Practice into Learning at UTS.* Sydney: University of Technology, Sydney.

Yeatman, A. (1994) *Postmodern Revisionings of the Political.* London: Routledge.

9

Learning to Work, Working to Learn: Theories of Situational Education

Mark Tennant

What you learn is bound up with what you have to do.

(Scribner 1985: 200)

Introduction

For a variety of reasons explored elsewhere in this volume, universities are increasingly under scrutiny to provide education that is more relevant and pertinent to the needs of employers. This often means providing a more situational form of education which is less abstract and discipline-bound and closer to the issues to be found in work contexts. It is often suggested that the contemporary workforce needs to be clever, adaptable and flexible. Such a workforce is one which can quickly and willingly apply existing knowledge and skills to new situations, and one which is prepared to acquire new learning as the circumstances warrant, and capable of doing so. There is an expectation that both formal education and workplace training should produce the kind of learning that allows such adaptability and flexibility.

Largely because universities have lost their monopoly over the accreditation, production and distribution of knowledge, and because business and industry are becoming more adept at providing learning opportunities in the workplace, universities are developing more of a market focus. One symptom of this is a focus on professional and vocational practice with new forms of 'flexible' delivery designed to capture expanding global and local student markets. Indeed, the university sector is beginning to reconfigure itself within a lifelong learning framework, with a focus on learning rather than education, workplace problems rather than traditional disciplines. Furthermore, there is a recognition of the need for multiple re-entry points into the university across the lifespan. Within this context new partnerships between universities and public and private sector organizations have emerged which attempt to address the learning needs of the workforce. A common element in such partnerships is learning in the workplace. This may vary from using workplace experiences to provide a context for academic study to much more radical models of work-based learning where the work itself becomes the curriculum. My interest in this chapter is the changing nature of education and how its interface with workplaces produces, presupposes or otherwise shapes new learner identities and pedagogical practices.

Self-work and learning

If we think of conventional university education as being in the liberal tradition (see Symes in this volume), then education is said to lead to a greater awareness of self through cultivating an identity which is independent, rational, autonomous, coherent and socially responsible. Such a view of identity has been strongly challenged in recent years from a range of different theoretical positions, largely because it is seen as overly static and essentialist, and thus ignores the socially constructed nature of identity. At the very least the increasing pluralization of society has challenged any pretence that universal social and normative frames of reference can provide unchanging anchoring points for identity. Indeed, increasing social and cultural mobility has begun to erode the possibility of developing an identity built on any singular and stable socio-cultural community. This has meant that the fashioning of identity has become an individual reflexive enterprise, a lifelong learning project in which the person (or 'subject') incorporates experiences and events into an ongoing narrative about the self. This view of the self as a story or narrative seems to cut across theoretical and disciplinary boundaries in the social sciences and humanities (White 1989; Giddens 1991; Beck 1992; Freeman 1993; Gergen and Kaye 1993; McAdams 1996). The main theoretical tension, however, concerns whether such self-narration should or could be targeted towards the construction of a stable, coherent, bounded identity; or whether such a project is a chimera, neither desirable nor possible in a world of multiple and shifting, open-ended and ambiguous narratives and identities.

The shift of learning to the workplace heightens this tension, partly because the contemporary workplace demands a more flexible and mobile self, and partly because learning in the workplace is predicated on the capacity for self-reflection on workplace experiences. The learner/worker is in a rather contradictory and ambiguous position as they grapple with intersecting versions about what it means to be effective in the workplace. For example, there are local and particular situated knowledges that must be mastered; at the same time, there is a demand for flexibility and mobility that implies generic attitudes and skills. Then there is the academic recognition of workplace experiences to 'make them count' for educational credit. Performance in the workplace and the gaining of educational qualifications become the markers of personal development and fulfilment. Thus a better worker is a better person in the broader sense, and the route to this better-ment is the capacity to manage and fashion one's identity as worker/learner: as a kind of 'entrepreneur of the self'. As Usher and Solomon observe:

> ... the management of subjectivity, the discursive construction of workers as 'subjects' of a particular kind, is now more than ever before an essential element of governmentality and the central task of organisations ... this is not simply a matter of manipulation or a systematic and deliberate shaping of the subjectivity of workers ... it is the very stimulation of subjectivity, the emphasis on the self, on knowing and managing the self and on self-change, which is the way of maximising capacities and dispositions in the workplace ... it then becomes easy enough to take this a step further and see work as a source of learning, as meaningful and as essential to self-fulfilment.
>
> (1999: 158)

Education built on workplace learning promotes this kind of self-management and self-reflection; not for the purposes of discovering who one is, but for creating what one might become in a strategic, tactical and political sense. In this scenario, exactly what constitutes 'strategic, tactical and political' is contestable, particularly in relation to whether the point of reference is the individual, the organization, or the broader public do-main. Jansen and Wildemeersch highlight the likelihood of narrow, inward-looking institutional 'references' dominating:

> This means that the tasks and aims that modern institutions set for themselves are delimited by their *internal* criteria of what is useful and effective ... A striking effect of this on personal development is that one learns to define personal responsibility in technological rather than moral terms. To act in a responsible way comes to mean to execute loyally, effectively, and efficiently procedures and operations that serve the achievement of institutional objectives.
>
> (1998: 222)

As a consequence, argue Jansen and Wildemeersch, questions are never raised concerning the social usefulness of institutional values, norms and products. This leads to a growing sense of collective irresponsibility, just at a time when it is important for institutions 'to carry moral responsibility for what happens to society and to the population in general' (1998: 222). Jansen and Wildemeersch argue that self-work must entail questions such as 'how should we live?' and 'how can we develop morally justifiable forms of life in a post-traditional social order?' And so they point to the danger of educational processes that simply help the learner to act as an entrepren-eur of the self within an 'enterprised culture', which is a privatized activity, necessarily divorced from collective issues of justice, democracy and com-munal life.

While this objection has merit, and therefore needs to be addressed, it partly rests on the assumption that there is a new type of identity which will emerge in the guise of the 'learner/worker'. This is an identity which is fairly fixed and stable (within the allowable parameters of flexibility) and into which neophyte learner/workers can be inducted. But this is a mis-reading of what it means to be an entrepreneur of the self, where the emphasis is not on unearthing who one is as a learner/worker or on getting the identity right, but rather on inventing, modulating and multiplying one's relationships as a learner/worker. In exploring new ways of relating to others, a multiplicity of self-accounts or narratives is invited, a particular account coming into play in a particular relationship. This idea of self-narration changing according to the relationship in which one is engaged illustrates a shift in focus from individual selves coming together to form a relationship, to one where the relationship takes centre stage, with selves being realized principally as the by-products of relatedness. Thus it is a misconstrual to regard shifting self-narratives as somehow self-serving or deceitful: it is simply to recognize that each portrayal of self operates with the conventions of a particular relationship. As Gergen and Kaye intimate, such is '. . . to take seriously the multiple and varied forms of human con-nectedness that make up life . . .' (1993: 255). Thus there is no necessity to search for an invariant or definitive story about this new kind of learner/worker; indeed such a singular narrative would restrain and limit the capa-city to explore different relationships. The pedagogy of workplace learning, then, should more properly be based on the kind of self-reflection which opens up different ways of punctuating workplace experience and which exhibits a readiness to explore multiple perspectives and endorse their coexistence. Such an approach will enable learners to construct things from different viewpoints, releasing them from the limiting narrative beliefs pro-vided by either the organization or the educational institution.

What then are some of the issues and points of contest that can serve to provide an ongoing critique of the learner/worker? I have identified four such issues. These are explored below.

Workplace learning skills

Educators have long been concerned with developing the learning skills of students. This is a response to a commonly held view that teachers cannot be expected to teach everything, and therefore students need to be given the wherewithal to manage their own learning. It entails the development of a set of generic learning skills, but the skills identified are often only applicable to formal learning situations. The following are the typical skills that are often cited (see Smith 1990):

- learning from instruction (listening, taking notes, summarizing, questioning);
- performing assigned learning tasks (understanding the purpose of a task, following instructions, anticipating the kinds of responses required);

- relating practical experiences to the material being taught and applying the principles derived from theory and research;
- basic learning skills such as finding information, organizing and categorizing thoughts, reviewing material for examinations, developing exam technique;
- learning how to generalize and when to generalize.

The shift to learning from experience in the workplace requires a reconceptualization, or perhaps more accurately an additional set of skills and attitudes regarding learning. These include:

- the ability to analyse workplace experiences;
- the ability to learn from others;
- the ability to act without all the facts available;
- the ability to choose among multiple courses of action;
- the ability to learn about organizational culture;
- the ability to use a wide range of resources and activities as learning opportunities;
- the ability to understand the competing and varied interests in the shaping of one's work or professional identity.

Learning from workplace experience also entails the identification and creation of opportunities for experiences from which new learning will flow. This may involve the learner/worker volunteering or seeking out special projects or assignments in the workplace, being active in suggesting initiatives in which they may be involved, negotiating with supervisors for more varied tasks and responsibilities, or creating new ways of carrying out routine tasks.

Billett (1994), in his investigation of workplace learning in a mining and secondary processing plant, found that the informal elements of the learning system were the most valued by operators in assisting with workplace tasks and the resolution of problems encountered. An interesting aspect of this investigation is the rating of the utility of different learning resources for the development of different types of knowledge (propositional knowledge, procedural knowledge and dispositional knowledge). The data obtained support the perceived potency of 'everyday activities', 'observing and listening', and 'other workers' as sources of all three types of knowledge. Billett, however, warns that while informal learning clearly supports the development of higher order procedural knowledge, workers express concern about the possibility of developing conceptual (propositional) knowledge through informal means only. There is therefore scope for making the tacit understandings of skilled workers more explicit, which may mean periods of formal instruction. This provides justification for work-based learning: in situ learning alongside more organized activities provided by an established institute of higher learning such as a university.

The new learner, then, needs to develop a set of skills and attitudes relating to learning from experience in the workplace. The pedagogical expertise of the educator takes on a new significance in this context: it shifts from being a content specialist towards helping learners to acquire the capacity to reflect on their experiences. There now exists a body of literature relating to learning from experience which outlines a variety of approaches that take experience as the raw material to be analysed through 'critical reflection'. Such reflection involves abstracting legitimate knowledge which can be used for credit in a formal course. This might include identifying unexamined and distorting psychocultural assumptions in order to promote 'perspective transformation' (Mezirow 1991), or unmasking power relations with a view to consciousness raising (see Hart 1991). This literature tends to be focused on either the liberatory and empowering potential of critical reflection or the management of experience for more effective workplace performance and/or for academic credit. By and large it takes experience as given and in need of interpretation, recognizing the inevitable contestation in any interpretation or 'reading' of an experience.

Where learning from workplace experience is formalized for academic credit, no doubt there will be different renderings of experience depending on one's point of view: from the learner, the organization, or the educational institution providing the credit. The new learner thus needs to understand the interests served by a particular interpretation of experience, and have the capacity to negotiate a preferred interpretation. Thus while it is important for the new learner/worker to develop learning skills appropriate to the workplace, the skills themselves need to be interrogated and the learning emanating from them problematized and open to different interpretations. The pedagogy is such that new learning skills are acquired, multiplied and problematized simultaneously.

The new teacher–learner relationships

The shift to workplace learning is symptomatic of a general shift from 'education' to 'learning'. This is accompanied by the increasing importance and centrality of the 'learner' as opposed to the 'teacher' in the pedagogical relationship. Of course the idea of learner-centredness and the changing 'teacher–learner' relationship it implies is not new. The literature in adult education, for example, has placed much emphasis on the importance of establishing an appropriate adult teacher–learner relationship, with the learner at its centre. Freire's distinction between 'banking education' and 'problem-posing education' (1974) and Knowles's ideas (1990) of the 'learning facilitator' as opposed to 'teacher' are illustrative of attempts to reconfigure the teacher–learner relationship. In such conceptions, learners are given more power and responsibility over what they learn and they are crucially seen as producers of knowledge. This is certainly the case with workplace learning, but with the additional complexity of a shifting interplay between learners as producers of knowledge, as consumers of learning, and as performers of skills and attitudes. The teacher in these circumstances can take up a number of positions. These include an arbiter of what constitutes worthy knowledge, a guide who assists learners to 'learn from experience', a measurement specialist who monitors performance, a facilitator who processes the concerns and interests of learners, or a critical commentator who addresses issues of power and authority. Of course a further complexity is that those who are learners in one context (or moment) may become teachers in another. In many instances teachers of adults are the subordinates of their learners in the larger organizational or professional context. This role flexibility, indeed ambiguity, is a feature of most workplace learning situations.

The teacher–learner relationship in workplace learning is clearly one that is shifting and constantly open to negotiation. In this scenario learner/workers seem to be empowered in the sense that they are active, skilled subjects. But the accompanying self-regulation and surveillance is arguably disempowering. For instance, learners are co-opted (or perhaps duped) into managing themselves in line with both organizational and educational requirements. In these circumstances the real skill of the new learner is to find spaces for 'self-creation' among the contested meanings of experience that are bound to emerge from the different perspectives of the employer, educator and learner. Thus new learners need to be able to critique the discourse of experiential learning while paradoxically adopting this discourse. That is, they must maintain a sceptical and questioning attitude to the various ways in which learner/workers are positioned and experience is reconstituted as learning. A corresponding role for the teacher is to adopt the discourse of workplace experiential learning while simultaneously engaging in a critique of this discourse with the learner/workers. The teacher–learner relationship, then, is best seen as centred on the co-construction of new learner/worker identities.

The learner as producer of knowledge

Traditional education, separated from the workplace, has always been prepared to be 'against' the workplace with its narrow, often short-term interests, its lack of concern with social issues and its potential to manipulate, alienate and oppress the rights and selfhoods of workers. With newly emerging education/workplace partnerships, educational provision is more than ever 'with' the workplace, and the workplace is equally portrayed as 'with' the learner/worker. As mentioned earlier, resistance and contestation around identity and personal development in this situation becomes more problematic, or at least more complex and contradictory. On the one hand, there is an emphasis on the 'active' subject, which on the face of it appears 'empowering'. But on the other, it is now more than ever in the interests of active subjects to engage in their own surveillance, and to align themselves with the expectations and values of the new alliance between the employer and the educator. In this scenario there is a marked shift from the learner as a consumer of knowledge, to the learner/worker as a performer of knowledge and skill, the criteria for effective performance being negotiated between the education/workplace partners. The rhetoric of workplace learning, however, positions the learner/worker as a *producer* of knowledge. Exploring what it means to be a producer of knowledge, and whether there is a distinct 'kind' of knowledge involved, is a crucial element of the pedagogy of workplace learning. This is partly because it opens up new possibilities for narratives about the learner/worker which provide a counterpoint to the potentially dominant 'performance' narrative of the employer/educator alliance.

An objection frequently raised about the kind of knowledge which is produced through workplace experience is that it is often local, contingent and private, and perhaps uncommunicable in a public sense. It thus functions to complement and enrich codified knowledge gained through formal study. For example, an autoclave operator in a chemical processing plant may have some formal knowledge about chemical reactions, the operation of autoclaves, and procedural knowledge of the operation of particular brands of autoclave. But they will also develop considerable knowledge about how particular autoclaves in a particular plant operate, with all their idiosyncrasies. It is this more localized knowledge which is crucial to the effective performance of the plant, but it may not be able to be codified and transferred to others. There is no substitute for experience. Similarly a paediatrician may enrich their clinical knowledge and practice through having children, but what is gained can only be gained through the experience of having children, and in no other way. In such instances, so the argument goes, the only indicator that knowledge has been produced is one's performance. But while it is true that the totality of experiences cannot be taken on by others, experiences can nevertheless be talked about, compared, theorized and problematized. Workplace pedagogy can be directed towards this end. It is not so much performance that matters: it is how one's engagement with practice produces new ways of thinking about a problem or issue.

Perhaps the best illustration of the production of knowledge through reflection on workplace practice is the development of psychoanalytic theory at the beginning of the twentieth century in Vienna. Much of the theorizing grew directly from clinical practice, and with sharing clinical and theoretical insights with others so engaged. Effective performance in the form of clinical success, although relevant, was not used as the benchmark for the production of knowledge; more important were the observations and connections made within and between case studies within an emerging theoretical framework. In this way the knowledge produced went beyond performance and beyond the experiences of any single clinician. Such examples (and they are legion in the history of the professions) suggest that what is needed is an adequate pedagogy of the workplace that focuses on the production of knowledge and which goes beyond the local, contingent and private.

The 'situatedness' of the learner

One important impetus for linking education more closely with the workplace has comes from the steadily growing acknowledgement of the value of context in learning. In work-based learning, where work is the curriculum, context is all. The learner, and the learning, is thus thoroughly situated. Now, there are different theoretical 'takes' on what it means to be a situated learner. Perhaps the most radical of these is that of Lave and Wenger (1991), whose views are useful as a counterpoint for exploring what it means to be 'situated'. For them the essential thing about 'situated' learning is that it involves participation in communities of practice. At first this participation is peripheral, but it increases gradually in engagement and complexity until the learner becomes a full participant in a community of practice.

Learners can be characterized as having increasing access to participating roles in a community of practice:

> ... the skillful learner acquires something more like the ability to play various roles in various fields of participation. This would involve things other than schemata: ability to anticipate, a sense of what can feasibly occur within specified contexts ... a prereflective grasp of complex situations ... timing of actions relative to changing circumstances: the ability to improvise.
>
> (Lave and Wenger 1991: 20)

In Lave and Wenger's analysis, learning is not so much a matter of individuals acquiring mastery over knowledge and processes of reasoning; it is a matter of co-participants engaging in a community of practice. The focus is thus on the community rather than the individual. Far from eclipsing the person, they claim the person in this community is a 'person-in-the-world', not an isolated individual, but a 'whole person' who is a member of a socio-cultural community.

The closest Lave and Wenger come to articulating a pedagogy of workplace practice is in their concern with identifying the conditions which distort or enhance learning in communities of practice. For example, the prospects of learning from practice are diminished where there is conflict between newcomers and masters, bosses, or managers; similarly, learning is distorted when there are strong asymmetrical master–apprentice relationships. Legitimate peripheral participants need broad access to arenas of mature practice and they need fewer demands on their time, effort and responsibility for work than full participants. Finally, the socio-political organization of practice needs to be 'transparent', only in this way can learners develop as full participants. For as Lave and Wenger (1991: 101) argue:

> To become a full member of a community of practice requires access to a wide range of ongoing activity, old timers, and other members of the community; and to information, resources, and opportunities for participation.

The focus is thus on the structuring of a community's learning resources. Apart from this there appears to be little scope for workplace pedagogy. For example, they reject the idea of learning from reflection on practice or action as misconstrued mainly because there is a difference between talking about practice from the outside and talking within it:

> In a community of practice, there are no special forms of discourse aimed at apprentices or crucial to their centripetal movement toward full participation that correspond to the marked genres of the question–answer–evaluation format of classroom teaching . . . For newcomers then the purpose is not to learn *from* talk as a substitute for legitimate peripheral participation; it is to learn *to* talk as a key to legitimate peripheral participation.
>
> (Lave and Wenger 1991: 108–9)

The idea then of discourse about practice as somehow distanced from practice or standing outside it is alien to their analysis. Discourse itself is seen as a social and cultural practice and not a kind of second order representation of practice. It follows that it is not possible or desirable to go beyond the 'situation given' and extract from experience that which is decontextualized, abstract or general. Lave and Wenger argue that:

> . . . even so-called general knowledge only has power in specific circumstances . . . abstract representations are meaningless unless they can be made specific to the situation at hand . . . Knowing a general rule by itself in no way ensures that any generality it may carry is enabled in the specific circumstances in which it is relevant. In this sense any 'power of abstraction' is thoroughly situated, in the lives of persons and in the culture that makes it possible.
>
> (1991: 33–4)

There are a number of difficulties with this extreme position. First, it leaves no scope for recognizing the kind of learning which transports one to a different time and space, to escape the 'situatedness' of one's life, which is clearly a desirable facet of at least some learning. Second, it fails to recognize the possibility of arranging learning situations that support more general learning, such as that advocated by others (Greeno *et al.* 1993; Greeno 1997). They argue, in relation to the transfer of learning, that it is not a matter of learners acquiring abstract knowledge and procedures that are applied to many situations. Instead, it is a matter of 'learning to participate in interactions in ways that succeed over a broad range of situations' (Greeno, 1997: 7). A third problem with Lave and Wenger's analysis is that there seems to be no scope for critique and change in communities of practice – for standing outside the framework and taken-for-granted assumptions of the community. While the academy may be critiqued for reproducing the social order, on the face of it, it is more 'world open' than a community of practice which contains within it the 'secrets' of practice which can only be attained through peripheral participation. Finally there seems to be no recognition of the existence of a plurality of situated knowledges. These objections leave the door open to develop a pedagogy which focuses on the situatedness of the learner but which in many respects goes beyond the situation, exploring other contexts, other stories, broader interests and other places.

In conclusion

As universities embrace more situational forms of education as exemplified in work-based learning, the new learner is invited to participate in manifold forms of self-work. In responding to this invitation, the task is not to 'discover' oneself, but to explore multiple stories with a view to opening up new relationships: with co-workers, co-learners, teachers, supervisors, employers, and so on. This is a relational view of the self that implies a pedagogy of self-reflection that insists on maintaining a permanent critique of oneself as a learner and worker. Work-based learning needs to ensure that its participants have enough scope to engage in such a critique.

References

Beck, U. (1992) *Risk Society: Towards a New Modernity*. London: Sage.

Billett, S. (1994) Situated learning – a workplace experience. *Australian Journal of Adult and Community Education*, 34 (2), 112–31.

Freeman, M. (1993) *Rewriting the Self: History, Memory, Narrative*. London: Routledge.

Freire, P. (1974) *Pedagogy of the Oppressed*. Harmondsworth: Penguin.

Gergen, K. and Kaye, J. (1993) Beyond narrative in the negotiation of therapeutic meaning, in K. Gergen (ed.) *Refiguring Self and Psychology*. Aldershot: Dartmouth.

Giddens, A. (1991) *Modernity and Self-Identity: Self and Society in the Late Modern Age*. Cambridge: Polity.

Greeno, J. (1997) On claims that answer the wrong questions. *Educational Researcher*, 26 (1), 5–17.

Greeno, J., Moore, J., and Smith, D. (1993) Transfer of situated learning, in D. K. Detterman and R. J. Sternberg (eds) *Transfer on Trial: Intelligence, Cognition, and Instruction*. Norwood, NJ: Ablex.

Hart, M. U. (1991) Liberation through consciousness raising, in J. Mezirow (ed.) *Fostering Critical Reflection in Adulthood*. San Francisco, CA: Jossey-Bass.

Jansen, T. and Wildemeersch, D. (1998) Beyond the myth of self-actualisation: re-inventing the community perspective in adult education. *Adult Education Quarterly*, 48 (4), 216–26.

Knowles, M. S. (1990) *The Adult Learner: A Neglected Species*. Houston, TX: Gulf Publishing.

Lave, J. and Wenger, E. (1991) *Situated Learning: Legitimate Peripheral Participation*. Cambridge: Cambridge University Press.

McAdams, D. (1996) Personality, modernity, and the storied self: a contemporary framework for studying persons. *Psychological Inquiry*, 7, 295–321.

Mezirow, J. (1991) *Transformative Dimensions of Adult Learning*. San Francisco, CA: Jossey-Bass.

Scribner, S. (1985) Knowledge at work. *Anthropology and Education Quarterly*, 16, 199–206.

Smith, R. (1990) *Learning to Learn across the Lifespan*. San Francisco, CA: Jossey-Bass.

Usher, R. and Solomon, N. (1999) Experiential learning and the shaping of subjectivity in the workplace. *Studies in the Education of Adults*, 31 (2), 155–63.

White, M. (1989) *Selected Papers*. Adelaide: Dulwich Centre Publications.

10

The Organization of Identity:
Four Cases

Clive Chappell, Lesley Farrell,
Hermine Scheeres and Nicky Solomon

Since businesses can no longer be solely about profit . . . they are now in competition with churches, governments, and universities in the framing and conduct of social and moral agendas.

(Gee *et al.* 1996: 32)

Introduction

When we think of workplace restructuring we generally focus on macro-organizational change, the kinds of organizational changes that occur when companies adopt a global orientation. We think, for instance, of moves to shift business functions to remote sites, to downsize and reorganize the workforce. In focusing on the macro level, however, it is easy to lose sight of the micro-processes that constitute, and are constituted by, these macro-level changes. In this chapter we argue that macro-level changes in the workplace always entail, and may even be said to rely on, changes in the micro-processes of work, the ways that individuals do their work, relate with one another and access and produce 'knowledge' day by day. We argue that these changes are discursively mediated and contested (Casey 1995; Farrell 2000; Scheeres 1999), and that they involve profound changes in the social relationships of the workplaces. According to Gee *et al.* (1996), 'What we are really talking about here is the textual creation of . . . new social identities.'

What is interesting, from our point of view, is that economic restructuring entails the restructuring of the workforce as well as the workplace; it involves the restructuring of working identities, working knowledges and working relationships. Our focus in this chapter is, therefore, on the micro level of workplace restructuring. We are interested in the ways that workers at several sites construct and reconstruct their identities from the discursive resources available to them, in a context of rapid and profound change. We present four cases that, though in some respects different, have critical features in common. The first involves the identities of educational practitioners in a university. The second looks at the identities of vocational education and training teachers in publicly funded colleges. The third focuses on the identities of workplace educators and the last on those of workers in a post-Fordised factory. Each case draws on recent research conducted by the authors.

In each case, workplace education and training play a critical part, reflecting the prominence that learning and knowledge have gained in workplaces over the past decade. We are interested in workplaces where learning is explicitly acknowledged as a work practice, where 'learning is the new form of labour' (Zuboff 1988: 395) and where in Senge's formulation 'people are continually learning how to learn together' (1992: 3). This has significant implications for the individual and collaborative construction of working identities. In each case, too, our focus is on the production of knowledge and identity, highlighting the way in which, in new workplaces, '. . . knowledge processes are of crucial importance and the dominant conditions of production have become discursive' (Casey 1995: 10).

Identity and the new production of knowledge

Our interest in identity reflects recent debates in the human and social sciences concerning identity. The concept of identity has been labelled a fiction, an invention of modernity and has been rejected by some theorists (Rorty 1989; Bauman 1996). Others support the concept and suggest that its existence enables new and imaginative representations of the self to be created (Elliott 1996). Social theorists such as Giddens (1991) and Beck (1992) reconfigure identity as a reflexive rewriting of the self, made possible by the continuous self-monitoring processes characteristic of late modernity. Hall (1996) calls for a radical reconceptualization of notions of identity that shifts it away from a focus on the individual and recognizes the nexus between identity formation and discourse within a socio-political context.

This identity–discourse connection is of particular significance. It not only suggests that the new knowledge discourses are working to change the identities of workers as learners and educators, but also that traditional knowledge discourses construct learners and educators in particular and site-specific ways. As a consequence, a number of tensions have been created at the micro level, as the 'new knowledge' workers renegotiate a sense of who they are in restructuring workplaces.

The identities of learners and educators are now challenged by contemporary discourses that, in one way or another, disturb traditional ideas about what counts as knowledge. While these discourses often emphasize the crucial importance of knowledge in contemporary societies (Castells 1993), at the same time, and somewhat paradoxically, they question the adequacy and utility of the content, organization, production and transmission of knowledge found in modern educational institutions.

Many of these new discourses appear to unsettle modern understandings of knowledge by reversing the traditional binaries that privilege one form of knowledge over its 'other'. Today, epistemological discourses emphasize knowledge constructed as practical, interdisciplinary, informal, applied and contextual over knowledge constructed as theoretical, disciplinary, formal, foundational and generalizable. While there is considerable discussion about how this emphasis has come about, we focus on the consequences of this discursive shift for the identities of learners and educational practitioners. Learners and educational practitioners are in no small measure constructed by and through knowledge discourses. Furthermore, the different institutional sites in which learners and educational practitioners undertake their knowledge work are also constructed and reconstructed by these same discourses.

From a postmodern perspective, one of the effects of globalization on knowledge production is manifested in a shift in interest from knowledge for its social and cultural significance to an understanding of knowledge as a commodity. In terms of the latter, knowledge is valued in economic terms and for its exchange value. This is accompanied by a generalized doubt about any universal truth-claims and a radical change in questions about what is worthwhile knowledge. As Lyotard (1984) argued, the questions have shifted from 'is knowledge true?' to 'what is its use and how will it enhance the performance of people and organizations?' These kinds of questions are a discursive mechanism for linking education with economic goals. In other words, such questions result in education being connected to the production of specific forms of knowledge that are needed for staying competitive in the globalized marketplace (Edwards and Usher 2000). The recognition that knowledge has exchange value has important consequences for a range of workplaces including universities and factories.

At the same time, the contemporary reconfiguration of knowledge in economic terms (where 'worthwhile' knowledge is understood in terms of its contribution to efficiency and productivity), is manifested in a valorizing of knowledge that is produced outside the academy – one significant site being the industrial workplace. It is now commonplace for contemporary work to be named as 'knowledge work' and for some employees to be called 'knowledge workers' (Senge 1992). As Gee *et al.* suggest, 'What is important is not the material product or the brute service . . . rather it is the knowledge it takes to innovate, design, efficiently produce, market, and transform products and services as symbols of identity and lifestyle in a high risk world' (1996: 28).

The discourses of organizational learning emphasize 'ongoing' learning and signal the transitory nature of knowledge in workplaces and the importance of situated formal and informal learning. The usefulness of knowledge is increasingly short-term in the new workplace where processes and structures are in a constant cycle of change. While at times specialist knowledge can be brought into such a workplace, the really useful knowledge is often not transferable but is generated on-site in a context of application and constant adaptation.

Case 1: Changing academic identity

The central focus of this first case is on the identity of academics as they confront major challenges faced by contemporary universities. As many writers have demonstrated, globalization has contributed to significant cultural changes to the academy, academic writing and academics (Scott 1995; Edwards and Usher 2000). Our interest is in the way these processes create particular sets of conditions that contribute to the construction of new and different textual practices, new kinds of knowledge and subjects.

The argument here is that the ambiguous and complex effects of globalization set up intertextual conditions that involve various and different kinds of language games that contemporary academics play. Important to our argument, though, is that while the globalization discourses provide the rules *for* playing these games, they do not prescribe the rules *of* the games, which are constantly being reworked as academics acquire new roles and positions.

Of course there is a danger that this discussion over-simplifies the ambiguous effects of globalization on the university and academic roles. It is necessary therefore to precede this discussion with an acknowledgement that there is no single response to globalization by educational institutions. The power of national and institutional structures means that they are indeed able to produce significant variations in the way globalization discourses are instantiated. In recognition of this, we draw attention to the fact that the following discussion is constructed from a particular writing position – one that has emerged through particular sets of social and textual experiences in our work at a technological university in Australia. This position has, however, been constructed through an engagement with a broader intertextual field, namely, the writings of academics in other institutional and national circumstances who are likewise engaging in a critical theorization of the current changes and challenges that they face. We therefore tentatively suggest that our discussion of the relationship between the textual production of knowledge in the contemporary academy and the construction of new subjects may well be the common experience of many academics.

These interrogations of knowledge production are manifested in the recent analysis of changing research practices by a number of theorists. For example, Stronach and MacLure (1997) describe contemporary research practices in terms of three research games. Their description captures the overall shift from a lengthy disciplinary-bound research process (Game 1) to a more accelerated and abbreviated version (Game 2) and then to the fragmented, performative research that has become structured around 'business ethos' (Game 3). The knowledge produced through this third game is less resilient, more transient and tends to be more socially accountable.

Furthermore, these descriptions of such diverse research practices come at a time when academics are experiencing the effects of a shift towards knowledge production outside the academy. The descriptions above offer an explanation for the diversity of research questions and educational initiatives now being explored. They also illuminate the emerging challenges to existing epistemological and methodological practices that are being constituted through new forms of textualism.

Changing subjects in the academy

The recognition of the multiple sites of knowledge production challenges both the university's idea of itself as the primary site of knowledge and the academic's idea of herself or himself as the primary producer of knowledge. This has contributed to a kind of 'identity crisis' for both the academy and the academic. An important manifestation of this is the fact that academics now find themselves playing different knowledge games. Some of these games relate to the emergence of 'knowledge production' and 'knowledge management' as academics confront questions about conventional notions of what is legitimate knowledge.

Other sets of games relate to the academic's increasing involvement with organizations outside the academy, in collaborative research and educational programmes. In these games, academics are participating in new partnerships, alignments and networks that further contribute to the blurring of the boundaries between the academy and other organizations and thus to the 'realization' of education. As academics cross into the real world, they are also confronting and constructing new ways of being. This is a consequence of playing new games that involve new rules, new boundaries, and sequences of textual and social processes, new performances and interactions with different players. In emerging collaborative arrangements with organizations and government bodies, there may or may not be an agreement as to which game is being played. Yet at the same time in these arrangements participants are playing for their own stakes. Moreover the existing textual practices and rules through which these stakes are played are always in a process of being reworked.

But they are also one of the seemingly counter-intuitive effects of globalization on the production of knowledge, that is, the influence of the local and the way globalization actually stimulates the diversity and hybridity of knowledge production – what Stronach and MacLure (1997) refer to as the 'unruliness of knowledge'. This 'unruliness' is one of the 'un/anticipated' consequences of governmentality. It can be understood as resulting from the ambiguous and complex effects of the state's control of higher education through policy that has introduced a new un/ruliness into knowledge production. On the one hand, there is a reduction in government

resourcing of higher education that is supposed to encourage market efficiency but, on the other, constructs technologies that tightly regulate what
counts as legitimate or worthwhile knowledge. These include increasing
funds for collaborative research such as the Australian Research Council
(ARC) Strategic Partnership with Industry, Research and Training (SPIRT)
grants as well as the development of highly specific criteria for funding
research.

In Australia, as elsewhere, the research audit exercise is a technology of
power that attaches differential weighting to particular kinds of outcomes
and performances, with a corresponding downgrading of others. This regulatory exercise has several effects. It can be seen as a counterbalance to the
'freeing-up' of knowledge production manifested in the new collaborative
research and teaching initiatives and a generalized legitimization of knowledge produced outside the academy. Importantly, in addition, it heightens
the accountability of academics, since it is not only a means for rewarding
outputs but also an instrument of state performativity – a technology that
responds to the need 'to show people what we do'.

The demonstration of 'what we do' is subjected to the employment of
highly regulated categories. Specified performance measures literally cat-
egorize and count 'outputs' in a way that makes them auditable. This
auditing draws attention to the diversity of regulatory mechanisms that are
now used to govern at a distance. In line with Miller and Rose's arguments,
the research exercise can be understood as an intellectual technology that
renders aspects of existence amenable to inscription and calculation. It is
a discursive technology that pushes academic writing 'in (to) a particular
conceptual form and (makes it) amenable to intervention and regulation'
(1993: 79).

It is not difficult to understand this government technology as an exercise serving to increase the diversity of research activity. The exercise is
a mechanism that not only measures and counts but also influences the
nature of research activity and its outputs. It is a form of surveillance that,
through self-regulation, attempts to construct particular kinds of academic
work. These technologies certainly pull towards an 'economy of the same'
as they seek to shape, normalize and instrumentalize the conduct of academic 'labour'. However, at the same time, these technologies open up all
kinds of textual and subject possibilities. While academics argue against,
and experience, the limitations of the state's research exercises, the opening up of modes of knowledge production has created new types of textual
opportunity. The conditions of postmodernity have constrained writing practices through increased state interventions, but these same conditions have
also constructed new spaces resulting in more diverse academic writing and
a reidentification of the academic.

As indicated above, the dislocation and 'un/ruliness' of knowledge has
brought to the surface a contestation about what constitutes worthwhile
knowledge and this has had an effect on academic research, academic texts
and subjects. This has been in terms of an investigation of new sites and

new modes of knowledge production that in turn has led to a questioning of accepted epistemological and methodological paradigms. Academics across disciplinary areas are exploring and writing about new knowledge and new modes of knowledge production as they come to terms with their new academic identities.

Case 2: Identifying as a vocational teacher

The discourses of new vocationalism that emanated from the OECD (1989) should have heralded a renaissance in public vocational education and training. This is, after all, the educational sector that has always laid claim to a close and explicit relationship with the world of work. Further Education (FE) in the United Kingdom, Technical and Further Education (TAFE) in Australia and Community Colleges in the United States, for example, have all, in different ways, constructed an educational identity through their provisioning of vocational knowledge, workplace learning and industrial skill. Generally, this identity has also constructed vocational teachers as industry experts who pass on their vocational expertise to students in the various courses offered by these institutions. This educational sector has also generally deployed knowledge discourses that privilege practical, applied, contextualized and interdisciplinary knowledge over knowledge that is theoretical, pure, general and disciplinary.

However, recent research suggests that these institutions and their teachers are not experiencing any policy-driven reinvigoration. Indeed, many commentators suggest that public vocational education is now in crisis (Grubb 1996; Chappell 1999; Shain and Gleeson 1999). They point to the reduction in government funding and the marketization practices that are now endemic in these institutions. They also suggest that increasing competition for students from private providers, together with the encouragement of industry-delivered and accredited vocational training programmes, are all contributing to this crisis.

While not denying the impact of these policy-driven changes on the public provision of vocational education, the argument pursued here is that these institutions and the teachers that work within them also face unsettling times, brought on by the emergence of new knowledge discourses. These new discourses not only undermine the traditional knowledge discourses that underpinned the sector, but also work to change the identity of TAFE teachers. These effects are explored in relation to one group of training teachers working in a TAFE college in New South Wales.

Talking-up vocationalism

When teachers speak of their work in TAFE they place a great deal of importance on the industrial experience they bring with them to the institution.

They commonly speak of 'knowledge of industry', 'workplace knowledge', 'technical competence', 'knowledge relevant to industry' and their 'practical experience' of work. They talk about bringing 'real-world' examples to the learning process or, as one teacher put it,

> TAFE pays me for my practical knowledge and skills gained through my work experience. Students in our courses aren't interested in theory, but want to know if it works in practice. I always have to make this connection and use real case studies and examples to illustrate what I mean.

By emphasizing the practical over the theoretical, TAFE teachers construct an identity that is different from the identities of other educators, such as university academics. TAFE teachers generally lay no claim over the disciplinary knowledge that grounds much of the curriculum in higher education and indeed curricula in schools. Rather they claim specialized vocational knowledge and expertise gained through their experiences in particular industries and occupations. And unlike academics they make no claim to the production of new knowledge but rather the application of existing knowledge at work.

However, TAFE teachers reveal that this claim to the possession of specialized, vocational knowledge and its application is also deeply problematic. TAFE teachers speak consistently of the need to 'keep up to date' with industry and to maintain their 'industrial expertise'. They explain this need in terms of maintaining their credibility with students:

> I'm really scared that I will lose the relevance and currency of my practical experience. I'm just really scared about my credibility with the students; you know, five years down the track and I haven't worked in the industry for five years.

This commonly expressed view suggests that teachers believe their legitimacy, particularly in the eyes of students, is dependent on their industrial expertise and that this constitutes a distinctive occupational identity. The discourse of industrial expertise therefore does discursive work for TAFE teachers similar to that which disciplinary knowledge does for academics and school teachers.

This similarity however is only a partial one. In the world of the TAFE teacher the ability to 'keep up to date' is given additional importance because many TAFE students are not only learners but are, at the same time, workers. Thus they are able to make an ongoing evaluation of the industrial expertise of the TAFE teacher. The utility and currency of the vocational knowledge and skills that TAFE teachers share with their students can be tested immediately by students in their working lives. It is in this sense 'practical' knowledge and is judged not in terms of its claims to generalizable 'truth' as in the case of disciplinary knowledge but rather its performativity. Consequently, a TAFE teacher's credibility as an 'industry expert' is always open to question and further compounded by their location at a college rather than a workplace.

This location puts pressure on the discourse of industrial expertise that TAFE teachers use to construct a legitimate educational identity. As a location it is characterized by discourses that are different from those circulating in other workplaces. These discourses, for example, work to formalize 'industrial expertise' by deploying traditional curriculum technologies that compartmentalize such expertise into subjects, hierarchies, sequencing strategies and levels of achievement. They impose particular pedagogical and assessment frameworks on the learning process, and through these disciplining discursive practices they reconstruct the contextualized knowledge of work into the generalized vocational knowledge of a given occupation.

As a consequence TAFE teachers use the discourses of working knowledge to construct a legitimate occupational identity that is different from the identity of other teachers. However, at the same time, TAFE teachers draw on educational discourses to reinforce their identity as professional educators. They undertake teacher-education programmes which foreground traditional curriculum practices. They are encouraged to theorize their pedagogy through the research discourses of educational psychology, sociology and philosophy. All of these discursive practices have themselves been based on traditional views of knowledge which privilege that which is formal, theoretical, generalizeable and foundational. But these sit uncomfortably with the knowledge that is necessary in a rapidly changing workplace.

Case 3: Workplace educators as discourse technologists

A prominent feature of the contemporary workplace seeking to engage with the global economy is the emergence of what Fairclough calls the 'discourse technologist' (1996: 73). Discourse technologists are 'expert outsiders', people who are *in* workplaces (for a time, at least) but not *of* them. They are most commonly consultants, people employed on a contractual basis to bring about specific changes in work organization. They may be employed to establish a new department, to oversee organizational restructuring or to review the practices to which a company adheres. However specific their duties might appear to be they have a generic function within a workplace. They have two major tasks. The first is to 'shift the policing of discourse practices from the local to the transnational level' (Fairclough 1996: 73). The second is to give the legitimacy of 'science, knowledge and truth' to organizational practices that were formerly executed by individuals at the local level. In other words, what discourse technologists have in common is that they are employed to intervene actively in the discursive construction of knowledge and identity in local workplaces in ways that will reduce the influence of persistent local discourses and increase those of emerging transnational discourses. Discourse technologists are one of the conduits through which economic globalization is being funnelled.

In many ways workplace literacy educators can be considered prototypical 'discourse technologists'. They are 'expert outsiders', employed in workplaces on a contractual basis with highly specific briefs. Sometimes they are required to prepare workers for certification (like the Base-level Vehicle Builders Certificate), and at others they are employed to deliver targeted programmes in, for instance, Occupational Health and Safety. Workplace educators are generally understood to be concerned with developing the skills and competencies of workers in the restructuring workplace. They are acknowledged as agents of globalization, but only in so far as they are understood to be increasing the skill base of workers and so contributing to the development of the more flexible workforce Australia needs if it is to attract the business of global corporations. While this may, and usually does, involve intervention in the discursive practices of work, this has been seen as incidental; the explicit focus of the literacy educator is generally understood to be concerned with increasing the skill base of the workforce. The line between workplace literacy education and other forms of workplace education is increasingly blurred, with literacy educators often taking on the role of organizational change agents and content-oriented workplace educators increasingly focusing on the language practices associated with new knowledge (Sefton *et al.* 1994).

Workplace literacy educators are, however, in a slightly different position from other workplace educators. They are explicitly charged with intervening directly in the discursive practice of (some) workers. However, the public and professional rhetoric presents workplace literacy education as an intervention in the discursive practice of work that is at worst neutral and at best benign. The purpose of workplace literacy education is to expand the linguistic repertoires of workers and, therefore, to extend the opportunities available to them in the globalizing workplace. If, however, workplace educators as a group can be considered discourse technologists, then they are primarily concerned with changing what counts as working knowledge, not simply extending it. This is not merely a matter of emphasis. Changing the basis of legitimacy from the local to the transnational, and shifting knowledge claims from concrete and localized 'experience' to abstracted claims to 'science', 'knowledge' and 'truth', involves profound changes to work practice and to the ways that working relationships and working identities are constructed at the local level. It goes to the heart of the way that power is produced and mediated in workplaces through workplace education.

There are, as we demonstrate below, good reasons to argue that workplace educators do indeed act as discourse technologists, at least some of the time. However, this does not mean that they have comprehensive control of the discursive practice of the workplace. Local workplaces are heteroglossic sites (Farrell 1999) and what counts as legitimate working knowledge is contested moment by moment in routine workplace interactions.

To understand how this happens we focus here on a brief exchange between Sally (a pseudonym) who is a workplace educator chairing a team meeting, and Bill, a warping shed supervisor at Australian Fabric

Manufacturers (AFM), using transcript material from the Textual Practice of Competence Project (an Australian Research Council project described in Farrell 2000).

In this transcript segment Bill is invited to describe the work that he has executed in claiming the expenditure of $20,000 on new equipment for the warping shed. He describes working with Margaret (another workplace educator) to do the calculations on which the claim is based:

> *Bill:* Yeah. Me and Margaret, yeah, got together and I've worked out quite a bit lost downtime and costing unloading.

While Bill acknowledges Margaret as a co-worker on the project he clearly identifies himself as primary in the process of knowledge production ('I've worked out'). In response, Sally immediately raises the question:

> *Sally:* To what extent are you following the framework of that, that eight-step guideline that Andy put out originally in that, in the book where . . . particularly step 7 where it's got the action plan and it's got, um, Who? When? Where? and so on. Are you using those at all?

There are a number of points to note about this question. First, Sally is intervening directly and explicitly in the discursive production of knowledge, rejecting Bill's formulation and ignoring the substantive issues Bill raises ('lost downtime'). Second, although framed as a question her comment asserts the primacy of the written text, and of a specific generic structure. Third, the 'eight-step guideline' to which she refers is a problem-solving protocol mandated by a global company. The company, with a head office in the US, demands that remote supplier companies provide written evidence that their protocols have been adopted (Farrell 2000). Sally is explicitly 'shift [ing] the policing of discourse practices from the local to the transnational level'. In doing so she is also intervening to shift the basis of legitimacy within AFM from Bill's claim ('I've worked out') to a highly generalized claim to 'science, knowledge and truth' ('Who? When? Where?') as it is formulated in an *Eight-Step Problem Solving Plan.*

Bill, however, explicitly rejects this shift. Calling on traditional workplace discourses he asserts the primacy of embodied knowledge and himself as the principal epistemological actor:

> *Bill:* No, I'm just using this one [points to his head].

Sally does not persist with her alternative here:

> *Sally:* Yeah

and Matt acts as mediator:

> *Matt:* Baz filled one in.

It is interesting to see the way that Matt repositions the abstract, written, *Eight-Step Plan* in this brief turn. First, he reassigns responsibility for formulating knowledge in this way from Bill to Bill's colleague, Baz. In doing so he implies that the knowledge producer does not need to be the person who writes the knowledge down. He separates the intellectual work (working things out) from the act of writing (filling forms in). Second, he discounts the importance of the plan in the processes of knowledge production by referring to it as a form, not a structure for problem solving, merely paperwork. Sally picks up this reference in her next turn:

Sally: Ah, yeah. So you're following that paperwork there?

Bill emphasizes the distinction between knowledge production and the production of an externally mandated written text by disclaiming any knowledge of the *Eight-Step Plan*, locating that responsibility with Margaret, the workplace literacy educator:

Bill: Yeah. I don't know. Are you Margaret? [loud laughter]

and Sally accepts this distinction, for the moment:

Sally: I'm sorry, I've asked the wrong person.

It is not writing itself that is the issue for Bill here, however, although both Matt and Sally have expressed the view that Bill's literacy skills 'aren't up to it':

Bill: I'm just writing it all out and giving it to Margaret. That's all.

Bill writes frequently in other aspects of his work and has written out his calculations and his arguments. He regards this writing as private, however, an 'aid to working things out'. He gives this writing to Margaret to transform into the public, abstracted and, to him, irrelevant, *Eight-Step Plan*.

Workplace educators like Sally certainly do take up 'new work order' discourses (Farrell 1999) in which they are positioned as discourse technologists, conduits of economic globalization and brokers of transnational workplace discourses. The very act of chairing the team meetings, to which she accedes, at least some of the time, positions Sally as an agent of economic globalization within AFM. That she also actively intervenes in the processes of production also assists to 'shift the policing of discourse practices from the local to the transnational level'. There are, however, other discursive resources available in team meetings, and the workers, including Sally, take them up as this transcript segment demonstrates. Persistent workplace discourses remain powerful at local sites; they are rarely silenced when new discourses are introduced. Local workplaces, like AFM, are 'heteroglossic sites' in which persistent and transformative discourses engage 'noisily' with each other (Threadgold 1997).

Fairclough (1996) argues that the shift in the policing of discursive practice from the local to the transnational level relies on the 'expert outsider', the discourse technologist. Here we are arguing that workplace educators are indeed positioned as 'expert outsiders' in workplaces and that 'new work order' discourses partially determine what counts as working knowledge and working identity. Other discursive resources are available to workers and workplace educators, however, and these provide alternative working knowledges and alternative working identities.

Case 4: Factory workers as change facilitators

The last case refers to workplace educators who work in a factory as learning 'facilitators'. They have been drawn from within the ranks of their organization and may be employees who have worked for years on a production line, or have been leading hands or supervisors. They are now engaged in moving from the production line to the meeting room – from being doers to becoming talkers. This move, which involves the valuing of new kinds of knowledge by managers and employers, is constructing new kinds of identities and the (re)formation of social relations. These, coupled with new knowledge and modes of knowledge production, are the focus of ongoing negotiation and struggle in the workplace.

The same globalizing forces impacting on other workplaces are prevalent in the site for the fourth case. These have produced a new work order characterized by a shared vision among the employees of the company. Workplaces are organizing themselves into teams and introducing team meetings across all levels of the enterprise as part of the consultative and participatory processes associated with learning organizations. In such organizations employees are expected to learn to be effective team members who can successfully participate in a range of activities and interactions that have been added to their job descriptions.

The construction of the competent worker, therefore, includes knowledge, skills and attitudes which foreground social relations as much as the physical work of the production line. Problem solving, consultative committees, quality circles, formal and informal on-the-job training all involve consultation as well as reading and writing. This textualization of the workplace is a significant shift in industrial work practices and assists to discursively construct and value new forms of working knowledge.

The focus in this case is the introduction of participatory and consultative processes into a workplace and the impact that they have on the 'being' of managers and employees (du Gay 1996). The discourses of workplace reform often overlook their impact upon the subjectivities of the workers. For example, industry-based competency standards and the attendant competency-based education are constructed as sets of practices that can be 'taxonomized', listed and taught discretely and rationally, often through handbooks and manuals whose implementation leads to the 'production' of a competent worker. The major consideration for workers is how to get from point A to point B as quickly as possible.

One handbook suggests that 'few groups are blessed with flawless members'. It indicates that 'many groups will find that it is much easier and more profitable to restructure the group than to reconstruct each other's personalities' (Bolman and Deal 1991: 116). This kind of analysis demonstrates some understanding that there may be a question of the restructuring of the identities of workers involved – how they are expected to 'be', at work. However, the 'problem' is also neatly avoided by positioning it as one concerning group dynamics only, which can be solved by changing the composition of the group.

The research site is one where the generation of new work practices and new identities are as much a part of the everyday as the processes of production. The workplace is a manufacturing enterprise in Sydney employing around 800 workers, a non-unionized workplace where up to 70 per cent of the production line employees are from language backgrounds other than English and about 30 per cent of the workforce is casualized.

The company brought in a new management team six years ago to restructure a previously family-owned business. This team followed a now accepted pathway of developing a mission statement and a set of core values as the basis of establishing of a new work culture. In this culture social identities of workers are constructed along with related social practices which the workers were expected to learn, demonstrate and value (Gee *et al.* 1996). The mission statement and core values were textualized in the workplace and reproduced on factory walls and flashed around in meetings, in training manuals and in company annual reports and their like. Through these various textualizations the workplace and the workers were defined in particular ways. The mission or goals of the workplace could only be attained if work practices were an integral part of the identity of each worker, part of their core 'being'. For example, there were meetings in which employees from different levels of the organization met and discussed the day-to-day organization of work, quality control and productivity levels in conjunction with the company's mission statement.

A major change was the creation of a new section or department comprising a manager and five facilitators whose function was to re-establish and organize workplace teams. The manager of these teams was selected by one of the executives of the company – he was rung at home on a Friday night and offered the job with the suggestion that it would be good for his career. The five facilitators had been leading hands under the old system and they went through a similar selection procedure. One of the facilitators described the process in the following terms:

A: I've got a good job for you – you're going to do this job in Plant 1.
B: But I don't know anything about it . . .
A: You'll be good . . . You'll be good.

This case draws attention to the changing subjectivities of these key people, as they assumed different roles in the company and struggled to reconstruct themselves in the light of their repositioning by management. Within the unit the discursive construction of selves is a central activity and emphasizes that 'it is the power relations rather than facts about reality which make things true' (du Gay 1996: 45).

The unit, comprising a middle-level manager and senior workers imbued with a range of responsibilities, occupies a unique position within the hierarchy of the organization. This often led to confusion among the senior workers about their power and location in the organization, explained in the following way by one of the facilitators:

> The unit manager comes under the production manager so he's higher than the plant manager, and we're supposed to come under him, but we are not higher than the team leaders. I don't think we're higher than the people on the floor. I think mostly my level's there on the factory floor . . . I don't think the plant manager has any authority over me . . . well, he sort of does.

And further, commenting on the operators' perception of their relationship with the facilitators:

> I think I get confused as to what they see me as . . .

For the members of management, questions about power and confusion regarding the unit are non-existent. It is a much simpler story: the creation of a new unit with specific functions working towards the common goal of improved productivity. They employ discourses of knowledge commodification with which they are familiar in the manufacturing industry, and apply them to the production of the new worker. Thus, the new workers of the unit need some new things – in this case, new knowledge regarding participatory and problem-solving activities as outlined in contemporary management theory and the literature on organizational change. A large consultancy company is called in for this purpose, to provide a 'train the trainer' programme. The company, an organization that audits the workplace, develops enterprise-specific training materials and carries out the training, remains linked to the unit and works closely with them as a knowledge packager and transmitter. The emphasis is on a rational, logical and linear development from a state of ignorance through a set of procedures towards enlightenment – a production pathway. The textuality of the training production is very corporate and glossy: slick manuals and computer-mediated presentations carrying the essential message: 'It is up to each individual to act; to learn; to make a difference. Follow these rules and you will be able to do it.'

The workers are perceived as free and active subjects who have individual choices. There is little understanding of the complexities of class, gender and ethnicity operating both within and outside the practices of the workplace. The facilitators are not expected to take cognizance of these complexities.

The management story foregrounds workplace practices which are linked to the human resource development literature where reforms are long-term and iterative. Strategies are discussed and solutions posed – assumptions of success, unproblematized in any way, predominate. When these ideas and practices are applied in a particular context they emphasize the streamlined solving of problems. Management aims at making the process appear as straightforward as possible (just as they do with the production process).

However, for the unit manager and the facilitators the story is a different one. As they struggle with their own identities, they recognize that the alignment of selves to the new work culture is not necessarily one where the prescriptions of the training manuals eradicate the glitches of making such changes. On the contrary, they may engage in ongoing discursive construction of how one's being can be renewed in the changing workplace. Thus the manager and facilitators constantly question and comment on what is going on.

It is not that the unit workers (dis)believe the truths set out in the manuals, but rather that they take these truths on board and go about their jobs within the parameters and constraints of a unit which sees itself as 'without power'. They themselves construct a workable reality and create new ways for people to be at work rather than merely reflecting upon their social world as given (du Gay 1996: 53).

It may be that the very location or (dis)location of the unit provides the opportunity for different approaches to developing workplace practices. As the members struggle with ways of being and the construction of subjectivities that are recognizable, credible and comfortable within the hierarchy of the organization, they realize that it is possible to work within the postmodern disorder. Their discourses include cries of confusion about their 'real place' in the organization, but they actively use this as a flexible position whereby they try out the new and different. On the one hand there is the plant manager's view of his position of authority as exemplified in the following observation:

> Whatever happens here on the shop floor . . . myself or my team leaders are responsible. We are the owners – they [the members of the unit] are there as a tool to help us get to our final destination.

On the other there is that of the facilitator:

> . . . the responsibilities aren't clear. The roles are not clear cut – perhaps they need to be a bit blurred because they are breaking down boundaries, old strict demarcations, but it does make things difficult. The facilitators see possibilities in the collaborations between management and the floor. They are central players in the breaking down of boundaries, and work as active subjects rejecting the dividing practices that were inherent in the 'old' work order.

Conclusion

Restructured workplaces and the discursive practices that have brought them into being have privileged new forms of knowledge. The academic monopoly over knowledge production has been challenged and many other work sites have become sites of knowledge production and circulation. This is resulting in organizations where knowledge is employed by all the actors in a workplace, and it is a significant part of their expertise. As the four cases in this chapter demonstrate, the discursive practices that construct these new forms of knowledge have disrupted the working identities of academics, vocational teachers, workplace educators and factory workers. However, as this chapter has also illustrated, this disruption reveals itself in quite different and specific ways, reflecting the character and different imperatives that are manifested in different worksites.

References

Bauman, Z. (1996) From pilgrim to tourist – or a short history of identity, in S. Hall and P. du Gay (eds) *Questions of Cultural Identity*. London: Sage.

Beck, U. (1992) *Risk Society: Towards a New Modernity*. London: Sage.

Bolman, L. and Deal, T. (1991) *Reframing Organisations: Artistry, Choice and Leadership*. San Francisco, CA: Jossey-Bass.

Casey, C. (1995) *Work, Self and Society: After Industrialism*. London: Routledge.

Castells, M. (1993) The informational economy and the new international division of labour, in M. Carnoy, M. Castells, S. Cohen and F. M. Cardoso (eds) *The New Global Economy in the Information Age: Reflections on our Changing World*. University Park, PA: Pennsylvania State University Press.

Chappell, C. (1999) The Policies and Discourses of Vocational Education and Training: Their Effects on Teachers' Identities. Unpublished PhD Thesis, University of Technology, Sydney.

Du Gay, P. (1996) *Consumption and Identity at Work*. London: Sage.

Edwards, R. and Usher, R. (2000) *Globalisation and Pedagogy: Space, Peace and Identity*. London: Routledge.

Elliott, A. (1996) *Subject to Ourselves: Social Theory, Psycho-analysis and Postmodernity*. Cambridge: Polity Press.

Fairclough, N. (1996) Technologisation of discourse, in C. Caldas-Coulthard and M. Coulthard (eds) *Texts and Practices. Readings in Critical Discourse Analysis*. London: Routledge.

Farrell, L. (1999) Reconstructing Sally: narratives and counter narratives around work, education and workplace restructure. *Studies in Literacy and Numeracy*, 9 (2), 5–26.

Farrell, L. (2000) Ways of doing, ways of being: language, education and 'working' identities. *Language and Education*, 14 (1), 18–36.

Gee, J., Hull, G. and Lankshear, C. (1996) *The New Work Order: Behind the Language of the New Capitalism*. Sydney: Allen & Unwin.

Giddens, A. (1991) *Modernity and Self-Identity: Self and Society in the Late Modern Age*. Cambridge: Polity.

Grubb, W. N. (1996) The 'new vocationalism' in the United States: returning to John Dewey. *Educational Philosophy and Theory*, 28 (1), 1–23.

Hall, S. (1996) Introduction. Who needs 'identity'?, in S. Hall and P. du Gay (eds) *Questions of Cultural Identity*. London: Sage.

Lyotard, J-F. (1984) *The Postmodern Condition: A Report on Knowledge*. Manchester: Manchester University Press.

Miller, P. and Rose, N. (1993) Governing economic life, in M. Gane and T. Johnson (eds) *Foucault's New Domains*. London: Routledge.

OECD (Organisation for Economic Co-operation and Development) (1989) *Education and the Economy in a Changing Economy.* Paris: OECD.

Rorty, R. (1989) *Contingency, Irony and Solidarity.* Cambridge: Cambridge University Press.

Scheeres, H. (1999) Restructured work, restructured worker. *Literacy and Numeracy Studies,* 9 (1), 27–38.

Scott, P. (1995) *The Meanings of Mass Higher Education.* Buckingham: SRHE/Open University Press.

Sefton, R., Waterhouse, P. and Deakin, R. (1994) *Breathing Life into Training: A Model of Integrated Training.* Doncaster, Vic.: National Automotive Industry Training Board.

Senge, P. (1992) *The Fifth Discipline.* Sydney: Random House.

Shain, F. and Gleeson, D. (1999) Teachers' work and professionalism in the post-incorporated further education sector. *Education and Social Justice,* 1 (3), 55–64.

Stronach, I. and MacLure, M. (1997) *Educational Research Undone: The Postmodern Embrace.* Buckingham: Open University Press.

Threadgold, T. (1997) *Feminist Poetics: Poesis, Performance, Histories.* London: Routledge.

Zuboff, S. (1988) *In the Age of the Smart Machine: The Future of Work and Power.* New York, NY: Basic Books.

11

Organizational Gothic: Transfusing Vitality and Transforming the Corporate Body through Work-based Learning

John Garrick and Stewart Clegg

I am here to do Your bidding, Master. I am your slave, and You will reward me, for I shall be faithful . . . Now that you are near, I await Your commands, and you will not pass me by, will You, in distribution of good things?

(Stoker [1897] 1993: 86)

The lifeblood of organizational change

The role of knowledge management has become the lifeblood of organizational change and development in post-industrial workplaces. Learning is a core component of organizational knowledge – directly related to the knowledge products of a company. Learning has been integrated into all aspects of organizational business through 'balanced scorecard' measurements and reward systems such as performance-related pay and generous 'employee stock options'. In return for these transfusions employees must be prepared to yield up their vital secrets: that knowledge at work which has hitherto been their private preserve, often their only source of resistance to organizational surveillance and control. Financial capital is in this way revitalized by the regular ingestion of knowledge capital.

However, in this chapter we will observe that transformation, as a metaphor, has a dark side, best represented in the genre of Gothic horror. Here, the world of everyday life struggles with the forces of transformation unleashed when dusk falls and the imagination roams fearful but free. The apogee of the genre was Count Dracula. As a being, he depended upon replenishing his vital life fluids by ingesting those of others. Thus, in this genre, transformation depends upon transfusion and transgression. Dracula's transgression is his nightly transformation into the Prince of Darkness, who relies on the blood transfusions of living souls. However, once transfused, these souls join the ranks of the undead – those permanently committed to further transformation through an endless round of transfusion.

At the base of these transformations is a transformation of value: from an individually tacit asset, knowledge is transformed into an organizationally explicit factor of production. Not just another factor of production but *the* factor – that which can sustain vitality, reproduce capital and provide competitive edge. But first individuals have to yield their vitality. One might say that vital insights that were once implicit in specific individuals have to become part of the transformative capacity of the organization – irrespective of where the vitality may have originated once they have achieved integration. Typically, the construction of these organizational relations is pastoral and romantic, embodied in managerial win/win solutions and benevolent outcomes where everyone is represented as profiting. From the dark side of the dialectic, however, things are seen differently. Once the individuals' intellectual capital is transfused their vitality becomes vulnerable. If one is not constantly engaged in the performativity of transforming oneself (as one simultaneously transfuses vitality into the organization), one runs the risk of being sucked dry, spat out, made anaemic and, finally, redundant.

The individual souls in the corporation that learn are those replenished through being sucked dry and recruited as brides and grooms to the new organizational Draculas. These are corporate bodies that sustain themselves through transfusing the vitalities of the individuals who comprise and relate to them, in a tantalizing and, for some, materially rewarding game of seduction. Thus, a Gothic spin on the transformation of organizations through knowledge management focuses on the dark side of the dialectic of individual learning, organizational knowledge and their management. As a way of managing organizational learning, pastoral/romantic metaphors are used to stress mutual reciprocity and care of the self. Such notions are implicit in knowledge management. By contrast, the Gothic perspective sees such transformations as unequal exchanges with eventually mortifying consequences, unless such transformations are associated with the creation of a plurality of organizational reciprocities rather than one-way exchanges.

In this chapter we examine some of the organizational effects of this human capital discourse as it conflates the terms 'knowledge' and 'assets' and redefines the validity of knowledge in terms of its business utility and financial value. Hence, our use of the metaphor of vampirism: it is only when 'personal knowledge' is measured – organizationally imbibed and banked – that it counts. It is the counting that provides vitality for the brides and grooms of the organizational Draculas. The pleasure of learning therefore has its price, as one would expect, for it is econometrics (increasingly via the balanced scorecard) that discursively constructs and brings about the integration into the organization of personal and tacit knowledge.

The 'Americanized' conditions of work

Production and work are extremely important in modern society at almost every conceivable level. People often define themselves, and are socially defined, by the types of work that they do (or don't do). What people do at work, or the work that is denied them, has a direct connection to individual identity formation. Yet most contemporary workplaces are in states of constant change. The old Marxist certainties that argued for the creation of a class consciousness seem increasingly arcane, as:

> Capitalism itself has undergone a process of profound restructuring, characterised by greater flexibility in management; decentralisation and networking of firms both internally and in their relationships to other firms; considerable empowering of capital vis-à-vis labour with the concomitant decline of influence of the labour movement; increasing individualisation and diversification of working relationships; massive incorporation of women into the pre-paid labour force . . . increasing geographic and cultural differentiation of settings for capital accumulation and management.
>
> (Castells 1996: 1–2)

In all advanced industrial societies vast changes in production and work have occurred in the decades since the 1950s. In the first instance these changes have been associated with the rapid development and expansion of electronic technology, particularly the development of automated production systems. Relatively simple forms of automation in the 1950s and 1960s were rapidly surpassed by advanced electronic production and information systems. Such systems now integrate a wide variety of workplaces: manufacturing plants, offices, banks, shops, hospitals and public organizations. Casey (1999: 16) points out that 'smart' machines and 'seeing' and 'sensing' robots are beginning to affect industry, commerce, work and learning. These developments influence all domains of production, and are not restricted to heavy industry or manufacturing. For the smart machine has permeated professional sites of work such as medicine, law, finance and architecture. Indeed, the new technologies affect our entire social lives in some way (Aronowitz and DiFazio 1994; Rifkin 1996). Increasingly, we work in changing contexts of increasingly global work.

Globalization, although 'Americanization' may be more apposite, refers to a pattern of events facilitated by technological changes, economic shifts and organizational restructuring and networking. It differs from internationalism in an important sense, that the nation-state has a diminished role. The rise of multinational and transnational corporations in recent years has been greatly facilitated by the capabilities of advanced information and communication technologies (ICT). Globalization points to the rising importance of the multinational and transnational corporations that now control a large percentage of the world's economy and exert considerable influence on national policy and legislation. Transnational business operations and *supranational* associations such as the World Trade Organization (WTO), World Bank, European Union (EU) and so on, have a very significant impact on the magnitude and pace of globalization. Petrella (1996) defines the characteristics of globalization in terms of:

- the internationalization of financial markets;
- internationalization of corporate strategies, and a commitment to competition as a source of wealth creation;
- worldwide diffusion of technology and related R & D knowledge;
- transformation of consumption patterns into cultural products with worldwide consumer markets;
- the internationalization of the regulatory capabilities of national societies into a global political economic system;
- the diminished role of national governments in global governance.

The social, economic, political and cultural implications of globalization are immense. For instance, the WTO inclusion (in November 1999) of the People's Republic of China, home to 25 per cent of the world's population, has enormous significance for expanding global market opportunities. Also, the emergence of regional blocs and 'global webs' are likely to continue indefinitely with many implications for work. These implications encompass the structuring of occupations and labour markets as well as the mobility of high-skilled labour (and immigration policies). Low-skilled, low-wage labour is increasingly likely to be marginalized in the core global economic blocs, as globally competitive markets for goods and services and the capacity to globalize an organization through the electronic integration of geographically dispersed employees develop rapidly.

In an era of expanding virtual work, e-commerce and e-business, employees across geographic locations can now access centralized databases for a wide variety of purposes. Universities, airlines, libraries, finance and information-based organizations, such as consultancies and law firms, have global computer access to their own and other contracted users' information 24 hours a day. Such access enables information-processing work to be conducted worldwide in minutes. On-line co-workers can now include employees across a range of geographical locations and managers. Thus, 'Human Resource Managers' and 'Organizational Developers' deal with newly decentred workplaces, where there are increased levels of out-sourcing and short-term contract work, as crucial boundary maintainers for an era of 'knowledge workers'.

Projections of work and employment

The transition to an informational society presents critical questions about the future of work for workers, managers, organizations and learning. Debates about future opportunities in work, or indeed of the role of work in our lives, are far from resolved. Projections of work and employment in the twenty-first century predict (for the United States) that the bulk of increased employment opportunities will be in service activities (Castells 1996: 221–7). Now, 'services' is a very broad category. Included is not only Masters of the Universe, with their MBAs, but also those involved in food and cleaning who service them; those involved in custodial services, who incarcerate them as well as those who prosecute and defend them. It also includes temporary work and out-sourced activities. Legal, health, engineering, architectural, educational and other services also comprise this increasingly important sector.

Growth in the retail division also comprises a significant area for new jobs. In keeping with the trend toward the informational society, manufacturing jobs will continue to decline, agricultural jobs in the developed world will decline even more dramatically (with the notable exception of urban-oriented agricultural services such as gardeners). Occupationally, there will be considerable growth for skilled professionals, technicians and semi-skilled service occupations. According to the influential forecasts of Castells, 'sales and clerical workers will remain relatively stable, and craft workers may actually increase their share of total occupational employment . . . representing a tendency to stabilise a central core of skilled technical or manual workers around craft skills' (1996: 224).

The situation in Europe, however, does not present the same optimism of increased employment opportunities. The recent European Union 'jobs strategy' document (CEU 1999) indicates that Europe continues to experience high unemployment even in high-tech countries such as Finland, Germany and the UK. Currently there are 35 million persons registered as unemployed in the European Union nations, with increasing concerns about 'precarious jobs and in-work poverty' (CEU 1999). The number of part-time jobs has grown while the number of full-time jobs continues to decline. Increased jobs in newly developing countries may be accounted for by both the globalization of manufacturing operations and the increase in part-time and women's employment.

Post-Fordist writers have consistently argued that the new labour market is one that presents increasingly polarized work opportunities – with a core and a periphery. What this means is that there are emerging primary and secondary labour markets defined almost entirely by access to educational capital and opportunities for learning. In addition, jobs are of a temporary nature, focusing on particular projects at particular moments in time. It is worth noting here that there is a growth of casual and part-time work and evidence that these forms of work represent an expansion of less desirable forms of employment – particularly in the secondary labour market. Correspondingly there are astonishing disparities in relative remuneration outcomes.

In Australia the number of part-time jobs increased about 300 per cent between the early 1970s and the early 1990s. Full-time jobs increased over the same period by only 20 per cent. Part-time work has increased from 16 per cent of total employment in 1978 to over 25.5 per cent in 1997. This trend has not been steady but accelerating, particularly since 1991. The most recent labour force statistics show an absolute decline in the number of full-time jobs available. By far the most significant characteristic of part-time workers is their sex. Underpinning this shift is the increasing requirement for 'emotional labour' in service industries, for example, in ensuring customer satisfaction and well-being. In Australia almost 75 per cent of people working part-time are women and, according to the Australian Bureau of Statistics, the majority of men who work part-time are full-time students (ABS 1997). The conditions of part-time work vary from country to country and from region to region, as does the proportion of those employed part-time. Part-time employees often find themselves unable to participate in work-based learning or training as such activities are designed around a full-time worker.

The distinction between full-time and part-time workers is of prime significance for work-based learning – especially if work is the curriculum. In contrast with the expectations of earlier generations of workers in many sectors of industry, in which employer initiatives in training and staff development were typical, workers in the current and coming generation are increasingly expected to advance *their own* education and skills training independently of employing organizations. This, of course, has important access and equity implications and raises the controversial questions related to both 'who gets educated' and 'who pays'?

Because employment security is on the wane in most economies, systems of wage determination and remuneration generally are becoming more performance- or productivity-related. We live, increasingly, in an era of enterprise governance characterized by various forms of employee participation, 'team-work' and 'empowerment'. These practices remain sporadic and, in Australia, lack a strong legislative basis (Kitay and Lansbury 1997: 222). One consequence of the absence of this is that work-based learning opportunities directly connect to enterprise governance, rather than government provision or citizen entitlement. In Australia (in direct contrast to both China and Europe), work-based learning opportunities are tied to private and self-investment as distinct from state subsidized education and training. In this context, the privileged discourses become the development of knowledge workers and the management of intellectual capital.

Knowledge management and intellectual capital

Recently, a considerable amount of attention has been paid to 'knowledge management' and 'intellectual capital' (Drucker 1995; Nonaka and Takeuchi 1995; Marsick and Watkins 1999). Human resource management and organizational development discourses increasingly talk about the *tangible outcomes* of learning organizations. Tying discussions to the nomenclature of capital is, in many ways, a shrewd move. Through this connection, knowledge becomes a product. Marsick and Watkins (1999: 207). Advocates of human capital theory, put it this way: 'The creation and management of knowledge within the system, and its contribution to knowledge outcomes are captured through the idea of intellectual capital.' They assert that measures for 'intellectual capital' have grown from dissatisfaction with conventional economic measures of value, for instance the (over-)reliance on financially based instruments for assessing the merits of training and development. American and European companies are increasingly questioning whether training and development should be treated as capital expenditure or as corporate overheads.

Many American businesses have already shifted from traditional cost accounting to 'activity-based costing' (Drucker 1995: 37). Value analysis, process analysis, quality management and costing become increasingly integrated through such shifts. They can also potentially combine management theory, organizational development and statistical thinking in the notion of continuous, lifelong learning. But who benefits from this lifelong learning? Advocates of human capital theory (Nonaka and Takeuchi 1995; Edvinnson and Malone 1997; Marsick and Watkins 1997) assert that many of the assets that individuals bring to the post-industrial organization are 'intangible' (or intangibles). This is premised on *personal knowledge* (what people bring to practical situations that enables them to think and perform) rather than codified (propositional) knowledge. The trick is to get such personal knowledge – which, Eraut claims, is 'not only acquired through the use of public knowledge but also constructed from personal experience and reflection' (1999: 3) – into systems and products that organizations create and use. For instance, at General Motors field technicians wear voice-driven PCs. When they complete a repair, they verbally describe the procedure, their words being transcribed automatically into electronic text files. 'The company plans to collect this information centrally over an intranet, enabling technicians at GM's headquarters to review the reports and decide whether to use the information to alter service procedures or add to training materials' (Burton-Jones 1999: 10). In this way personal knowledge, which includes propositional knowledge along with procedural and process knowledge, is assumed to add value to the organization.

In the industrial era, intangibles were identified as 'good will'. Strassman (cited in Marsick and Watkins 1999) describe intellectual capital in the post-industrial era in terms of three capital components: human, structural and customer. He makes the point that:

> Re-engineering and downsizing play a critical role in destroying knowledge capital. The people who possess the accumulated knowledge about a company are the carriers of Knowledge Capital. They are the people who leave the workplace every night and may never return. They possess something for which they have spent untold hours listening and talking while delivering nothing of tangible value to paying customers. Their brains have become the repositories of an accumulation of insights about how 'things work here' . . . Learning organisations extend capacity to use learning as a strategic tool to generate new

knowledge in the form of products, patents, processes and services; and to use technology to capture knowledge.

(Marsick and Watkins 1999: 208)

As we have argued, the trick seems to be drawing personal knowledge from people, either employees or those who will shortly be ex-employees (but don't know it), as well as customers and suppliers, and incorporating it in the explicit knowledge of the organization. This can happen by treating skills as part of knowledge rather than separate from it. This allows for representations of 'competence', 'capabilities' or 'expertise' in which the use of skills (and propositional knowledge) can be observed, integrated and incorporated into computerized systems – the new custodians of corporate knowledge. Metaphorically, organizations must become increasingly like latter-day, postmodern Count Draculas: disembodied entities who must continually ingest the vital fluids of others and then manage them. The individual soul in the organizational body that learns in this way is virtually sucked dry, with 'learning' almost entirely integrated into all aspects of organizational business. For the brides and grooms recruited to service the new Draculas there is, for some, pleasure and profit in learning the tricks of this service but, as we have noted, such learning has its price.

Nowhere is the transactional detail of the exchange between the tacit embodiment of knowledge and its disembodied and fluid re-rendering as 'intellectual capital' more apparent than in that discourse that makes such exchange its explicit target. In one of the more influential contemporary management accounting texts (Kaplan and Norton 1996: 59) are several examples of management in a range of corporations seeking to 'improve asset utilization' through incorporating knowledge creation and exchange as part of their mission. For these writers this means 'a reduction in cash-to-cash cycles of investment in physical capital . . . in favour of investments in intellectual and human capital such as skilled technologists, data bases, and customer-knowledgeable personnel'. Within this discourse, the 'intellectual' capital of employees is constructed in a very specific way whereby their intellectual and human capacities are integrated with financial objectives. In fact, it is only when this integration has occurred that personal knowledge can be adequately accounted for. 'The most desirable results remain in terms of profit margins or observable (measurable) outcomes – financial objectives represent the long-term goal of the organisation: to provide superior returns based on the capital invested in the unit' (Kaplan and Norton 1996: 61). Here, the measurement approach is that of 'the balanced scorecard' which aims to make financial objectives explicit by adding return on *knowledge assets* to the traditional return on *financial assets* in the organization's yearly accounting metrics. Again, it is worth pointing out that this human capital discourse conflates 'knowledge' and 'assets' in such a way as to reinscribe what constitutes 'valid' knowledge in favour of its business utility and financial value. Hence, the metaphor of vampirism: it is only when personal knowledge is organizationally transfused that it counts.

Although there are many difficulties in measuring intellectual capital, it is nevertheless a conceptual package that is now 'cool'. Its packaging has the effect of creating theory and jargon which can be used to prepare a work environment for workplace restructuring, the re-engineering of worker functions, so that they perform in an innovative new way and, in some instances, it can be used to prepare its unwitting victims for downsizing. This occurs in spite of Marsick and Watkins's (1999) concern that re-engineering and downsizing are destructive of knowledge capital.

Accumulating intellectual capital appears to be a re-engineered version of asset-stripping knowledge workers. Accumulation is largely defined externally to those who are expected to do the creating, innovating and activating. Proponents of liberal progressivism and human capital theories of 'empowerment' and 'self-direction' may deny this, but our argument is that practitioners are frequently presented with something that is meant to be 'new' – even exciting – something they have to 'learn about' and then implement. Indeed, employees in many contemporary organizations hear about new learning 'opportunities' through staff development calendars or electronically, via email broadcasts to staff. There is often an implicit managerial expectation that staff will avail themselves of the new offerings to develop themselves; if they do not, they may have to accept responsibility for their own professional demise.

Drawing from Foucault (1982) one should expect that such communication processes are precisely where discourses produce power. With the overlay of new global driving forces in technology, cross-border competition, de-differentiation and email systems, we now have, as an example of something new to learn about, the emerging discourse of 'capacity building'. This new offering is, in part, intended to help 'manage' intellectual capital:

> [T]he application of objective capacities implies relationships of communication (whether in the form of previously acquired information or of shared work): it is tied also to power relations (whether they consist of obligatory tasks, of gestures imposed by tradition, of subdivisions and the more or less obligatory distribution of labor).
>
> (Foucault 1982: 218)

The point of using Foucault here is to unmask the proposition that 'capacity building' is simply a more rational, objective process of adjustment to conditions of rapid economic and social change. Rather, it is an operation of technique built upon communications and the relationships of power – 'which are distinct from objective abilities' (Foucault 1982: 219). Fuelling institutional and work-based power relations are the interconnected discourses that circulate around the management of 'intellectual' capital: learning organizations, flexible learning, human and cultural capital, productive diversity, and capacity building. Within and through these discourses a managerial reinscription of the term 'intellectual' occurs: from a term of abuse, drawn from the dark-side, from the profane, it shifts from something that pointy-headed and unproductive people do to something that ennobles even the most mundane manager. It is a more pragmatic form of knowledge that is now in demand, valorized through market forces.

To be a knowledge worker now becomes a calling equivalent to a vocation: knowledge workers are required to help organizations and industries meet contemporary market challenges and the demand for new forms of 'capacity building'. In turn, universities – in flexible mode – can now offer suites of 'transdisciplinary' work-based learning programmes. The transformative power of the new intellectualism can reach out even to the previously spurned 'ivory towers'. It is not only managers who can reinvent their explicit selves by effecting the transformation from being managers to becoming Chief Knowledge Officers. The transformation occurs through the appropriation of tacit knowledge; with this trick even academics can convert their explicit intellectual selves into knowledge managers and entrepreneurial consultants. What joy! What symmetry! What a transaction! But at what, if any, cost? What boundaries are dissolving and what new capacities are being built through these exchanges?

The dissolving boundaries of organizational learning

There is no single definition of capacity building in organizations but it is generally related to the deliberate promotion of new connections and the dissolving boundaries between the public and private sectors. Multi-sectorial connections require employees to possess integrated communicative capabilities that are meant to enhance the transferability of skills and employability. Here, a shift in the relationship between the state and the community – in which the provision of services becomes a web of cooperating and interdependent structures – can be discerned. This 'web', if it is to operate successfully, requires a shift from the state, as a purchaser of services, to the state as a civic catalyst. And there are certainly dissolving boundaries between commerce, industry and education. Formal education can now be enacted through webs of interdependent structures that encompass both commercial and non-commercial activities. Work-based learning (WBL) is one example of this. For instance, in WBL three-way negotiation processes of management, university and participant (student) are required to establish mutually acceptable learning contracts. In such a scenario the dissolving boundaries of formal education provision are intimately connected with 'capacity-building' and indebted to market principles in both public (university) and private (business) sectors. The capacity building is accompanied by the language of flexibility in (lifelong) learning which, in turn, encompasses the possibility (and material reality) of work being the curriculum.

New partnering arrangements are characteristic of many contemporary government business practices throughout OECD nations. The UK Dearing Report (1997) and in Australia the West Report (1998) both emphasize the need for partnerships between higher education and industry, particularly in relation to the cooperative design and delivery of courses, as well as the need for financial partnerships. The Fryer Report (1997) in the UK went as far as to recommend a 'University for Industry' (which now exists) and the *franchising* of higher and further education.[1]

At present, the language-in-use about capacity building stresses:

- development and maintenance of partnerships across a range of work roles and structures;
- continuous reciprocal transfer of knowledge between structures;
- flexible and innovative problem solving;
- investments in social, human and economic capital.

As mentioned, a specific illustration of capacity building is the relatively new work-based learning credential. This entails the distribution of university qualifications that requires partnering arrangements between organizations, universities and individual participants. WBL involves the recognition of learning that occurs in workplaces in ways that enable the transformation of personal, everyday 'know-how' into observable, assessable, tangible knowledge. The way this occurs is by transforming what one does at work (performance) into named 'areas of learning' that can be used to acquire academic credit. In this way, a new incentive for staff is created that carries the obligation on the part of participants to articulate what they know and what they have learned about their work in measured ways. The degrees of learning are now deployed by organizations as components of reward systems – precisely to effect efficiencies in individual and organizational performance and to convert personally embodied intellectual capital into tangible outcomes for the corporate body.

The reciprocal transfer of knowledge (and responsibilities) between structures always have political and organizational limitations. For instance, the gathering of information about other organizations than one's employer can easily become an occasion for commercial exploitation. Nonetheless, capacity building extends some of the principles of the 'learning organization' in the seductive promise of delivering more 'holistic' community partnering arrangements between private companies and what, at present, remain ostensibly public sector organizations. We use the term 'ostensibly' advisedly: the sources of funding for entrepreneurial business schools, for instance, are rarely subvened by the public purse even when they remain part of institutions that are so subvened. We take no moral position on this. We simply note that the new techniques of knowledge management are capable of not only transfusing the vitality and transforming the corporate body of the clients of the new pedagogy of knowledge management – they also transform the corporate body that manages as well as that which is managing. Quite what, metaphorically, is sucking which vital fluid from whom is a matter of contention. Certainly, as the practice spreads, the life support systems should become intertwined, the transfusions and transformations more seamless, and the vampirism more rampant.

Such arrangements are perhaps best viewed against the contemporary backdrop of constant and unpredictable social and economic change. A significant aspect of 'constant change' is de-differentiation, or the breaking down, blurring and increasing permeability of boundaries and norms (Edwards and Usher 1998: 83). Postmodernity may well be premised on de-differentiation. As Clegg (1995: 11) points out, modernity, as the outcome of modernization, was premised on an increasing functional differentiation of phenomena. Postmodernization and postmodernity reverse the process, involving 'a blurring of boundaries between what, under a more modernist impulse, would have been constituted as distinct phenomena [for instance] between literature and theory, high and popular culture' (Lash 1988: 312). Based on this reading, capacity building (and the management of intellectual capital) can be viewed as postmodern practices premised on de-differentiation involving the blurring of boundaries between public/private responsibilities, as well as between contemplative/instrumental knowledge, education/training, self/other and so on.

The complexities of contemporary work radically challenge traditional approaches to education and training. The issues and problems of postmodernity generate new interpretive frameworks, new conceptual resources and strategies. For instance, Usher (1997: 99) asserts that there is a widespread belief that 'the education system [in the UK] has failed at all levels to produce a flexible, adaptable workforce motivated to learn throughout life'. An adequate preparation of people for the market now requires greater subtlety, flexibility, responsiveness and pragmatism. As a consequence of rapid change, skilled workers and trained employees may have to discard 'knowledge' recently developed and adopt new ways of doing things and 'knowing' about their work. Pragmatic 'know-how' is now a highly sought-after commodity. It is against this backdrop that capacity-building approaches begin to look desirable.

Capacity building is currently being promoted at the level of conceptual strategy in a range of government enterprises and private sector companies. Unlike earlier approaches to competency-based training,[2] capacity building focuses on the ways that workers need to think and *how workers need to be in the world*. In order to perform in the required ways for the high-tcch workforce, workers have to reconceptualize not only their tasks and roles but also themselves. Capacity building thus requires the construction of a workforce that can mobilize resources to match the unpredictable market at any given moment. It is our contention that the idea of using embedded work-based learning rather than more conventional 'formal' education is, in part, designed to achieve this flexibility.

With employees increasingly having to work across professional and disciplinary boundaries, as well as rapidly mobilize resources to survive (maintain their jobs), unprecedented opportunities and diversity are spawned. Individual career pathways and professional identities open up to multiple possibilities. In addressing such diversity, work-based learning does offer new educational possibilities for workers at various levels. The transfusions, it is claimed, can not only vitalize the corporate body but also, reciprocally, transform the embodied worker (see Kono and Clegg 1998).

The new partnering/team approaches that characterize some of today's so-called 'learning organizations' allow for conflicts to be redefined, with employees mobilized to be strategic problem solvers, as well as being more directly responsible for the achievement of desirable outcomes. Such redefining clearly contains the potential for significant benefits for both individuals and organizations, with employees being actively encouraged to learn and to solve problems at grass-roots or shop-floor levels. But, as we know from Foucault, power is not always repressive and where there is power, typically there is resistance. Worker/learners are not merely passive subjects having their professional identities shaped for them by ever more subtle refinements of managerial reward systems. They are active subjects making sense of the contradictions and tensions that permeate contemporary workplaces. Work-based learning possibilities are new ingredients that enable active subjects to become discursive creators.

The incorporation of workplace-based learning into university education is partly an economic and social response to changing ideas about the roles of universities. For instance, Senge and Kim (1997) assert that higher education today is marked by decreased funding, as well as a lack of political support from a general public suspicious of and ambivalent towards academic institutions. The arrival of the so-called 'knowledge era' thus presents a new set of hopes and challenges for these declining institutions to reinvent themselves in ways that renew their social legitimacy and generate resources.

Coffield and Williamson (1997) argue that one hope for the continued viability of university education lies in developing philosophical approaches aimed at increasing the facilitation of lifelong learning, as knowledge-based societies become the norm. The idea of complete workplace-based qualifications rests heavily on this expectation. Just as knowledge-workers who are recruited to the cause of making their tacit intellectual capital explicit are not passive victims but have to be actively seduced, so universities are not simply passive recipients of 'industry demands' but are also agents for change. Workplace-based learning programmes have been presented as a response to the rapid economic and social change – as one way of assisting in the corporate building of intellectual capital and capacity.

New 'legitimations' of knowledge at work

Vitalized organizations are those in which the power embedded in mundane knowledge, in ordinary employees and routine practices, is liberated to transform behaviour, decision making and values (Kono and Clegg 1998). Through work-based approaches to learning, formal education systems are playing an increasingly significant role both in this 'liberation' and in the economics of knowledge. Universities are being forced to reconsider their position in growing knowledge-based economies; growing not only in the sense of becoming larger in quantitative terms but also in the structural sense of growth. Universities are being recast as components in the architecture of economic growth. There is a general transformation of understanding of what counts as knowledge – more performative than contemplative ways of knowing become increasingly stressed (Barnett 2000). What defence is there now for the study of Classics or Greats in the boardroom? While Roderick West, the principal architect of the West Report, is a Classicist and ex-Headmaster of an elite Sydney private school, the values one would associate with this background were not particularly emphasized in the report that bore his name. Even many of those careers that have benefited from an older valorization of knowledge are today reluctant to support what have become clearly historical curiosities. Yet, performativity can marginalize far more contemporary claims to knowledge as well, against the claims of business and applied technique.

Gibbons *et al.* (1994) assert that we live in a performative era in which knowledge is legitimized in so far as it will enhance productivity, and improve economic competitiveness and personal effectiveness, thus representing a shift in focus on skills and skill formation. Consumer demand escalates for more operational and instrumental/pragmatic views of knowledge and, as argued by Garrick and Kirkpatrick (1998), universities no longer have a monopoly on the generation of knowledge. Their legislative monopoly may remain for a few years yet but, practically, they are now just one among many players in the knowledge industry. Like clerics, those legislators of pre- and early modernity, they can hang on in penury and diminished significance, or they can change their message for the postmodern era. To do the latter they are being required to respond to fundamental shifts in how we seek to know the world. Under challenge are ideas of how to shape and legitimize what counts as knowledge and truth. In recent decades the reality of the market has provided a framework for public education policies whose experience, for some people and providers in the system, has been traumatic. The adoption of such approaches is not unproblematic. Educational programmes that now see universities entering into contracts with business organizations have associated tensions. For instance, Garrick (1998: 111) points to the enhanced *incorporation* of workers into workplace culture – via the appropriation of Japanese industrial relations and management techniques – through seductive company reward devices. These devices now encompass, inter alia, formal accreditation in the form of work-based learning diplomas and degrees. Our argument here is not that there is something intrinsically wrong with such accreditation. On the contrary. But where the workplace becomes the curriculum it is important that the learner and the accrediting agency retain some scope to decide what constitutes valuable learning. In the liberal view of the university, the individual learner was encouraged to 'think critically'. Yet at the same time, the sovereignty of the corpus of knowledge was never completely in doubt. Knowledge was transmitted from the academic corpus to the undergraduate cadre and, at best, individually and playfully dissected in the tutorial.

One of the rites of passage of the first year undergraduate was the devalorization of everyday knowledge and the humbling of the learner as an apprentice in a vast hall of knowledge to which only the licentiate had the key. The definitions of what counted as knowledge were those of the reproducers of knowledge (for few were actually producers). The new regimes of knowledge management – manifest in the learning organization and work-based learning – transform the terms of the traditional epistemological trade. The traditional protectionist response of the academic reproducers is that the weighting of decisions will invariably favour the corporate body of the employing organization, via the senior managers, who negotiate the curriculum with the university. They are the people who define what life interests and knowledge are vital and then seek to transfuse it into 'value-adding' knowledge capital (as our earlier General Motors' example demonstrates). Our concern is that, once transfused, everyday working knowledge can be devalorized.

Who are the winners and losers in these transformations? This is not a straightforward matter to determine. At one level the individual employees are winners: what *they* know is taken seriously, codified and rewarded. But they no longer know it exclusively; it is no longer their resource – it becomes a corporate resource. Thus, work-based learning can be viewed as a key practice in transforming organizational politics. It evaporates many of the resources for zero-sum political games as they may have been played in the past – the politics of 'strategic contingency' (Hickson *et al.* 1971; Hinings *et al.* 1974). The reason is simple: the power resources are traded away. So, to the extent that the politics are transformed from negative to positive power then the corporate body may be said to be a winner: its energies are revitalized and its politics transformed. What is the score with the universities? They will need to give up their traditional politics as well. No longer do they dictate the terms of trade of knowledge in a one-way exchange from the mastery of their members to the dependency of their subject population. Instead, they enter into a three-way negotiation, in principle, of the terms of trade, with both the employee and the corporate body as partners. Thus, they lose the privilege of their monopoly position as it has traditionally been licensed. Note that they do so in a new way: in the past, in institutional arenas such as theology, accounting or medicine – the professions – there was always a corporate negotiation of the content of the curriculum. But it was an arms-length negotiation between the university and the peak professional bodies. Now the negotiation is with corporate bodies that inhabit interstices unrepresented by the professions in any corporate sense. To the extent that a part of the power of the universities was premised on their untrammelled monopoly of the terms of knowledge trade then these developments weaken their power. Now they must enter negotiations with those whom, once upon a time, would have been scorned as repositories of ignorance. For some types of faculty this poses problems. Those faculties, particularly in the so-called 'hard' sciences and business, who have seen their knowledge management as premised essentially on a 'Newtonian' model, have difficulties. No longer the monopoly producers of the equivalent of 'nature's message' they must share definition not only of the nature of fundamental problems but also the means of addressing them. No more is it appropriate to argue, from analytical premises, that 'we' know best and that the receivers of knowledge in its reproduction should accept it on our terms. Of course, to the extent that they embrace work-based learning principles, then they can be winners as well. But, for academics whose conceptions of the glittering prizes have been sharply conditioned by reward structures oriented to norms of scientistic practice, this may be a bridge too far and too difficult to make. After all, it is their authority that is on the line.

Corresponding with the increased focus on action and pragmatism is the growing recognition that it is important to manage intellectual capital. As a part of this management, we have referred to the emergence of capacity building and workplace-based learning programmes. These focus on 'how to' problem-solving activities and observable outcomes. Such major shifts in the roles and purposes of higher education are both cause and effect of change.

It is commonly argued, in a reflex of the critical tradition, that individuals in work-based degree programmes should not be made to feel afraid of examining the 'hidden curriculum' of the corporate body, such as the ways in which employees may be socialized to perform in particular ways at work. Of course, this may not always be easy as contemporary models of work-based learning tend to place supervisors or managers in the role of coach, mentor, instructor and, in some cases, assessor. With negotiated WBL degrees and diplomas, a new category of student is being created – one who is likely to approach university learning from a perspective shaped, at least in part, by the organization that employs them. This category of student is accompanied by issues related to the acculturation and socialization of workers into organizations, and indeed, some senior expectations that the student will be 'indebted' to the organization for providing them with the opportunity to get a degree. 'Learning' relationships can thus perpetuate and even magnify the organization's power relationships. Students learn a new kind of dependency even as their transfusions of knowledge enrich the organization on which they become increasingly dependent. The winners may be losers; the positive may be negative, the vitalization may be zero-sum.

Revenge of the goths

Knowledge is now widely described as an asset and a resource. Establishing an appropriate balance between theoretical/disciplinary-based knowledge and the practical know-how desired in the workplace presents a significant challenge to staff responsible for planning and implementing these 'flexible' initiatives. To assist in this endeavour it may be worth heeding Nonaka and Takeuchi's (1995: 21) theory of 'knowledge management' which suggests that:

> Knowledge, expressed in words and numbers, only represents the tip of the iceberg ... knowledge is not easily visible and expressible ... Whereas Westerners tend to emphasise explicit knowledge, and the Japanese tacit knowledge ... human knowledge is created through social interaction between the tacit and explicit.

The drive to promote learning at work is difficult to argue against. Would you rather be employed in an organization that discouraged learning? Nonetheless it is prudent to examine the ways in which the language of learning is used in workplaces. Although sometimes well meant, contemporary discourses of learning are increasingly driven by political imperatives, organization change, efficiency requirements, cost-effectiveness and market economics. These emphases are underpinned by a stress on 'manipulative techniques, ready-made structures, impoverished language, and delight in surface appearance ...' (Griffin, 1997: 5). Her concern here is that 'conceptualization' in this mode of knowledge production is downgraded in favour of a more simplistic information gathering.

Work-based learning is most certainly a creation of its time. As we have argued, such an approach is connected to new modes of knowledge production, capability and capacity building, enterprise governance and employees increasingly on the lookout for learning 'opportunities' through work. Seductive, shiny and bright, it encourages a reconceptualization of intellectualism – not so much as independence of the human spirit but as enslavement of their will to corporate purpose. What will be of interest to researchers will be the creative ways in which the individual 'will to power' fights back and creates its own space of resistance. For, as Foucault suggests, *we will.* And, after all, in every instance of the genre, Dracula is eventually destroyed.

But in this metaphorical tale, it is always worth asking what, or which organizational actor, is playing Dracula?

Notes

1. Perhaps, despite resistance based on sentimental attachment to what seem increasingly to be nostalgic models of Enlightenment education, McDonalds may become a model for the future university, if not *the* model (Pritchard and Willmott 1997). There is no apparent reason why this should not occur. Only a monopoly licence to practise, granted through parliament, stands in the way of this innovation. And, surely, such monopolies are a restraint on competition policy. If other monopolies, such as public utilities, are being sold off or managed by private 'consortia' in many domains, such as water, transportation, construction, health services, and secondary education, why not tertiary education?
2. Competency-based education and training (CBET) systems, the 'new vocationalism' (Usher 1997: 99), show serious deficiencies. For instance, competence is usually defined in terms of predominantly observable behaviour. This sometimes means that employees who have attained competency-based qualifications may still lack the broader skills required to perform confidently in specific contexts (Garrick

1998). When competencies are defined in narrow, mechanistic and task-focused ways, CBET cannot offer the desired 'learning' solutions sought by industry leaders, senior government officials and many educators. Although the limits of CBET are becoming increasingly clear, there remains a powerful acceptance of such approaches to education at a policy level throughout OECD nations and among influential industry groups and policy makers. Driving this acceptance is a perception that CBET has a crucial role in economic regeneration and competitiveness.

References

ABS (Australian Bureau of Statistics) (1997) *The Labour Force Australia.* Canberra: Australian Government Publishing Service.

Aronowitz, S. and DiFazio, W. (1994) *The Jobless Future: Sci-Tech and the Dogma of Work.* Minneapolis, MN: University of Minnesota Press.

Barnett, R. (2000) Working knowledge, in J. Garrick and C. Rhodes (eds) *Research and Knowledge at Work.* London: Routledge.

Burton-Jones, A. (1999) *Knowledge Capitalism: Business, Work, and Learning in the New Economy.* Oxford: Oxford University Press.

Casey, C. (1999) The changing contexts of work, in D. Boud and J. Garrick (eds) *Understanding Learning at Work.* London: Routledge.

Castells, M. (1996) *The Information Age: Economy, Society and Culture. Volume 1: The Rise of the Network Society.* Oxford: Blackwell.

CEU (Commission of the European Union) (1999) *Implementing the OECD Jobs Strategy: Assessing Performance and Policy.* Luxembourg: Office of the European Communities.

Clegg, S. R. (1995) *Modern Organisations.* London: Sage.

Coffield, F. and Williamson, B. (1997) Introduction, in F. Coffield and B. Williamson (eds) *Repositioning Higher Education.* Buckingham: SRHE/Open University Press.

Dearing, R. (1997) *Higher Education in a Learning Society: The National Committee of Inquiry into Higher Education.* London: HMSO.

Drucker, P. (1995) The information executives truly need. *Harvard Business Review* (Jan–Feb.): 35–44.

Edvinnson, L. and Malone, M. (1997) *Intellectual Capital: Realizing Your Company's True Value by Finding its Hidden Roots.* New York: Harper Collins.

Edwards, R. and Usher, R. S. (1998) Lo(o)s(en)ing the boundaries: from 'education' to 'lifelong learning'. *Studies in Continuing Education*, 20 (1), 83–103.

Eraut, M. (1999) Non-formal Learning in the Workplace: The Hidden Dimension of Lifelong Learning, Keynote address, International Conference on Research on Work and Learning, University of Leeds, September 10–12.

Foucault, M. (1982) The subject and power, in H. Dreyfus and P. Rabinow (eds) *Michel Foucault: Beyond Structuralism and Hermeneutics.* Brighton: Harvester Press.

Fryer, R. H. (1997) *Learning for the 21st Century. Report of the National Advisory Group for Continuing Education and Lifelong Learning.* London: HMSO.

Garrick, J. (1998) *Informal Learning in the Workplace: Unmasking Human Resource Development.* London: Routledge.

Garrick, J. and Kirkpatrick, D. (1998) Workplace-based learning degrees: a new business venture, or a new critical business. *Higher Education Research and Development*, 17 (2), 171–82.

Gibbons, M., Limoges, C., Nowotny, H. *et al.* (1994) *The New Production of Knowledge: The Dynamics of Science and Research in Contemporary Societies.* London: Sage.

Griffin, A. (1997) Knowledge under attack: consumption, diversity and the need for values, in R. Barnett and A. Griffin (eds) *The End of Knowledge in Higher Education.* London: Cassell.

Hickson, D. J., Hinings, C. R., Lee, C. A., Schneck, R. E. and Pennings, J. M. (1971) A strategic contingencies theory of intra-organizational power. *Administrative Science Quarterly*, 16 (1), 216–29.

Hinings, C. R., Hickson, D. J., Pennings, J. M. and Schneck, R. E. (1974) Structural conditions of intra-organizational power. *Administrative Science Quarterly*, 9 (1), 22–44.

Kaplan, R. S. and Norton, D. P. (1996) *The Balanced Scorecard.* Boston MA: Harvard Business School Press.

Kitay, J. and Lansbury, R. D. (1997) *Changing Employment Relations in Australia.* Melbourne: Oxford University Press.

Kono, T. and Clegg, S. R. (1998) *Transformations of Corporate Cultures.* Berlin: de Gruyter.

Lash, S. (1988) Post-modernism as a 'regime of signification'. *Theory, Culture and Society*, 5 (2–3), 311–36.

Marsick, V. J. and Watkins, K. E. (1997) Organisational learning: review of research, in L. J. Bassi and D. Russ-Eft (eds) *What Works and What Doesn't: Assessment, Development, and Measurement.* Alexandria, VA: American Society for Training and Development.

Marsick, V. J. and Watkins, K. E. (1999) Envisioning new organisations for learning, in D. Boud and J. Garrick (eds) *Understanding Learning at Work.* London: Routledge.

Nonaka, I. and Takeuchi, H. (1995) *The Knowledge Creating Company.* New York NY: Oxford.

Petrella, R. (1996) Globalization and internationalization: the dynamics of the emerging world order, in R. Boyer and D. Drache (eds) *States Against Markets: The Limits of Globalization.* London: Routledge.

Pritchard, C. and Willmott, H. (1997) Just how managed is the McUniversity? *Organization Studies*, 18 (2), 287–316.

Rifkin, J. (1996) *The End of Work: The Decline of Global Labor Force and the Dawn of the Post-Market Era.* New York, NY: Putnam Books.

Senge, P. M. and Kim, D. H. (1997) From fragmentation to integration: building learning communities. *The Systems Thinker*, 8 (4), 1–5.

Stoker, B. ([1897] 1993) *Dracula.* Ware: Wordsworth Classics.

Usher, R. S. (1997) Seductive texts: competence, power and knowledge in post-modernity, in R. Barnett and A. Griffin (eds) *The End of Knowledge in Higher Education.* London: Cassell.

West, R. (1998) *Learning for Life: Review of Higher Education Financing and Policy.* Canberra: Australian Government Publishing Service.

Index

The Society for Research into Higher Education

The Society for Research into Higher Education (SRHE) exists to stimulate and coordinate research into all aspects of higher education. It aims to improve the quality of higher education through the encouragement of debate and publication on issues of policy, on the organization and management of higher education institutions, and on the curriculum, teaching and learning methods.

The Society is entirely independent and receives no subsidies, although individual events often receive sponsorship from business or industry. The Society is financed through corporate and individual subscriptions and has members from many parts of the world.

Under the imprint *SRHE & Open University Press*, the Society is a specialist publisher of research, having over 80 titles in print. In addition to *SRHE News*, the Society's newsletter, the Society publishes three journals: *Studies in Higher Education* (three issues a year), *Higher Education Quarterly* and *Research into Higher Education Abstracts* (three issues a year).

The Society runs frequent conferences, consultations, seminars and other events. The annual conference in December is organized at and with a higher education institution. There are a growing number of networks which focus on particular areas of interest, including:

Access	Learning Environment
Assessment	Legal Education
Consultants	Managing Innovation
Curriculum Development	New Technology for Learning
Eastern European	Postgraduate Issues
Educational Development Research	Quantitative Studies
FE/HE	Student Development
Funding	Vocational Qualifications
Graduate Employment	

Benefits to members

Individual

- The opportunity to participate in the Society's networks

- Reduced rates for the annual conferences
- Free copies of *Research into Higher Education Abstracts*
- Reduced rates for *Studies in Higher Education*
- Reduced rates for *Higher Education Quarterly*
- Free copy of *Register of Members' Research Interests* – includes valuable reference material on research being pursued by the Society's members
- Free copy of occasional in-house publications, e.g. *The Thirtieth Anniversary Seminars Presented by the Vice-Presidents*
- Free copies of *SRHE News* which informs members of the Society's activities and provides a calendar of events, with additional material provided in regular mailings
- A 35 per cent discount on all SRHE/Open University Press books
- Access to HESA statistics for student members
- The opportunity for you to apply for the annual research grants
- Inclusion of your research in the *Register of Members' Research Interests*

Corporate

- Reduced rates for the annual conferences
- The opportunity for members of the Institution to attend SRHE's network events at reduced rates
- Free copies of *Research into Higher Education Abstracts*
- Free copies of *Studies in Higher Education*
- Free copies of *Register of Members' Research Interests* – includes valuable reference material on research being pursued by the Society's members
- Free copy of occasional in-house publications
- Free copies of *SRHE News*
- A 35 per cent discount on all SRHE/Open University Press books
- Access to HESA statistics for research for students of the Institution
- The opportunity for members of the Institution to submit applications for the Society's research grants
- The opportunity to work with the Society and co-host conferences
- The opportunity to include in the *Register of Members' Research Interests* your Institution's research into aspects of higher education

Membership details: SRHE, 3 Devonshire Street, London W1N 2BA, UK. Tel: 020 7637 2766. Fax: 020 7637 2781. email: srhe@mailbox.ulcc.ac.uk
world wide web: http://www.srhe.ac.uk./srhe/
Catalogue: SRHE & Open University Press, Celtic Court, 22 Ballmoor, Buckingham MK18 1XW. Tel: 01280 823388. Fax: 01280 823233. email: enquiries@openup.co.uk

CHANGING ACADEMIC WORK
DEVELOPING THE LEARNING UNIVERSITY

Elaine Martin

Higher education has changed enormously in recent years. For instance, it now serves a more diverse range of students and is under closer government scrutiny and control. There is consequently a significant number of academics who are uneasy with current values and practices and who work with them reluctantly. Universities may speak publicly of efficiency and effectiveness but they cannot function successfully if their academic staff are disillusioned.

Changing Academic Work explores the competing tensions in contemporary work: the need to balance individualism with collaboration; accountability with reward; a valuing of the past with preparation for the future. The aim is to help staff build a contemporary university which is as much a learning organization as an organization about learning. Elaine Martin develops a set of simple but sound principles to guide academic work and, through case study material, she provides engaging and convincing illustrations of these principles in action. She offers insight and guidance for academic staff at all levels who wish to make their working environment more satisfying and productive.

Contents
Preface – Changes in academic work – Experiences of change in academic work – Learning and teaching in higher education – Organizational change and learning organizations – Finding a way forward – Visions and missions and reality – Collaboration and independence – Accountability and reward – Encouraging change: valuing the past, preparing for the future – A final word: a better working life – Bibliography – Index.

c.192pp   0 335 19883 X (Paperback)   0 335 19884 8 (Hardback)

SKILLS DEVELOPMENT IN HIGHER EDUCATION AND EMPLOYMENT

Neville Bennett, Elisabeth Dunne and Clive Carre

The last decade has seen radical changes in higher education. Long held assumptions about university and academic autonomy have been shattered as public and political interest in quality, standards and accountability have intensified efforts for reform. The increased influence of the state and employers in the curriculum of higher education is exemplified by the increasing emphasis on so-called core or transferable skills; an emphasis supported by the Dearing Report which identified what it called 'key' skills as necessary outcomes of all higher education programmes. However, there is little research evidence to support such assertions, or to underpin the identification of good practice in skill development in higher education or employment settings. Further, prescription has outrun the conceptualization of such skills; little attention has been paid to their theoretical underpinnings and definitions, or to assumptions concerning their transfer.

Thus the study reported in this book sets out to gain enhanced understandings of skill acquisition in higher education and employment settings with the aim of informing and improving provision. The findings and analyses provide a clear conceptualization of core and generic skills, and models of good practice in their delivery, derived from initiatives by employers and staff in higher education. Student and graduate employee perspectives on skill delivery and acquisition are presented, together with a clearer understanding of the influence of contexts in skill definition and use in workplace settings. Finally, important questions are raised about institutional influences and constraints on effective innovation, and the role that generic or key skills play in traditional academic study, and in workplace effectiveness.

Contents
Generic skills in the learning society – A conceptualization of skills and course provision – Beliefs and conceptions of teachers in higher education – The practices of university teachers – Student perceptions of skill development – Employer initiatives in higher education – Employers' perspectives on skills and their development – The graduate experience of work – The challenges of implementing generic skills – Appendices – References – Indexes.

c.208pp   0 335 20335 3 (Paperback)   0 335 20336 1 (Hardback)

USING EXPERIENCE FOR LEARNING

David Boud, Ruth Cohen and David Walker (eds)

This book is about the struggle to make sense of learning from experience. What are the key ideas that underpin learning from experience? How do we learn from experience? How does context and purpose influence learning? How does experience impact on individual and group learning? How can we help others to learn from their experience?

Using Experience for Learning reflects current interest in the importance of experience in informal and formal learning, whether it be applied for course credit, new forms of learning in the workplace, or acknowledging autonomous learning outside educational institutions. It also emphasizes the role of personal experience in learning: ideas are not separate from experience; relationships and personal interests impact on learning; and emotions have a vital part to play in intellectual learning. All the contributors write themselves into their chapters, giving an autobiographical account of how their experiences have influenced their learning and what has led them to their current views and practice.

Using Experience for Learning brings together a wide range of perspectives and conceptual frameworks with contributors from four continents, and is a valuable addition to the field of experiential learning.

Contents
Introduction: understanding learning from experience – Part 1: Introduction – Through the lens of learning: how the visceral experience of learning reframes teaching – Putting the heart back into learning – Activating internal processes in experiential learning – On becoming a maker of teachers: journey down a long hall of mirrors – Part 2: Introduction – Barriers to reflection on experience – Unlearning through experience – Experiential learning at a distance – Learning from experience in mathematics – Part 3: Introduction – How the T-Group changed my life: a sociological perspective on experiential group work – Living the learning: internalizing our model of group learning – Experiential learning and social transformation for a post-apartheid learning future – Experiential learning or learning from experience: does it make a difference? – Index.

Contributors
Lee Andresen, David Boud, Angela Brew, Stephen Brookfield, Ruth Cohen, Costas Criticos, Kathleen Dechant, Elizabeth Kasl, Victoria Marsick, John Mason, Nod Miller, John Mulligan, Denis Postle, Mary Thorpe, Robin Usher, David Walker.

208pp   0 335 19095 2 (Paperback)